Think Яeverse!

Atare E. Agbamu, CRMS

Edited by
Eric C. Peck

The Mortgage Press Ltd.
Wantagh, New York
Copyright © 2008, Atare E. Agbamu, CRMS

Think Reverse!

Copyright © 2008, Atare E. Agbamu, CRMS

All Rights Reserved. No part of this publication may be reproduced or transmitted in any form or by any means, electronic or mechanical, including photocopy, recording or any information storage and retrieval system now known or to be invented, without permission in writing from the publisher, except by a reviewer who wished to quote brief passages in connection with a review written for inclusion in a magazine, newspaper or broadcast. Published by The Mortgage Press Ltd., 1220 Wantagh Avenue, Wantagh, N.Y. 11793, (800) 890-8090.

Visit our Web sites, www.thinkreverse.com and www.mortgagepress.com for more information on the subjects covered in this book.

Although the author and publisher have made every effort to ensure the accuracy and completeness of information contained in this book, we assume no responsibility for errors, inaccuracies, omissions or any inconsistencies herein. Any slights of people, places and/or organizations are unintentional. Please consult your financial advisor and/or tax preparer for appropriate advice.

ISBN 978-0-615-18730-3

Published in the United States by
The Mortgage Press Ltd.
1220 Wantagh Avenue
Wantagh, NY 11793

Cover design by Joey Arendt
Edited by Eric C. Peck

ATTENTION CORPORATIONS AND PROFESSIONAL ORGANIZATIONS: Quantity discounts are available on bulk purchases of this book for educational, gift or promotional purposes. In addition, on orders of 250 or more, we can customize the color cover to include your copy and your logo to identify your organization. For more information, contact: Joel M. Berman, Publisher, The Mortgage Press, 1220 Wantagh, New York 11793 or e-mail joel@mortgagepress.com.

Think Reverse!

Think Reverse!

Table of contents

Foreword *by Jim Mahoney* 9
Introduction 13
Acknowledgements 19
Dedication 25

Part I: The new pillar of retirement security

CHAPTER 1:	The new pillar of retirement security 29
CHAPTER 2:	Financial fuel for a longer ride......................................39
CHAPTER 3:	HECM: Uncle Sam's gift to older adults.......................51
CHAPTER 4:	HomeKeeper: Tearing down cash barriers to aging 65
CHAPTER 5:	Jumbos in Reverseland 73

Part II: Marketing reverse mortgages: It's all about education

CHAPTER 6:	A different kind of customer 85
CHAPTER 7:	Jason Miller needs help 97
CHAPTER 8:	The marketing basket...107
CHAPTER 9:	Become a rev-angelist 131
CHAPTER 10:	Marketing postscripts..143

Part III: Originating reverse mortgages

CHAPTER 11:	Essentials of reverse mortgage origination I 153
CHAPTER 12:	Essentials of reverse mortgage origination II 175
CHAPTER 13:	Laws and regulations in Reverseland 189
CHAPTER 14:	The road to Reverseland 205

Think Reverse!

Part IV: Enhancing freedom: The essence of reverse mortgages

**CHAPTER 15: Beyond our wildest imagination:
Profiles in satisfaction** 217

Part V: A new frontier in mortgage lending

CHAPTER 16: The new mortgage cheese 231

Appendix 245
Bibliography 297
Glossary of terms 303
Endnotes 313

Table of contents

Think Reverse!

Foreword
by Jim Mahoney

When I first began reviewing the contents of this book, I became quite jealous. You see, when my close colleagues and I first decided to enter the reverse mortgage business over a decade ago, there were no guidebooks and reverse mortgages did not boast the status of innovative financial tool these home loans enjoy today. In fact, it was quite a different time …

In the earlier days of the reverse mortgage industry, we were a small but passionate group, a group struggling to explain the concept of reverse mortgages to a skeptical senior audience jaded by too many predatory lending scandals than should ever have befallen their generation. Their adult children, accountants, lawyers, financial advisors—everyone who offers seniors advice, from their mailman to their butcher—had either no information on reverse mortgages or simply, misinformation. As a result, when asked about these unique home loans, most people spit back the signature comment on reverse mortgages of the 90s, "Oh yeah, those are the scams where they give you some money and then take your house."

Difficult … sure. But we knew that reverse mortgages offered a powerful solution for seniors faced with a wide range of financial concerns, from funding their retirements, to rising healthcare costs, to seeking the ability to maintain a certain quality of life while remaining in their homes.

Fast-forward to 2007, and it's an exciting time in this young industry. Since 2000, the industry's trade group, the National Association of Reverse Mortgage Lenders (NRMLA), has been instrumental in helping all of the participants unite to educate seniors, their children, advisors, mortgage professionals, lawmakers and the media on the facts about reverse mortgages. We focused on refining the numerous consumer safeguards built into reverse mortgages and worked hard to dispel myths and misinformation by launching an education campaign.

As a result, we have successfully elevated reverse mortgages from a suspi-

Think Reverse!

cious oddity to a credible financial solution. Mainstream media and personal finance experts now regularly present reverse mortgages as an important and viable financial option for seniors. As a result of this seven-year effort, reverse mortgages now present a compelling business opportunity—one that offers that rare satisfaction of 'doing good while doing well,' as reverse mortgages have a dramatic and positive impact on the lives of seniors.

There could not be a better time for professionals to explore the reverse mortgage business. The industry has firmly established the value and credibility of reverse mortgages through education, as well as strategic product design, and the establishment of best practices models and an industry code of conduct. While the demographics for forward mortgage are shrinking, according to some experts, the target audience for reverse mortgages (ages 62 and over) is growing as America ages. As an industry, we have enjoyed 50 percent-90 percent growth per annum over the last seven years, and even if this growth rate continues through 2010, we'll have only achieved five percent market penetration.

Perhaps the greatest advantage for professionals interested in developing a reverse mortgage business is that many of the start-up challenges any industry faces have been conquered, and now discussed in fine detail in this book. Whether you are new to reverse mortgages or already in the reverse mortgage business, this book has a lot to offer. Atare Agbamu has set down an impressive amount of information, from detailed product information to marketing and sales strategies, from crucial origination steps, to insights for understanding seniors. And he delivers it in an easy-to-read, simple-to-understand style that will make this book essential reading for all reverse mortgage professionals. Reverse mortgages are not that difficult, but they are quite different from traditional "forward" mortgages and other financial products. A dedicated reader will find that these chapters will accelerate his or her learning and speed up successful entrance into this exciting industry.

Jim Mahoney, co-founder and former chairman
Financial Freedom Senior Funding Corporation
Co-founder of the National Reverse Mortgage Lenders Association (NRMLA)

Foreword

Think Reverse!

Introduction

In *The 8th Habit*, author Stephen R. Covey says, every "new contribution" requires a "whole new preparation." My preparation for this book began in October 2001 when my friend and boss, Dan Mitchell, placed a stack of papers on my desk and asked me to "run with it." Unknown to me as a new hire, the company we both worked for then had just signed up with a reverse mortgage wholesaler. It wasn't clear why Dan tapped me to work on this new lending program for the company's Minnesota operations, but I went to work. My first task was to make sense of the papers.

Until that point in my residential mortgage lending career, I was unaware of "reverse mortgages." As I studied the papers, I was hooked, fascinated, and excited by what I was learning. Here is a home loan that provides older adult customers extra cash to spend any way they wish. They maintain physical and legal control of their homes and make no monthly repayments for as long as they live in their homes! It had a 'too good to be true' smell to it. I had to find out more.

After studying the product literature from Dan, I set about looking for more information about these loans. Out of curiosity, I picked up a textbook that we had used in March of 1999 in the National Association of Mortgage Brokers (NAMB) Residential Mortgage Lending (RML) School. The book covered the intricacies of residential mortgage lending, from application to servicing. To my surprise, all I found were three paragraphs on "RAM" or Reverse Annuity Mortgage, a precursor to modern reverse mortgages. Then, it hit me: Mortgage professionals are receiving outdated information on a crucial program. I saw a critical knowledge gap about these programs in the mortgage brokerage community and decided to learn more to help fill the gap.

This realization led to the inception of my nationally distributed column, "Forward on Reverse," in February of 2002. Two years later, my publisher, Joel M. Berman of The Mortgage Press Ltd., asked me to write a

Think Reverse!

book to guide mortgage professionals in marketing and originating reverse mortgages.

Think Reverse! is a road map into an exciting new frontier in residential mortgage lending —Reverse mortgages. Although there are some resources on reverse mortgages, they are primarily directed at educating consumers. Resources for educating mortgage professionals and other financial advisors are paltry to non-existent outside the industry. This book is an attempt to fill that void.

The growing ranks of wholesalers in Reverseland do a good job of training their correspondents. But with massive expansion of the industry on the horizon, even wholesalers' training capacity will require effective outside support. This book will aid the training effort.

The most effective way to educate consumers is to educate those on whom they traditionally rely on for mortgage finance advice—mortgage professionals and financial advisors, such as accountants, attorneys, financial planners and others.

Although it is improving, the level of reverse mortgage knowledge among these professionals today is unacceptable. For example, a customer of mine who was featured on NBC's Today Show in May of 2005 was advised by an otherwise competent financial planner that "there was no way" she could live in her home in a suburb of St. Paul, Minn. because she did not have enough Wall Street-linked assets. For a newly widowed spouse, mother and grandmother, it was a jarring piece of advice. If the advisor had reverse mortgage know-how, he could have given better advice. Thanks to a reverse mortgage we did for her, she is living in her home today, "financially covered," as she puts it. She's one of three fascinating and instructive profiles in Part IV of this book.

Today, older-adult customers are being directed into unsuitable forward mortgage programs. The story I shared in my column in *The Mortgage Press,* "Does John Neincash need mortgage payments?" is a case in point (see Appendix 4[a]). An experienced Twin Cities-based mortgage professional, dubbed "Peter Forward" in another column ("Harvesting cash for the golden years: To HECM or to HELOC?" [See Appendix 4[b]), put his own mother in a more costly home equity line of credit (HELOC) because he did not grasp the cost-benefit relation of reverse mortgages vis-à-vis HELOCs. A *Wall Street Journal* financial columnist misadvised readers in a January 2006 article.

The next source of headache for the mortgage industry will be *mortgage-product suitability* for older adults. This book will help forward mortgage

Introduction

professionals gain the know-how to serve aging customers and avoid ethical and legal problems.

Think Reverse! is organized into five parts and 16 chapters. At a time of uncertainty about retirement finance, I argued in Chapter 1 that a reverse mortgage is the new pillar of retirement security. Instead of expecting to collect fixed retirement benefits from one employer after 20, 30 or 40 years of service, you may want to focus on buying a home and building equity one mortgage payment at a time. Chapter 2 takes the view that with rising longevity, reverse mortgages supply extra financial fuel for a longer ride. Chapters 3, 4 and 5 offer overview of reverse mortgage programs: FHA's *HECM* or Home Equity Conversion Mortgage, Fannie Mae's *HomeKeeper*, Financial Freedom's *Cash Account Advantage*, Bank of America's *The Independence Plan*, Generation Mortgage's *Generation Plus*, and MetLife Bank's *Reverse Select*. And they anticipate program innovation.

The marketing chapters in Part II comprise the book's first core. Education is central to marketing reverse mortgages, but that education must begin with an understanding of aging and the aging consumer. Drawing heavily on the seminal work of David B. Wolfe and Robert E. Snyder in *Ageless Marketing*, Chapter 6 offers fresh insights into the aging customer, beyond conventional stereotypes. It's not enough to know an older customer's age, home equity position, income, zip code, and other data that can be fed into a computer. Your 62-year-old customer is not a 22-year-old version of herself. She's different. To market effectively to her, you must know what makes her different.

Chapter 7 builds on Chapter 6 by explaining values that are vital and unimportant to an aging customer. It underscores the influence of stories in marketing to older adults and explains how to find compelling stories. Chapter 8 introduces the reverse mortgage "marketing basket," consisting of advertising, lead generation, public relations, and networking. It shows how to deploy the *civic capital* of your company in marketing reverse mortgages. Chapter 9 is about lessons learned in marketing reverse mortgages since 1989. As an evolving area, it helps to have some field-tested lessons that apply across the reverse marketing landscape. Chapter 10 is a postscript to the marketing chapters, offering bite-size summaries to aid study. You may begin studying the marketing chapters from the postscript; however, to get full value, you must study Part II entirely.

Part III is the book's other core. Chapters 11 and 12 cover the elements of reverse mortgage origination. Chapter 13 summarizes laws and regulations critical to successful reverse mortgage origination and offers some dos' and

Think Reverse!

don'ts. Chapter 14 is a road map to reverse country. Readers of my column across the country often ask: "How do I get into reverse mortgages?" This chapter explains various levels of participation and provides guidance and resources for newcomers.

Part IV/Chapter 15 introduces the reader to three engaging and instructive profiles. The first is a widow, mother, and grandmother in Cottage Grove, Minn. Her determination to remain in her home, against the advice of a knowing but reverse-mortgage-ignorant financial advisor, led her to reverse mortgages and to me. She was featured on NBC's Today Show in May of 2005.

There is the story of two spirited ladies in Marshall, Texas. Extra cash from a reverse mortgage helped them turn their dreams into reality.

Finally, the riveting account of a civic-minded couple in Hampstead, N.H. completes the profiles. They say the extra cash has taken the "shackles" off their hands, giving them freedom to add to the lives of others in their community. These profiles illustrate the *essence* of reverse mortgages.

Part V/Chapter 16 is about change. Reverse mortgages represent a seminal opportunity for mortgage professionals. What we are losing on the forward mortgage side due to structural demographic shrinkage in younger markets, we are gaining on the reverse mortgage side because of structural expansion in older-adult population. However, to take advantage of the opportunity, we must be prepared, first by becoming aware of the opportunity and second, by training ourselves in reverse mortgage lending.

The language of reverse country is different. A glossary is included to unlock concepts critical to understanding these special home loans.

The appendices offer more resources to help you. Appendix 1 is a transcript of my conversation with Stephen A. Moses, a champion of long-term care reform in America. Moses shows the relationship between long-term care reform and reverse mortgages and offers marketing insights for reverse mortgage professionals. Appendices 2(a)(b) presents my 7-Point ReverseTalk™. This one-page tool will help marketer and audience focus on experiences extra cash from reverse mortgages can make possible. Appendix 2(c) explains how to get broadcast coverage on a small budget. Appendix 2(d) is a sample press release. Appendix 3(a) shares the perspective of a reverse mortgage originator with a background as a Certified Financial Planner (CFP) and a forward mortgage originator. Appendix 3(b) is a sample requirement for reverse mortgage correspondent. And Appendix 3(c) shows the steps to terminating a reverse mortgage loan when last customer dies. There's more. Welcome to the reverse mortgage experience!

Introduction

Think Reverse!

Acknowledgements

First, I give thanks to our heavenly Father, the Almighty Author and Creator of all. So, to Him alone is the glory (Soli Deo Gloria) for this work.

Many kind and thoughtful people aided the researching and writing of this book. As you read on, please help me thank the following people:

My wife, Efe, and our three winsome children—Awesiri, Akporefe and Tejiri—for their love, understanding and support …

My cousin Henry Agbamu of Lagos, Nigeria, for unceasing encouragement over the years and for his example …

My dear friend, Femi Olowu, for his friendship and encouragement; Femi is a prince among friends …

Samuel Olugbade and Margaret Adeola Adedeji, our dear family friends, for wise counsel, prayers, generosity and encouragement. Bro. Gbade is a prince among friends …

Our family friends, David and Remi Iselewa, Diesode and Denise Omenih, Daniel and Angela Ugwumba, Greg and Cindy Doyle (Greg is a prince among neighbors), Stacy and Scott Hanson, and Peter and Michelle Atakpu, for encouragement …

My friends and former owners of Credo Mortgage, Dan and Cari Mitchell, for inviting me to join their team in 2001, for introducing me to reverse mortgages and challenging me to "run with it," for creating and modeling a strong culture of learning and ethics at Credo Mortgage, and for their

Think Reverse!

unceasing encouragement …

My dear friend and editor at *The Mortgage Press*, Eric C. Peck, for helping to launch my column in 2002, for remaining a steady source of encouragement and for keen editorial judgment; Eric is a prince among editors …

Andrew T. Berman, the marketing chief at *The Mortgage Press* for helping to launch my column nationally. Andrew and Eric saw back then that no one was writing regularly about reverse mortgages in the national mortgage media, and decided to change that with my column; for young mortgage media leaders, they were years ahead of their peers …

My publisher, Joel M. Berman, for his confidence in me and for inviting me to write this book, for framing its practical focus on marketing and originating reverse mortgages, for his infectious enthusiasm for this book, and for his encouragement …

Annette Lee, a former reverse mortgage counselor at Senior Housing Inc. in Minneapolis for supporting my initial reverse mortgage education, for her kindness and for introducing me to the work of Ken Scholen, the father of reverse mortgages in America …

Gretchen Carlson of Community Education in South Washington County (Minnesota) for reading parts of the manuscript and offering suggestions …

Evelyn Pallas, a former reverse mortgage counselor at Community Action for Suburban Hennepin in Hopkins, Minn., for supporting my early education in reverse mortgages. Before she retired a few years ago, Evelyn was the dean of reverse mortgage counselors in Minnesota. Her extensive knowledge of reverse mortgages was always available to me …

Industry leaders Sarah Hulbert, Jim Mahoney, Paul Franklin, Barbara Franklin, Peter Bell, David Carey, Kathleen Hardy, Jeff Taylor, Jim Milano, Darryl Hicks, Patrick McEnerney, John Nixon, Craig Corn and Liz Scholz for aiding my research, granting interviews and enduring endless e-mail queries from me …

Special thanks to Sarah Hulbert, Jim Mahoney and Paul Franklin for reading the manuscript and suggesting improvements. Jim and Sarah's contribution

Acknowledgements

to this book is invaluable. Despite their responsibilities, they read every chapter and offered suggestions …

My friend, mentor and co-author of the pioneering book, *Ageless Marketing*, David B. Wolfe, for intellectual generosity, mentorship, reading and commenting on the marketing chapters; David Wolfe's work [Developmental Relationship Marketing or DRM] is the foundation of 21st century marketing; stumbling on *Ageless Marketing* through Peter Bell of NRMLA was one of the blessings of researching and writing this book …

Industry masters Deanne Opstad, Connie Osman, Sherry Apanay, Jenny Gattrell, Melissa Entin and Diane Byrnes for sharing their knowledge and insights with me; Deanne (dean of industry's underwriters) read the origination chapters and suggested improvements; Jenny Gatrell (authority on the Cash Account Advantage) reviewed my take on her specialty; Diane Byrnes contributed the life-planning scenarios in Chapter 5; Sam Avaiusini and Erik Anderson aided my research on The Independence Plan; Heather Papineau prepared key charts …

Edward J. Szymanoski Jr. of HUD, one of HECM's inventors, for giving me access to his seminal papers on HECM design and answering my endless questions, enhancing my understanding of HECM's structure, supporting my ongoing HECM research, and contributing some charts to this book …

Lawrence Jensen, CFP, owner of Jackson Funding LLC in Walpole, Mass., for sharing his insights as a reverse mortgage lender with financial planning and forward mortgage experience …

Justin Meise of River Communications in New York, a firm with much experience marketing reverse mortgages, for reading the marketing chapters and offering insightful suggestions …

Patrick Martyn, executive director of the Minnesota Mortgage Association for reading the manuscript and suggesting improvements and for his enduring moral support …

Rebecca Selby, owner of White Consulting, a PR and marketing consulting firm in Minneapolis, for contributing a feature on how to get broadcast access on a slim budget …

Think Reverse!

Therese Cain, executive director of Little Brothers—Friends of the Elderly, my long-time colleague in service of lonely and isolated elders in the Twin Cities, for unceasing encouragement and support, for reading the manuscript and suggesting improvements, for helping me begin the writing of this book by suggesting Maria Johnson as my research support; for being a tough, incisive, but gentle, idea-sparring partner, for her keen editorial judgment over the years ...

Maria Johnson of Do Good.Biz in Minneapolis, for giving me able research support, for her patience, encouragement, and creativity; Maria is a princess among research support and her contribution to this book is priceless ...

Dory Lidinsky, a former colleague at Credo Mortgage, for helping with illustrations, for her willingness to help whenever I ask ...

Craig Wanamaker, my colleague at Credo Mortgage for his ceaseless affirmation and encouragement, for wisdom and humor, for praying with me and for me, for connecting me with the Rev. Tom Parrish, who provided solid counsel at the beginning ...

My colleagues at Credo Mortgage: Mary Peterson, Gunnar Nelson, Jim Betzold (former), Jackie Irene, Margaret Oibrekkenn (former), Craig Patterson, Dave Patterson, Chris Corpooral and Mitzi Mitchell for encouragement ...

And finally, my mini-congregation brothers and sisters at Hope Church, Oakdale, Minn., for their fellowship, prayers and encouragement ...

Although I received generous support in researching and writing *Think Reverse!,* any error in it is my responsibility. Thank you very much for picking up this book.

Atare E. Agbamu, CRMS
Oakdale, Minn.
August 2008

Acknowledgements

Think Reverse!

Dedication

With love, to the memory of my father …
Olorogun Dick Aduaren Agbamu (1910-1967) of Uvwie, Urhoboland, Delta State, Nigeria

And to my mother …
Florence Shobode Erakpoweri

Think Reverse!

Part I

The new pillar of retirement security

The new pillar of retirement security: *Chapter 1*

Financial fuel for a longer ride: *Chapter 2*

HECM: Uncle Sam's gift to older adults: *Chapter 3*

HomeKeeper: Tearing down cash barriers to aging: *Chapter 4*

Jumbos in Reverseland: *Chapter 5*

Part I: The new pillar of retirement security

Chapter One
The new pillar of retirement security

Opening quotes ...
"... my hope is that this idea [reverse mortgage] will eventually become a pillar of security for older Americans and a foundation for greater dignity, hope and financial independence for their retirement years."
—**Jack Kemp, Secretary of Housing and Urban Development (1989)**

"His house was a focal point for his community. Listening to his stories, I realized that the house was more than four walls and a roof. It was his life, it was his past, and it was his future. The reverse mortgage allowed Arthur to stay in his home. He harnessed the power of this loan to achieve financial security and independence and to preserve his memories."
—**Michael G. Fitzpatrick, Congressman, 8th District of Pennsylvania (2005)**

Chapter 1 objectives
After studying this chapter, the reader will be able to:
- Know what drove reverse mortgage evolution in the U.S.
- Define a reverse mortgage
- Get a sense of reverse mortgage early history in the U.S.
- Name four reverse mortgage programs and their owners
- Know industry participants
- Appreciate the potential size of the reverse mortgage market
- Recognize seven common myths versus facts about reverse mortgages

Tapping home equity to address need among elders
Meet John and Jenny Hudson. John is a retired electrician and Jenny worked as a secretary for a small Twin Cities medical device company that was gobbled up in the merger-mania of the 1980s. The Hudsons are in their 80s. John

Part I: The new pillar of retirement security

is in a wheelchair and is on several medications for multiple sclerosis and other ailments. Jenny has had a hip replacement, followed by a double bypass.

John and Jenny have a combined monthly income of $2,600. Their mortgage and credit card payments amount to approximately $1,500 per month. Their monthly medication bills total $800, leaving them only $300 to live on. Their St. Paul home is valued at $220,000.

For a 78-year-old widow, Greta (Aunt Greta) Snyder is in remarkably good health. What is not so good is Aunt Greta's financial health. She's in foreclosure. The St. Paul resident has not made her mortgage payment of $300 for seven months. Her principal balance is $28,000. To do some necessary repairs to her well-kept 1950s home, she took out a home equity loan of $20,000 three years ago. The monthly payment on the home—equity loan is $350. She is three months behind. Her sole source of income is her Social Security. She gets $750 per month. Her home is valued at $190,000.

Sixty-seven-year-old Alan and 66-year-old Amy Kaiiser live in a breathtaking canyon home in Irvine, Calif. In June of 2006, their home was appraised for $4.1 million. Made up of stocks, mutual funds, treasuries and corporate bonds, their nest egg was valued at more than $1.7 million as of December 2006. The Kaiisers operate a small family jewelry business that Alan inherited from his late father. They are beginning to think about retirement, but want to completely remodel their canyon dream home before they retire because it is where they plan to stay for life. They need some serious cash.

While going through their mail one evening, Alan noticed a brochure for a reverse mortgage known as the Cash Account Advantage from a company called Financial Freedom. He called Amy and they went over the brochure together. They were excited by what they read. It seemed like the perfect solution to their need for cash to do the home remodeling they desired before retiring.

The next day, Alan Kaiiser called Financial Freedom to speak with a reverse mortgage specialist. Amy was in on the conversation. They were given a refresher on reverse mortgages, including the pros and cons on all available programs. In the end, given the value of their home, the size of their outstanding mortgage balance (approximately $360,000), and the annual positive cash flow from getting rid of their monthly mortgage payments (approximately $30,000), they decided to take the Cash Account Advantage credit line reverse mortgage.

In about four weeks from date of their call to Financial Freedom, they secured a $660,000 Cash Account Advantage or "jumbo" reverse mortgage, paid off their $360,000 mortgage balance, leaving them with $300,000 that they promptly used to do the remodeling they had planned for their home.

The Hudsons, Greta Snyder, and the Kaiisers are assumed names for older adult customers whose stories I have become familiar with as a reverse mortgage originator and student since 2001. They are rich in home equity, yet lacking in cash.

The need to combat cash-poverty among America's older adults who have huge home equity wealth, but lack the extra cash that often makes the difference between living well and living poor, drove the development of reverse mortgages in this country beginning in the 1970s.

What is a reverse mortgage?

A reverse mortgage is a home-equity loan for homeowners 62 and older. It helps seniors to turn a part of the equity in their homes into tax-free cash without having to sell the home, give up title or take on the obligation of new monthly mortgage repayments.

John and Jenny Hudson used a reverse mortgage to payoff their mortgage and credit card debts, increasing their spending money by $1,500. In addition, they have $20,000 in a reverse mortgage credit line they can draw on for large unforeseen expenses.

Greta Snyder used a reverse mortgage to halt foreclosure proceedings by paying off her mortgage debts. She has full use of her Social Security income, plus more than $60,000 in a reverse mortgage credit line. Alan and Amy Kaiiser used a reverse mortgage to make one of their retirement dreams—remodeling their Canyon home—come true.

The Hudsons, Greta Snyder and the Kaiisers are not isolated stories among America's older adult population. For them and many others in similar situations, a reverse mortgage is, in Jack Kemp's words, "a new pillar of security ... and a foundation for greater dignity, hope and financial independence in their retirement years."

U.S. beginnings

In 1961, Nelson Haynes of Deering Savings and Loans of Portland, Maine, made the first reverse mortgage loan on record in the U.S. to Nelle Young.

Beginning in the 1970s, through the 80s, and into the 90s, the quest for "new financial instruments for the aged" stimulated much research and experimentation in academia and in the marketplace. Conferences on aging and home equity were organized and recommendations were made for program development. Congressional committees heard testimonies from the

Part I: The new pillar of retirement security

leading minds in the field. Learned papers on using home equity for seniors were published by reverse mortgage pioneers such as Ken Scholen, Yung-Ping Chen, Jack M. Guttentag, Maurice Weinrobe, Bruce Jacobs and others.

Early reverse mortgage programs were developed in Ohio—Equi-Pay, the first reverse mortgage loan program, launched by Arlo Smith of Broadview Savings and Loan in 1977; California—the San Francisco Reverse Annuity Mortgage or RAM program in 1981; Massachusetts—the Massachusetts Elderly Equity program in 1986) and Virginia—the first reverse mortgage line of credit in 1988, among others. The search eventually led to the development of the Federal Housing Administration's (FHA's) Home Equity Conversion Mortgage (HECM) in 1989.

With the FHA-insured HECM showing commercial promise, Fannie Mae launched its own proprietary program, the Homekeeper in 1995. To address the needs of homeowners with higher-end homes, Financial Freedom Senior Funding Corporation introduced a jumbo program, the Cash Account in 1996 (now Cash Account Advantage); Reverse Mortgage of America (bought by Bank of America in 2007) rolled out The Independence Plan in 2006. Since 2007, other proprietary products have come into the market. For more on the early history of reverse mortgages in the U.S., visit Ken Scholen's Web site www.reverse.org/history and read his foundational books.

Participants in the reverse mortgage industry

The participants in the reverse mortgage industry are HUD/FHA, Fannie Mae, Ginnie Mae, lenders (wholesale and retail) and correspondents.

- **The U.S. Department of Housing and Urban Development (HUD)** developed HECM following an act of congress. It regulates the program and provides essential insurance to protect HECM borrowers and lenders. For example, only an FHA-approved lender's employee may take the HECM application. If a lender fails to make payments to a borrower, HUD/FHA steps in to ensure that the borrower continues to receive cash.

- **Fannie Mae** is one of the largest investors in HECM. It continues to play a vital role in the evolution of the industry.

- **Lehman Brothers** is a major force in the secondary market for jumbo

The new pillar of retirement security

(high-end home loans) reverse mortgages. It pioneered the securitization of reverse mortgages in 1999.

- **Bank of America** is an investor in reverse mortgages. It issued the first HECM Mortgage-Backed Security (HECM MBS) in 2006. In 2007, it acquired Reverse Mortgage of America to become a major force in the origination and servicing of reverse mortgages.

- **Ginnie Mae** launched the first standardized HECM Mortgage-Backed Security in 2007. Its goals are to increase liquidity, bring in new lenders, drive down borrowing costs and develop a strong secondary market for reverse mortgages. With its "full faith and credit" guarantee behind HECM lenders, reverse mortgages are ready for the skies.

- **Lenders** are the loan funders, using, wholesale and retail channels to produce loans. In 2008, some major lenders are Wells Fargo Home Mortgage, Financial Freedom Senior Funding Corporation, Bank of America, MetLife Bank, World Alliance Financial, Liberty Reverse Mortgage, Omni Home Financing, First Mariner Bank, Urban Financial Group, Generation Mortgage Company, American Reverse Mortgage, M&T Bank, Academy Mortgage, James B. Nutter and Company, Pacific Reverse Mortgage, and others. For a list of NRMLA-member lenders, go to www.reversemortgage.org/locatealender/tabid/255/default.aspx.

- **Servicers** are the major wholesalers. They manage closed loans for investors.

- **Correspondents** originate reverse mortgage loans for wholesalers, similar to mortgage brokers in the traditional forward mortgage industry.

- **HECM Advisors** are state-licensed mortgage professionals—mortgage brokers, lenders or small community banks—who assist borrowers independently to obtain HECMs through lenders or correspondents. There is speculation that FHA may eliminate the HECM advisor role.

- **Counselors:** There are HECM and HomeKeeper counselors. Jumbo lenders use HECM or some independent counselors. Federal law says HECM customers must receive counseling from HUD-approved counselors.

Part I: The new pillar of retirement security

The senior market

For the size of the reverse mortgage market in the U.S., let's look at some numbers assembled by the Administration on Aging:

- The population of 65-plus-years-olds numbered 35.6 million in 2002, an increase of 3.3 million or 10.2 percent since 1992.
- Americans aged 45-64 who will reach 65 over the next two decades increased by 38 percent
- More than two million people celebrated their 65th birthday in 2002.
- The 65-plus demographic will more than double to 71.5 million by 2030.
- The 85-plus segment will increase from 4.6 million in 2002 to 9.6 million by 2030.
- One in every eight persons or 12.3 percent of the population is an older person.
- 21.8 million households are headed by seniors and 80 percent were owners.
- 73 percent of senior homeowners in 2001 owned their homes "free and clear."

Industry analysts believe there are over 21 million older adults homeowners and that 60 percent of the market is between 65 and 70. According to the Reverse Mortgage Market Index (RMMI), home equity held by seniors aged 62 and older is more than $4 trillion in 2008.

Seven common myths vs. facts

The market is enormous. Many older adults and their advisors know about reverse mortgages today, but some myths persist among mortgage professionals, lawyers, accountants, and even among skilled financial advisers, as we shall see later. Let's look at seven myths and related facts:

Myth #1: The lender will take my home while I am living there, and I'll have no place to live.
Fact: This is not true. The lender puts a lien on the house to secure the loan as with any home equity loan, forward or reverse. The home belongs to the borrower. The homeowner can sell and move on any time. All they need to do is pay off the loan and the lien is gone.

Myth #2: My heirs will be liable for whatever I owe beyond the value of my home.
Fact: This is also untrue. A reverse mortgage is a non-recourse loan, which means the lender is forbidden by law from looking beyond the home's value to satisfy the cash it loaned the customer.

The new pillar of retirement security

Myth #3: The home must be "free and clear" for the borrower to qualify for a reverse mortgage.
Fact: No, it doesn't. People with existing mortgages can qualify for a reverse mortgage. In fact, many seniors use reverse mortgages to get rid of the traditional forward monthly mortgage payment obligation.

Myth #4: Reverse mortgages are for older adults in dire financial situations
Fact: Many older adults have used the extra cash from reverse mortgages to pay for lifestyle needs such as vacations, college tuition payments for their grandchildren, to gain free time for community service, and to buy a new home. Multi-millionaires in California and other states have used reverse mortgages (see Chapter 5).

Myth #5: Reverse mortgages are very risky.
Fact: Yes, they are more risky for lenders, not for consumers. They are the most consumer-friendly home-equity loans around, fortified with a host of anti-predatory features to protect consumers.

Myth #6: Reverse mortgage closing costs are too high.
Fact: Yes, they are high in the first couple of years and then start dropping. The benefits are higher in contrast with "cheaper" forward home equity loans or lines of credit.

Myth #7: The lender will take part of the appreciation in my home.
Fact: There is no shared appreciation feature in today's reverse mortgages. The appreciation in home value belongs to the homeowner.

More than 40 years since the first reverse mortgage loan in the U.S. was originated and almost 20 years since HUD rolled out HECM, the myths remain. You should recognize them for what they are and convey the facts to your customers.

In Chapter 2, we take a deeper look at reverse mortgages.

Resources
- Ken Scholen, *Reverse Mortgages for Beginners* (Apple Valley, MN: NCHEC Press, 1998), pages 108-123
- For more reverse mortgage history, visit www.reverse.org
- National Reverse Mortgage Lenders Association, www.nrmlaonline.org

Part I: The new pillar of retirement security

The new pillar of retirement security

Part I: The new pillar of retirement security

Chapter Two
Financial fuel for a longer ride

Opening quotes ...
"Happiness in retirement can depend in large measure on whether retirees have enough money to enjoy themselves and 'live well.'"
—**Rhonda Whitenack**

Chapter 2 objectives
After studying this chapter, the reader will be able to:
- Describe how reverse mortgages can enhance the new longevity
- Explain the basic building blocks of reverse mortgages
- Understand applicant, as well as property, qualifications
- Discuss the factors influencing how much a borrower gets
- Name cash advance options
- Describe the factors that may cause the lender to call a loan
- Explain specialty or public reverse mortgages

Longevity: The biggest change
If you were asked to mention the most remarkable change engines of the 20th century, you would probably list mass production of cars, aviation, radio, television, space exploration, computers, the Internet, and other notable progress in science, medicine, pharmaceuticals and the arts.

One historic change that may escape your census is the advancement in longevity. We are living longer, adding productive years and improving lives due to progress in medicine, nutrition, public health, and sanitation.

For much of human history, life expectancy at birth was just under 18 years. Plagues of all sorts, infectious diseases, violence, and wars cut life short. A very lucky few lived to 40, 50, 60 or even 70 years of age. In the last 1,000 years, the average life expectancy moved from 25 years to 47 years in

Part I: The new pillar of retirement security

1900. It has zoomed to about 81 years for men and 83 years for women today in the U.S.[1]

From 1900-2000, for example, the number of Americans 65 years of age and older jumped almost 12 times from 3 to 35 million. According to numbers compiled by the Administration on Aging, that number will more than double to 71.5 million by 2030, a mere 22 years from now (see Figure 2.1 below). Just think about it for a minute: It took 100 years to grow the 65-plus age group from 3 to 35 million; it will take about 23 years to more than double that number! During this period, those 85-plus will jump 109 percent from 4.6 million to 9.6 million. There is no question that longevity is one of the biggest changes of modern times. *(See Figure 2.1)*

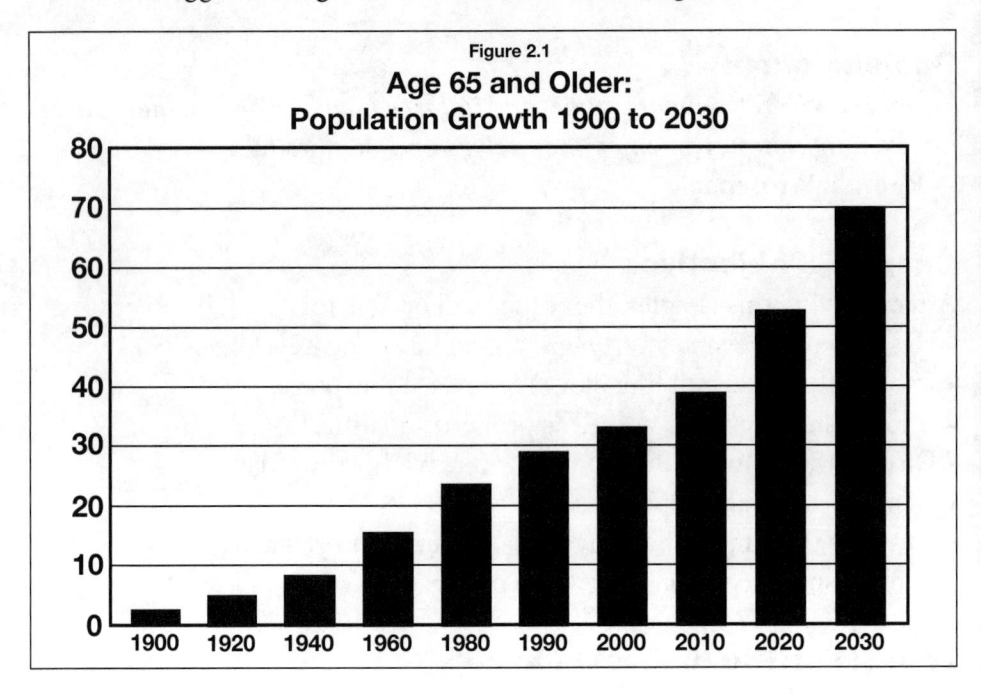

Figure 2.1
Age 65 and Older: Population Growth 1900 to 2030

More financial fuel for the longer ride

Traditionally, financial fuel for the retirement years came from sources such as pension, Social Security, IRS, 401K, stocks and bonds. The home, while making up almost half of most retiree's retirement assets, was considered illiquid. You could not easily turn it into cash. *Home equity was a very valuable asset, but it was not cash.*

With traditional *defined benefit* pension, you serve the company for 30 or 40

Footnote
1-AARP's *Home Made Money* (2003), pages 20-21.

Financial fuel for a longer ride

years and collected a set pension for life. In the era of *defined contribution* plans, workers and companies often do not hang around long enough for workers to qualify. The workers who qualify have the responsibility of managing their own 401K plans. It is not surprising that 45 percent of all workers in a 2004 survey say they have total assets of less than $25,000, outside their homes. Workers who own stocks and bonds are tied to the fortunes of the financial markets. *(See Figure 2.2)*

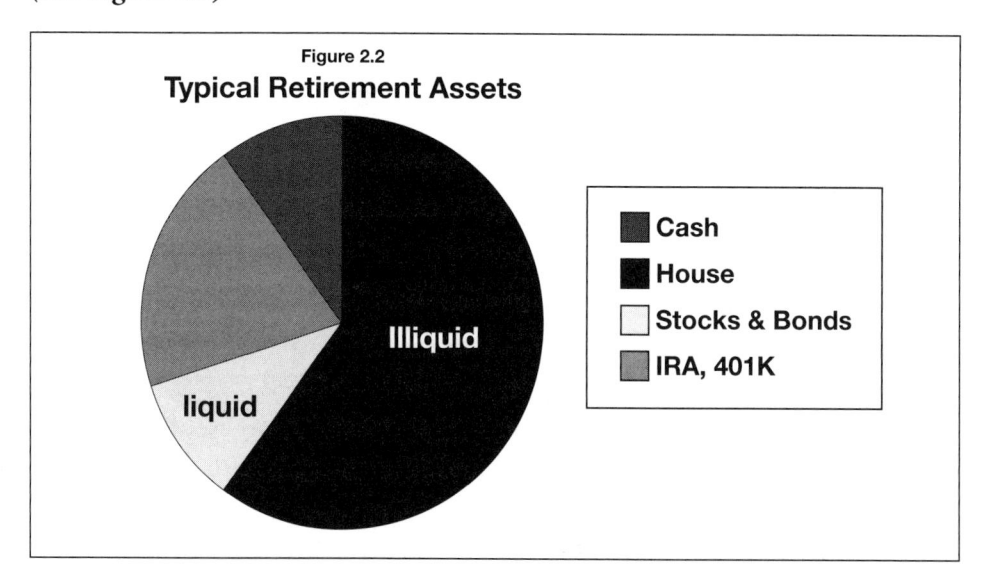

Figure 2.2
Typical Retirement Assets

[Pie chart showing Illiquid and liquid portions, with legend: Cash, House, Stocks & Bonds, IRA, 401K]

Social Security retirement benefits are the only income source for 20 percent of retirees who are 65 and older. The average monthly Social Security check for a retired worker is approximately $900. A couple gets about $1,525. It's not surprising that many older adults, according to a study by New York City-based think tank, Demos, are loading up on credit card debt.

A key to unlocking the financial fuel pump

By far, the largest asset most retired people have is their home. Until now, retired homeowners with huge home equity have had two ways to get cash from their homes: they can sell their home for cash or they can take out a home equity loan or a line of credit. But they will have to qualify on credit and income. They have to deal with monthly payments. For those retirees who do not want to move from their homes or take on the burden of monthly mortgage payments that come with traditional "forward" home equity loans or lines of credit, *a reverse mortgage is the key to unlocking the financial fuel pump.*

Part I: The new pillar of retirement security

Home equity into tax-free cash

So, what is a reverse mortgage again? Let's recall the definition of a reverse mortgage from Chapter 1.

A reverse mortgage is a home equity loan for homeowners 62 and older. It helps seniors to turn a part of the equity in their homes into tax-free cash without having to sell the home, give up title or ownership, or take on the obligation of new monthly mortgage payments.

Let's look at the parts of this definition:
- A home equity loan
- Helps senior homeowners, 62 and better
- Turns part of home equity into tax-free cash
- No giving up title to their homes
- No selling their homes
- No taking on the burden of new monthly mortgage payments

Let's ask another question: What makes reverse mortgages different from other home loans?

The DNA of reverse mortgages

Basic building blocks of reverse mortgages are as follows:
- Converts home equity into cash
- Pays the borrower
- No monthly repayments
- Loan advances are tax-free
- Credit not often required
- Income not required
- Borrower retains title and possession
- Lender puts a lien on the property
- Debt rises, equity falls
- Must be first lien loans
- Home value limits debt
- Non-recourse loans
- Flexible cash advance choices
- Line of Credit often grows
- Lump-sum repayment
- Consumer education required

Financial fuel for a longer ride

1. **Converts home equity into cash:** A reverse mortgage turns home equity into cash for homeowner 62 or older.

2. **Pays the borrower:** Lender pays the borrower. It is the opposite (reverse) of traditional borrower/lender relationship.

3. **No monthly payment:** Borrower makes no monthly repayment for as long as the home is their primary residence; there is no worry about missing payment and losing the home because there is none to make.

4. **Loan advances are tax-free:** The IRS considers payments borrower receives from a reverse lender as a loan advances; therefore, no tax is due.

5. **No income or credit to qualify:** With traditional mortgage lending, a lender checks your income and your credit to qualify you for a loan. Generally, with a reverse mortgage, income and credit are irrelevant, but there is a slight exception for the FHA-insured reverse mortgage called Home Equity Conversion Mortgage or HECM. If your customer defaults on any federal debt, it may prevent them from getting the HECM loan. With a satisfactory payment agreement with the federal agency your customer owed, the HECM may be allowed.

6. **Borrower retains title and possession:** In a reverse mortgage, borrower keeps title and possession of property. Because borrower is owner, not the bank or lender, borrower is responsible for paying property taxes and homeowner's insurance.

7. **Lender puts a lien on property:** As with a traditional forward mortgage, in a reverse mortgage, the bank or lender puts a lien on property to secure loan's repayment.

8. **Debt rises, equity falls:** A reverse mortgage is a "rising-debt/falling equity loan." As the bank or lender pays you, your debt rises and your equity in the home falls. Again, this is the reverse of what happens in a traditional forward mortgage where, as you make monthly cash repayments, your equity rises and your debt falls each month until the debt is paid in full and the house is "free and clear." With a reverse mortgage, you are using cash advances from lender to take out equity; with a traditional forward mortgage, you are using cash payments to lender to build up equity.

Part I: The new pillar of retirement security

9. **Must be a first lien:** A reverse mortgage must be in a first lien position. If there is a lien on the home, it must be paid off or, in the case of single-purpose reverse mortgages, subordinated or placed in a lower lien position. As the industry evolves, we could see emergence of second lien reverse mortgages.

10. **Home value limits debt:** A reverse mortgage debt can never be greater than the value of the home securing the debt. This is one of several safety features built into it. For example, if the lender advances $200,000 and, at the end of the loan, the home appraises for $150,000, the lender can only collect $150,000 from the borrower or her estate, not a penny more! With HECMs, the lender can file an insurance claim with FHA to make up the difference.

11. **Non-recourse loans:** Reverse mortgages are non-recourse loans. Lender can only look to the value of the home to satisfy reverse borrower's debts. The lender cannot touch any other assets borrower owns. Again, this is part of a system of safeguards designed into these special home loans. This feature protects borrowers and their heirs.

12. **Flexible cash advance choices:** Reverse mortgage borrowers can receive their available home cash in a lump sum payment at closing. They can get equal monthly payments for a specified period (for example, 10 years); this is called a "term payment." They can receive equal monthly payments for as long as they live in the home; this is called a "tenure payment." They can set up a reverse mortgage creditline that can be used as needed; or they can opt for a combination of a creditline and term or a creditline and tenure.

13. **A line of credit that often grows (HECM and jumbos, except Home-Keeper):** A reverse mortgage creditline, specifically the creditlines of FHA-insured HECM and proprietary jumbo reverse programs grow over time, making more cash available for the borrower. This feature assumes home appreciation and aging customer. Fannie Mae's Homekeeper is an exception. It has a flat creditline.

14. **Lump sum repayment:** You gradually pay off your traditional forward mortgage in monthly installments. With a reverse mortgage, payment is due in one lump sum when: (1) Last borrower moves out for more than 12 months; (2) Last borrower sells home; and (3) Last borrower dies.

Financial fuel for a longer ride

15. **Consumer education:** Reverse mortgage customers are required to receive consumer education. For HECMs, consumer education is provided free by HUD-approved reverse mortgage counselors. For Fannie Mae's Homekeeper program, counselors can be HUD-approved or Fannie Mae-approved. And for the proprietary jumbos, independent counselors are available. Some jumbo lenders use FHA-approved counselors trained in their programs.

Available programs

Besides FHA-insured HECM and Fannie Mae's proprietary HomeKeeper, some programs and their owners include Cash Account Advantage (Financial Freedom), The Independence Plan and Senior Equity Maximizer (Bank of America), Generation Plus (Generation Mortgage Company), Reverse Select (MetLife Bank), Cash Keeper (Sun West Mortgage), and Simple60 and Equity Plus Advantage (World Alliance Financial).

Applicant qualifications

Generally, an applicant must meet the following tests:

- Be 62 or better; where there are two or more borrowers, the youngest must be 62 (some programs have lowered age-eligibility to under 62);
- Own the home "free and clear" or with enough equity for reverse mortgage to pay off your existing mortgage;
- Home must be primary residence; they must live in it more than six months in a year (second homes are eligible for some jumbo programs);
- Applicant must receive consumer education.

Property qualifications

Depending on program chosen, the following property types *may be* eligible:
- Single family residence
- One- to four-unit dwelling with the borrower occupying one unit as a main residence
- Condominium units
- Planned Unit Developments (PUDs)
- Manufactured homes on permanent foundations
- Second homes
- "Gentleman" farms (hobby farms)
- Excess acreage property

Cooperative units are now eligible for HECM loans. Owners of co-ops in

Part I: The new pillar of retirement security

New York State can qualify for Cash Account Advantage, Generation Plus, Reverse Select, Cash Keeper, Equity Plus Advantage, Fixed 4 Life XL, Flex XL and others. In Chapters 3, 4 and 5, we will see program-specific property qualifications for HECM, HomeKeeper and jumbos.

How much can a borrower get?

Amount of cash a reverse mortgage borrower gets depends on:
- Age
- Home value/built-up equity
- Home location (HECM only)
- Current interest rates
- Type of reverse mortgage program chosen
- Interest rate adjustment period selected
- Number of borrowers (HomeKeeper and jumbos)

Age: While 62 is the minimum age for these loans, as a rule, the older the borrower, the more they get. For example, a 72-year-old will get more than a mere 62-year-old. Actuarial assumptions about life expectancy drive this basic rule.

Home value/built-up equity: The more valuable your home is and the more equity you have accrued, the more you can borrow.

Home location: At the time this book was printed, it was not clear whether the Housing and Economic Recovery Act of 2008 (signed into law on July 30, 2008) authorized a single national HECM loan limit. If it does, it may have a floor of $417,000 and a ceiling of $625,000. If it doesn't, we are back to the usual area-by-area arrangement.

Current interest rates: Again, as a rule, when current interest rates are low, you can borrow more. When they are high, you get less cash.

Type of reverse mortgage program chosen: In the low-end program group, FHA's HECM gives the borrower more money than Fannie Mae's Homekeeper. If your property is valued at $625,000 and above, jumbos may give you more.

Interest rate adjustment period selected: Within FHA HECM, monthly adjusting option gives your borrower more money than annually adjusting because monthly adjusting has a lower interest rate.

Financial fuel for a longer ride

Number of borrowers: The number of borrowers is irrelevant with HECM, but they impact available equity with HomeKeeper and jumbos.

Cash advance options

Your reverse mortgage customer has five cash advance options (a.k.a. payment plans) as follows:

1. Customer may receive net available cash as a *lump sum* at closing;
2. Customer may choose a fixed amount (say, $900) for a fixed number of years (say, 10 years). This is called a *term* option or plan;
3. Customer may get a fixed amount ($500) for as long as she lives in her home as a primary residence. This is a *tenure* plan;
4. Customer may put her entire net cash in a *creditline* where she can access her cash as needed; or
5. Customer may take a combination of term and creditline or *modified term* or tenure and creditline, or *modified tenure*.

A different line of credit

HECM and jumbo reverse mortgage creditlines are designed to grow, making more equity available for your customer. Homekeeper has a flat creditline.

Payback time

A reverse mortgage is a loan against borrower's home. It is repayable when last borrower moves out of home for more than 12 months, sells home or dies. Lender has the right to call the loan or declare it 'due and payable' if any of the following events occur:

- Bankruptcy
- Failure to pay property taxes or homeowner's insurance
- Failure to maintain home, causing deterioration of home value
- Donation or abandonment of home
- Fraud
- Eminent domain or government wants the home for public purposes
- Renting part of the home
- Adding a new owner to the title
- Changing the home's zoning classification
- Taking out new debt against the home that jeopardizes the reverse mortgage's first lien position (in HECM's case, first and second lien positions)

Part I: The new pillar of retirement security
Specialty reverse mortgages
HECM, Homekeeper, jumbos and others to come are marketplace reverse-mortgages that borrowers can use to meet any need. There are two specialty or single-purpose reverse mortgages older adults can use to pay property taxes and to repair or improve their homes: Property Tax Deferral (PTD) loans and Deferred Payment Loans (DPLs).

Property tax deferral (PTD) loans
Property tax deferral (PTD) loans are designed for seniors to pay their property taxes by some state and local governments. Qualifications for these loans change from state to state and from county to county, but borrowers in most cases must be 65-plus years of age and have low- to moderate-incomes. They may not be available in all states.

Deferred payment loans (DPLs)
Similar to PTDs, DPLs are given to seniors for repairs and home improvements. They are project-specific, such as roof repair, heating, stairs, floors, plumbing, storm windows, insulation, ramps, rails and grab bar installation. These so-called public reverse mortgages are the lowest cost reverse mortgages your customers will find, but they are unavailable to all older adults and are restricted to specific purposes. Repayment is usually not due until borrower sells property.

Resources
- Ken Dychtwald, *Age Power*: www.agewave.com
- Demos: www.demos.org
- Administration on Aging: www.aoa.org

Financial fuel for a longer ride

Part I: The new pillar of retirement security

Chapter Three
Uncle Sam's gift to older adults

Opening quotes ...
"HECM ... revolutionized the industry."
—**Sarah F. Hulbert**

"If you are not in the HECM business, you are not in the reverse mortgage business."
—-**James A. Brodsky**

Chapter 3 objectives
After studying this chapter, the reader will be able to:
- Explain role of HECMs in the reverse mortgage industry
- Know HECM-specific applicant and property qualifications
- Describe HECM cash advance options
- Appreciate how customer needs influence cash advance options
- Discuss three HECM scenarios
- Explain how HECM creditline works
- Describe HECM creditline growth formula
- Know the elements of HECM's costs
- Explain the function of HECM's Upfront MIP
- Define ten key HECM concepts
- Explain HECM's rapid reduced-cost refinance
- Discuss HECM's refinance anti-churning disclosure
- Explain five-times and within-five-years HECM refinance rules
- Advance 10 reasons for HECM's market dominance
- Offer seven reasons for concern about HECM
- Discuss anticipated HECM program changes

Part I: The new pillar of retirement security

HECM rules the reverse space

In U.S. reverse mortgage industry, FHA-insured Home Equity Conversion Mortgage (HECM) rules. It enjoys a dominant market share, estimated at over 95 percent. Because of its vigorous market position, HECM has become synonymous with reverse mortgages.

Created under the Housing and Community Development Act of 1987 (Public Laws 100-242, 02/05/1988), HECM is the only reverse mortgage backed by the federal government. The federal agency that brought HECM to life is the U.S. Department of Housing and Urban Development through its Federal Housing Administration unit. So, you will see it referred to as FHA's HECM or HUD/FHA HECM.

FHA supports the market in HECM reverse mortgages by insuring lenders and borrowers against loss. For lenders, FHA insurance picks up the difference if they lend more than the house is worth at loan's maturity. For borrowers, FHA insurance ensures that the cash advances they receive from lenders will continue even if lenders go belly up. Through the HECM insurance fund, the U.S. government is lender of last resort on HECM loans.

HECM applicant qualifications

To qualify for a HECM loan, applicant and co-applicant:
- Must be 62 or older; with multiple borrowers, the youngest must be 62;
- Must either own home "free and clear" or have an existing mortgage that can be paid off or subordinated;
- Must live in the home as a primary resident; and
- Must receive HECM-specific consumer education from a HUD-approved housing counseling agency (where the borrower lacks legal capacity, consumer education can be done with a power of attorney or a court-appointed conservator/guardian).

Issues that can disqualify a borrower from getting a HECM loan include the following:
- Default on debt to any federal government agency such as the Small Business Administration (SBA), Federal Student Loan Administration, VA-guaranteed loans or IRS tax liens.
- Being on HUD's Limited Denial of Participation (LDP) list or on the list of persons suspended, excluded or debarred from HUD and other federal programs by the General Services Administration (GSA).

Uncle Sam's gift to older adults

HECM property qualifications

An applicant's home must be:
- A single family residence;
- One- to four-unit dwelling with borrower occupying one unit as a primary residence;
- A condominium unit;
- A unit in a Planned Unit Development (PUD) or in a Master Planned Communities;
- A manufactured home with a permanent foundation, built after June 15, 1976;
- A property held in a living trust that meets HUD's requirements

HECM lending limits

Amount an applicant gets from a HECM loan depends on:
- **Age:** older customer gets more
- **Home value:** More valuable homes get more
- **Home location:** FHA's county-by-county lending limits rule; could change soon
- **Interest rates:** Lower rates give customer more
- **Adjustment Period Selected:** Monthly adjusting ARMs give more cash than annually adjusting; monthly rates are lower

(See Figures 3.1 and 3.2)

Figure 3.1
HECM Principal Limit Factors
for Selected Ages and Interest Rates

Interest Rate*	Age of Borrower at Loan Origination		
	65	75	85
7.0%	0.489	0.609	0.738
8.5%	0.369	0.503	0.660
10.0%	0.280	0.416	0.589

*Expected Rate (e.g., 10-Year Treasury Rate + Lender's Margin)

→ Factor increases with age

↓ Factor decreases with interest rate

Source: HUD

Part I: The new pillar of retirement security

Figure 3.2
How Principal Limit Factors Determine Payment Limits
75 Year Old Borrower and 7 Percent Expected Interest Rate

Appraised Value & Maximum Claim	$100,000.00
Times Principal Limit Factor	0.609
Initial Principal Limit	**60,900.00**
Less:	
Upfront Premium	(2,000.00)
Loan Closing Costs	(3,000.00)
Servicing Fee Set Aside	(4,084.96)
Initial Cash to Borrower	(1,815.04)
Net Principal Limit	**50,000.00**
Maximum Monthly Tenure Payment (without a line of credit)	367.20
Maximum Line of Credit (without monthly payments)	50,000.00

Source: HUD (PD&R)

Figures 3.1 and 3.2 illustrate how a principal limit factor, based on a borrower's age and current interest rate, combines with other data to arrive at how much a borrower gets from a HECM loan. The principal limit factors are set using unique computer software that makes HUD's expected revenues (from borrowers' premiums) equal its expected costs (HUD's payments to lenders when a borrowers' longevity or home-value declines result in losses). The HUD software uses complicated guesses about house-price growth, death and move-out rates to generate these factors.

Because other data needed to determine how much a borrower gets (such as their starting home value and their lender's loan fees) differs for each loan, the final loan amount calculation is customized for each borrower.

When your HECM software gives you those neat numbers on paper, *these are the drivers*. A list of principal limit factors at various interest rates and borrower's age is available for review in Appendix 20 of the HECM Handbook 4235.1 Rev.1. See link below:

www.hud.gov/offices/adm/hudclips/handbooks/hsgh/4235.1/index.cfm

HECM Cash Advance options
An HECM borrower can get her cash out as a:
- **Lump sum** at closing;
- Fixed monthly advances for a fixed period or (**term**);
- Fixed monthly advances for as long as the borrower lives in her home as a principal residence or (**tenure**);
- **Creditline** for borrower to use as needed;
- Combination of a term and a creditline (**modified term**); or
- Combination of tenure and a creditline (**modified tenure**).

So we have *lump sum, term, tenure, creditline, modified term* and *modified tenure* as cash advance choices available to borrowers under the HECM loan.

Personal needs determine cash advance options
Generally, cash advance option depends on borrower's need or needs. For example, if a customer's income from pension, 401K, IRA, or Social Security is insufficient to meet her monthly expenses, she might consider a term or a tenure cash advance plan. If customer is concerned about her ability to deal with unforeseen large bills, she may select a modified term or a modified tenure option. A term option usually offers more monthly cash because it is for a period, say seven years. While a tenure option normally gives less monthly cash because tenure is for an indefinite period, a lump sum cash advance choice is good for someone who wants to make her home age-friendly. Whatever the customer's needs, HECM cash advance options are designed to address them. Let's look at three scenarios.

HECM scenario number one: Low monthly income
Challenge: Bob Tupack's monthly income is $900 from Social Security. Because of the third constant in life—inflation—his monthly expenses have jumped to $1,200 a month, a budgetary shortfall of $300.
Solution: Mr. Tupack takes a modified tenure giving him an extra $400 a month to meet the shortfall with a creditline for big-ticket needs when they arise.

HECM scenario number two: No savings for contingencies
Challenge: Julie Rossner has a monthly income of $2,500 and expenses of $2,200. She has a little monthly surplus, but she has no savings for emergencies in case the furnace goes out or a leaky roof needs fixing.
Solution: A HECM loan gives her $95,000 and she puts it in a growing HECM creditline. Bye-bye worry.

Part I: The new pillar of retirement security

HECM scenario number three: Serious cash for major home modification

Challenge: John Bullcock wants to make his bathroom and his kitchen wheelchair-accessible. His monthly income of $1,900 is fine. Average estimate for all the work he intends to do came to $35,000. He has only $4,000 in savings.

Solution: A HECM lump sum gives him the money he needs for home modification. He leaves the balance in a creditline.

How HECM creditline works

HECM creditline is a unique feature. Unlike forward home equity lines of credit or HELOCs, it is engineered to grow monthly, thus increasing home equity available to customers for conversion into cash. The growth is ***not*** like earning interest on a certificate of deposit. ***It is home equity growth***. For older adults on fixed incomes, it is a significant device. How does this home-equity-growth machine work? It is simple ... *the HECM creditline is designed to grow by one twelfth (1/12) of the going note rate, plus 50 basis points.*

For example, Alan Cashmore opted for a HECM creditline in a recent reverse mortgage transaction. The net available cash to 79-year-old Mr. Cashmore was $120,000. His loan balance at closing was $20,000 (he took out $12,000 cash and incurred $8,000 in HECM costs). The going rate on the $20,000 loan balance is 3.5 percent. Meanwhile, Mr. Cashmore decides to put the remaining equity ($100,000) in a HECM creditline, growing at 1/12 of four percent (3.50 + 0.50)/12 = 0.33 monthly. Thanks to the $12,000 cash he took out at closing, his regular Social Security and pension checks, and his own considerable dollar-stretching skills, Mr. Cashmore didn't have to touch his HECM creditline for a while. Let's see how the $100,000 in equity grows in six months:

- Month 1: $100,000 x 0.0033 = $330 + $100,000 = $100,330
- Month 2: $100,330 x 0.0033 = $331.09 + $100,330 = $100,661.09
- Month 3: $100,661.09 x 0.0033 = $332.18 + $100,661.09 = $100,993.27
- Month 4: $100,993.27 x 0.0033 = $333.28 + $100,993.27 = $101,326.55
- Month 5: $101,326.55 x 0.0033 = $334.38 + $101,326.55 = $101,660.93
- Month 6: $101,660.93 x 0.0033 = $335.48 + $101,660.93 = $101,996.41

As our calculation shows above, after six months, Mr. Cashmore's HECM creditline would have grown by almost $2,000! Calculation assumes stable initial interest rate over the six months period, but we know

Uncle Sam's gift to older adults

the world works differently. Whenever rates go up or down, growth multiplier (**0.0033**) will change, but the *basic growth formula* remains constant as follows:

HECM Creditline growth formula
Initial interest rate   3.50 percent
+
50 basis points   0.50
=
HECM creditline growth rate of four percent
Growth rate divided by 12 months (4 percent/12 = 0 .0033 or growth multiplier)

HECM borrower costs
HECM costs include the following:

Origination fee
The Housing and Economic Recovery Act of 2008 (signed into law July 30, 2008) has introduced a new formula for calculating HECM origination fees as follows:
The HECM origination fee is two percent of first $200,000 of maximum claim amount (MCA), plus one percent of the balance above $200,000. Fee is capped at $6,000. For example, if the MCA is $275,000, origination fee will be calculated as follows:

    A. First $200,000 x 2%   = $ 4,000
    B. Balance $75,000 x 1%   = $ 750
    C. Total origination fee   = $ 4,750

Closing costs
Standard mortgage closing costs in the customer's locality.
Other closing costs:

- Appraisal
- Title insurance
- Credit report
- Document preparation
- Recording fees
- Escrow/settlement fees
- Flood certification fee
- Attorney's fees
- Title examination fee
- County tax
- State stamp taxes
- Termite inspection fee

Initial mortgage insurance premium (Initial MIP)
Two percent of lending limit or appraised home value. Borrower pays FHA

Part I: The new pillar of retirement security

to insure the continuation of cash advances in case lender defaults. It protects lender against home-price decline at maturity.

Monthly mortgage insurance premium (Monthly MIP)

The monthly MIP is 0.50 percent of loan balance. To use Mr. Cashmore's example again, the monthly MIP would be 0.50 percent of $20,000 = $100/12 or $8.33 per month. Fee goes to HUD.

Servicing fee

Servicing fee ranges from $30-$35 a month. For fixed-rate HECMs where servicing fee is not built into the rate, the fee can be up to $30 per month.

Interest rates

Interest rates are pegged to the LIBOR (London Interbank Offer Rate) and the CMT (Constant Maturity Treasury) indices, plus a margin set by investor. FHA forbids the commingling of indices. If you use LIBOR to calculate the expected rate, it is LIBOR for the note rate, same for CMT.

Monthly ARM

One-month LIBOR or one-month CMT + margin (there is no annual interest rate cap, but there is a lifetime cap of 10 percent above the initial rate).

Annual ARM

One-year LIBOR or one-year CMT + margin (there is an annual interest rate cap of two percent and a lifetime cap of five percent above the initial rate).

Fixed-rate HECM

Fixed-rate HECMs are available. With fixed-rate HECMs, the expected rate is also the note. If the lender uses seven percent to calculate the principal limit, the note rate must be seven percent.

Switching between ARM and fixed

Unless borrowers want to refinance their HECMs, FHA disallows switching from ARM to fixed and vice-versa.

Uncle Sam's gift to older adults

HECM ARMs

HECM ARMs	Eligible index types	
	Periodic adjustments	**Expected average mortgage interest rate**
Monthly adjustable	1-month CMT	10-year CMT
	1-year CMT	10-year CMT
	1-month LIBOR	10-year LIBOR swap
Annually adjustable	1-year CMT	10-year CMT
	1-year LIBOR	10-year LIBOR swap

Source: FHA

Repaying the HECM

HECM loan is repaid in one lump sum when last borrower sells home, moves out, or dies. Other events may give lender the right to declare HECM loan "due and payable" as follows:
- Allowing the home to deteriorate, except for normal wear and tear;
- Failing to live in the home for more than 12 months in a row;
- Neglecting to pay property taxes or hazard insurance;
- Violating terms of loan agreement; or
- Filing petition for bankruptcy.

Defining key HECM concepts

HECMs and reverse mortgages have spun new concepts and brought new vocabulary into residential mortgage lending. Below are some concepts that will enhance your understanding of the HECM loan:

■ **Maximum claim amount (MCA)** is the top amount FHA will insure a loan for in a county. This amount, which changes from county to county and increases every year, may be the appraised value of the home or it may be more or less. Check your county's loan limit at https://entp.hud.gov/idapp/html/hicostlook.cfm. At industry's urging, HUD has asked Congress to set one national lending limit for HECM. Change could come in 2007.

Part I: The new pillar of retirement security

- **Principal limit (PL)** is the top dollar amount available to customer before loan costs are deducted.

- **Net principal limit (NPL)** is the amount available to customer after loan closing costs and liens are deducted.

- **Expected rate (ER) (expected average interest rate)** is the rate used to decide how much a HECM customer can borrow. It is based on 10-year U.S. Treasury Note plus a margin.

- **Initial interest rate (IIR)** is the rate actually applied to a HECM customer loan balance (note rate). It is based on the one-year U.S. Treasury Bill plus a margin.

- **Servicing fee set-aside (SFSA)** is non-cash equity reserved to pay monthly servicing fees for projected life of loan. SFSA could be eliminated; it's confusing to customers.

- **Unpaid principal balance (UPB)** is the loan balance that will have to be paid at maturity. Also called loan balance …

- **Initial mortgage insurance premium (IMIP)** is premium HECM customer pays FHA for insuring cash advances will continue if lender defaults; it also protects lender against home price decline at maturity. It's two percent of lending limit or maximum claim amount (MCA).

- **Monthly mortgage insurance premium (MMIP)** is another insurance fee. It is 0.50 percent of the outstanding balance every month divided by 12. Again, using the Alan Cashmore example above, it will be $20,000 X 0.50 = $100/12 = $8.33. So, $8.33 is added to Mr. Cashmore's outstanding balance every month and remitted to FHA.

- **Total annual loan cost (TALC)** is to HECMs and reverse mortgages what the annual percentage rate (APR) is to traditional forward mortgages; it is more rigorous than APR. It helps customers compare costs on a "grape to grape" basis.

HECM's rapid reduced-cost refinance

In traditional forward mortgage universe, when interest rates fall, whether or

Uncle Sam's gift to older adults

not there is a parallel rise in home values, refinance activities increase because homeowners want to reduce their mortgage financing costs. When interest rates fall and home values rise, home equity increases. Until April 26, 2004, HECM customer could not take advantage of increased equity in her home through a refinance as a forward mortgage customer could easily do. On that day, HUD authorized HECM refinance that is not only faster and cheaper, but also safer.

To make it faster, HUD said *borrowers could skip required HECM counseling if three conditions were met* (See conditions for safety below). To make it cheaper, HUD decreed that *initial mortgage insurance premium should apply only to the additional maximum claim amount* (MCA, see key concepts). For example, when 76-year-old Paul Hauser took out a HECM loan for the first time in May 2001, his maximum claim amount (MCA) was $110,000 and his original principal limit (PL) was $65,000. Thanks to low rates and home-price appreciation in his suburban Twin Cities' county, by June 2004 when he decided to refinance, his maximum claim amount has jumped to $220,000 and his principal limit is now set at $130,000. So, initial mortgage insurance premium will apply to the difference between Mr. Hauser's original MCA $110,000 and the new MCA $220,000 ($220,000-$110,000 = $110,000). Therefore, FHA two percent initial MIP applies to $110,000, not $220,000. We'll do the refinance calculation in Chapter 12.

To make HECM refinance safer, HUD decreed as follows:

The financing HECM lender must provide the HECM borrower a new piece of paper called **HECM Anti-Churning Disclosure form** (HUD Form 92901). Basically, this form tells the customer that lender will not encourage revolving-door refinance that benefits lender at the customer's expense.

The 5-Times Rule: Refinancing HECM lender must ensure that additional principal limit (benefit to customer) exceeds total refinance costs five times.

The Within-5-Years Rule: The HECM refinance must be within five years of the original HECM loan.

The three conditions must be met for HECM counseling requirement to be waived for a refinance. Waiving the HECM counseling makes the HECM refinance process faster; however, HUD does not want to sacrifice safety for speed. So, it ingeniously linked them! For HECM lenders who want a quicker refinance process, the rules are clear: Make sure customer gets anti-churning disclosure, make certain customer's principal limit exceeds refinance costs at least five times, and certify that refinance transaction happens within five years of original HECM loan.

Why HECM loan is strong

Below are reasons for HECM's market leadership:

- Federal government insurance guarantees borrower will receive cash, even if lender goes belly up;
- No monthly repayment burden, freeing up cash flow for better quality of life in one's slow-down years;
- Tax-free cash with some strings attached;
- Free up cash flow by paying off forward mortgages, credit cards and other debts;
- Variable interest rates with caps, linked to U.S. Treasury index and margins set by Fannie Mae;
- Provides more cash than alternatives in low-to-moderate reverse market;
- Flexible cash advance options;
- Innovative creditline;
- Financed closing costs;
- Loan balance limited by home's value (protects other assets and heirs);
- No income or credit qualification (except credit review for federal-debt delinquency);
- Homeowner retains title and possession of home;
- Required consumer education by HUD-approved counseling agencies to confirm consumers make informed decisions; and
- Rapid, reduced-cost, churning-proof refinance.

Some reasons to pause

Here are reasons to pause:

- A rising debt loan means home equity will decline … heirs may have no home to inherit;
- Expensive for short-term (less than five years) use;
- No single higher national loan limit restricts loan size, this complicates marketing and administration;
- Lack of awareness among seniors and their advisors persists;
- Delinquent federal debt prevents access to program;
- Counseling requirement may slow process;

- HECM loan process can be slow;
- Program is too dominant in the market (could discourage competition);
- Government regulations and controls stifle program innovation; and
- HECM loan is not durable (when last customer leaves home for healthcare facility for more than 12 months, lender may call loan).

HECM changes ahead

HECM loan is the reverse mortgage industry's bread and butter. We have seen why it is strong above. Strong as it may, HECM needs improvement. We can expect the following changes in the coming months:

- ■ **Volume cap removal:** Federal law setting up the HECM program capped origination volume at 250,000. The industry could reach that limit before you read this sentence. Volume cap removal is vital to industry, and it will be removed.
- ■ **Reduced initial MIP:** HUD could reduce initial MIP to one percent from two and increase annual premium from 0.5 percent to a higher percentage to help combat HECM's association with high upfront costs.
- ■ **HECM for home purchase:** HUD has also proposed legislation that will add a home purchase program. Expect it.

Together, these anticipated changes could strengthen HECM's hold on the reverse mortgage market and provide a template for expected private-label program development in the months ahead. For now, as NRMLA's general counsel has said: "If you are not in the HECM business, you are not in the reverse mortgage business."

In Chapter 4, we look at Fannie Mae's HomeKeeper.

Resources
- HUD: www.hud.gov/buying/rvrsmort.cfm
- AARP's Home Made Money: www.aarp.org/revmort
- Fannie Mae's Money From Home: www.efanniemae.com/lc/publications/borrowers/pdf/moneyfromhome.pdf
- NRMLA: www.nrmlaonline.org
- www.hecmresources.org

Part I: The new pillar of retirement security

Chapter Four
HomeKeeper: Tearing down cash barriers to aging

Chapter 4 objectives
After studying this chapter, the reader will be able to:
- Discuss differences between HomeKeeper and HECM in borrower and property qualifications, cash advance options, and costs
- Explain how HomeKeeper for Home Purchase works
- Advance three reasons for HomeKeeper
- Offer three reasons to pause for HomeKeeper

A new home, a mortgage and no monthly payments
Linda Loaner wants to be closer to her only daughter and grandchildren in Arizona. At 79 years of age, she is in reasonably good health, except for recurring bouts of arthritis, which her doctor says could be better managed in a warmer climate. Thanks to careful planning by her late husband, Larry, Mrs. Loaner's savings and income are strong. Although she loves the Twin Cities area that she has lived in for more than 50 years, she longs to be near her daughter and grandchildren in sunny Tempe, Ariz.

Except for a small lien, her home is paid for. Mrs. Loaner, like many people her age, does not want to worry about any new mortgage payments, even if she could qualify for one. While she wants to be closer to her daughter, she does not want to be a burden on her by moving in with her and her family. Linda wants to own her own place closer to her daughter, but does not want to exhaust her savings or the sale proceeds from her Twin Cities home.

As industry leading as the FHA's HECM is, it does not address the needs of customers like Linda Loaner or the higher loan-limit needs of older adults with property values higher than the uneven county-by-county loan limits of HECM. With higher national HECM loan limits coming, this may no longer be the case, except

Part I: The new pillar of retirement security

for multi-million dollar homes. To meet these market needs, Fannie Mae launched the HomeKeeper reverse mortgage in 1995. In 1998, the secondary mortgage market colossus offered the *HomeKeeper for Home Purchase*, a program tailor-made for older adults like Linda Loaner. Before we return to Mrs. Loaner's scenario, let's take a closer look at Fannie Mae's HomeKeeper reverse mortgage.

HomeKeeper customer qualifications
HomeKeeper customer must:
- Be 62 or older like HECM's
- Own the home "free and clear" or carry a mortgage balance that can be paid off with a HomeKeeper loan, similar to HECM;
- Make home her primary residence, like HECM;
- Limit number of borrowers to three (HECM has no limit on number of borrowers);
- Keep property taxes and hazard insurance current, similar to HECM;
- Attend reverse mortgage consumer education using Fannie Mae's curriculum.

HomeKeeper property qualifications
To qualify for a HomeKeeper reverse mortgage, a property must:
- Be a one-unit, single-family residence, like HECM;
- Be a condominium unit or a unit in a planned unit development (PUD) that meets standard Fannie Mae guidelines; or
- Be a property held in a trust or controlled by a power of attorney that meets Fannie Mae's guidelines.

Factors affecting HomeKeeper's loan amount
The following factors determine a borrower's loan limit:
- Age (or ages) of borrowers.
- Number of borrowers.
- Adjusted property value.

The exact relationship of these factors in calculating borrower's lending limit is known to Fannie Mae. What is known is that the higher the property value, older and fewer the borrowers, the more they get. All property values are adjusted to conform to Fannie Mae's annually adjusted loan limits. For 2008, it is $417,000. If borrower's home appraises for $470,000, it will be "adjusted" to $417,000, thus the "adjusted property value" factor. Homes that appraise below the limit need no adjustment. *(See Figure 4.1)*

Homekeeper: Tearing down cash barriers to aging

Figure 4.1
HomeKeeper Borrowing Power

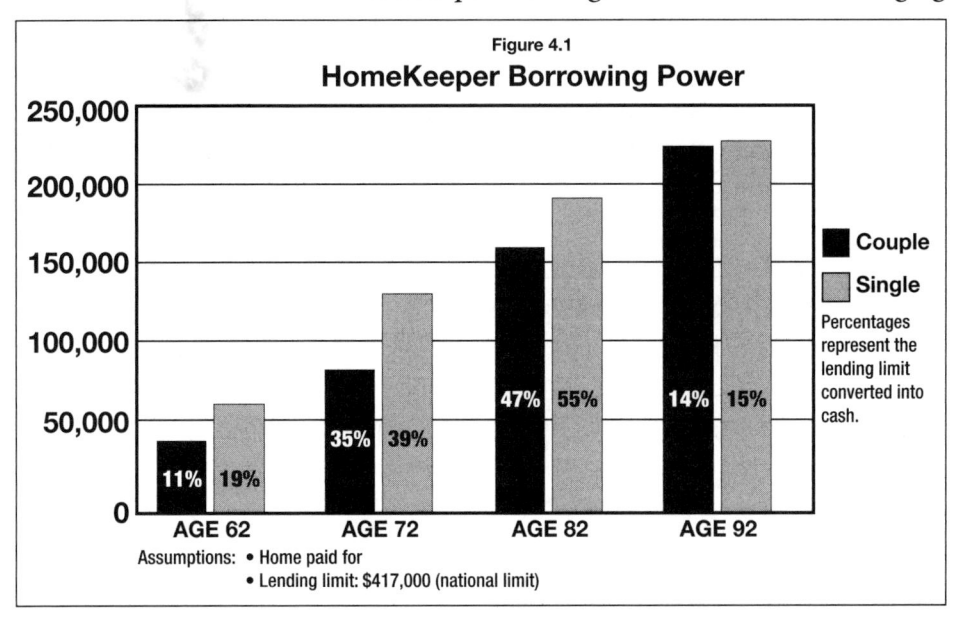

[Bar chart showing borrowing power for Couple (black) and Single (gray) at ages 62, 72, 82, and 92. Values: Age 62 — 11%, 19%; Age 72 — 35%, 39%; Age 82 — 47%, 55%; Age 92 — 14%, 15%. Percentages represent the lending limit converted into cash. Assumptions: Home paid for; Lending limit: $417,000 (national limit).]

With the HomeKeeper *(See Figure 4.1)*, the single borrower gets more than the couple. For example, at age 62, a single borrower gets nine percent; at 72, the difference is four percent; eight at 82 and one precent at 92.

HomeKeeper's cash advance options

A HomeKeeper customer can take out cash in three ways:
- **Tenure option**: Equal monthly payments for as long as home is principal residence.
- **Creditline**: Unscheduled payments as needed.
- **Modified tenure**: A combination of a tenure and creditline options.

HomeKeeper has no term option and its creditline does not grow like HECM's. ance options are as flexible as HECMs. There is an interesting twist to the HomeKeeper cash advance system: payment suspension. A HomeKeeper customer can ask lender to suspend her monthly advances to conserve *principal limit*. As with HECM, she can make partial prepayment at any time to increase her principal limit.

If a HomeKeeper customer goes to Las Vegas and hits the jackpot, she may use part of her gambling windfall to reduce her loan balance, but she must leave at least $50 in loan balance or HomeKeeper loan would end.

Similar to HECMs, HomeKeeper cash advance options were designed to meet cash needs of customers. A customer needs to supplement her Social Security or pension checks with regular, predictable cash income; she

67

Part I: The new pillar of retirement security

would choose a tenure option. Those who want some cash cushion against large unexpected bills such as roof repair or the purchase of a new car may opt for a combination of creditline and tenure (modified tenure). And others who have strong and secured monthly cash incomes may choose the creditline option.

HomeKeeper closing costs
HomeKeeper closing costs consists of:
- Origination fee. Fee is $2,000 or two percent of adjusted property value or the purchase price.
- Standard real estate closing costs in local market.

Key HomeKeeper concepts
Adjusted property value
Adjusted property value is the portion of a property's appraised value used to decide borrower's principal limit in a HomeKeeper loan. It is the appraised value or Fannie Mae's national loan limit. The 2006-2007 lending limit for single family homes is $417,000. If a property appraises for $470,000, it will be "adjusted" to $417,000.

Suspension
HomeKeeper's cash advance options include a suspension feature, giving HomeKeeper customer the option to suspend loan advances from lender. This feature helps the borrower to conserve equity and reduce costs.

Partial repayment
The partial repayment feature in Fannie Mae's HomeKeeper creditline allows the borrower to partially repay the borrowed cash and then draw the cash again, just like a traditional forward mortgage home equity line of credit.

The standard HomeKeeper loan is a conventional supplement to the HECM loan. It was designed to serve the cash needs of older adults similar to HECM.

Buy a home in reverse
HomeKeeper for home purchase was created for older adults like Linda Loaner. She wants to move closer to her family in a warmer climate. It is also good for customers who want to downsize into age-friendly homes or move into new homes with less maintenance headaches.

Homekeeper: Tearing down cash barriers to aging

How HomeKeeper for home purchase works

Let's return to the Linda Loaner scenario to illustrate how the HomeKeeper for home purchase works:

- At 79-years-old, Mrs. Loaner now lives in a Twin Cities home valued at $150,000.
- Custom-built, age-friendly home she wants to buy in Tempe costs $170,000.
- After sales commission, she had $140,000 left.
- She wants to buy the Tempe home outright, but does not want to deplete her savings.
- She also does not want the burden of new monthly mortgage payments.

So, she applied for a HomeKeeper for home purchase.

Using the Tempe home price as the basis for the loan amount calculation, the reverse mortgage loan officer punched into the computer $170,000, her age (79), the number of borrowers, one and voila! She qualified for $88,400. She took out $81,600 from her bank account as a down payment and closed on the Tempe home.

At closing, she receives a deed to her new home. HomeKeeper for home purchase funds are taken out as a lump sum from the HomeKeeper creditline. The benefits of this innovative loan for Mrs. Loaner include:

- A brand new home in warmer climate close to her family.
- No monthly mortgage payments (she's responsible for taxes and hazard insurance)
- $58,400 in the bank from her Minnesota home sale ($140,000-$81,600)
- She bought a new home and got a reverse mortgage financing in one transaction, one set of closing costs. *(See Figure 4.2)*

Figure 4.2
HomeKeeper for Home Purchase:
The Linda Loaner Case

- Net cash from sale of former Twin Cities home $140,000.
- Price of Tempe, AZ new home is $170,000.
- At 79, Mrs. Loaner qualifies for $88,400 purchase money reverse mortgage based on Tempe home price and her age.
- She takes difference $81,600 from $140,000 in the bank.
- Buys Tempe home for $170,000 ($88,400 plus $81,600).
- No money mortgage payment for as long as she lives in Arizona home.

Part I: The new pillar of retirement security

Except for required verification of assets for downpayment (in this case the $140,000 sales proceed from her Twin Cities home), underwriting Home-Keeper for home purchase is the same as standard HomeKeeper. There is no income or credit requirement.

While Mrs. Loaner puts down the exact difference between the appraised value of the Tempe home ($170,000) and the HomeKeeper loan she qualified for ($88,400), she had the option of putting down more and leaving some cash in her HomeKeeper creditline. As we know, HomeKeeper creditline is flat; so, Mrs. Loaner is better off leaving her cash in a savings account.

Why consider HomeKeeper

HomeKeeper has the same DNA as other reverse mortgages. Its strengths are as follows:
- It has a single higher national loan limit;
- Fannie Mae stands behind every HomeKeeper loan;
- Closing costs are lower than HECM's;
- Its payment suspension and partial repayment options encourage equity conservation, giving its cash advance system some flexibility;
- It is a conventional supplement to government-insured HECM;
- Its consumer education rule is more flexible than HECM's; allowing even for lender's staff to provide consumer education.

Reasons for a pause

HomeKeeper option offers some reasons for a pause as follows:
- Its principal limit tends to be smaller than HECM's despite its higher national loan limits;
- Its creditline is flat, subjecting its buying power to the cash-corroding impact of inflation;
- Its interest rate is higher than HECM's;
- Although it is as widely available as HECM and owned by a secondary market colossus with unparalleled marketing resources, HomeKeeper enjoys less than five percent market share;
- It cannot be done on a two- to four-unit property even with the owner occupying one unit as a principal residence;
- With repairs "greater than 15 percent of the adjusted property value, the property is not eligible until those repairs are completed."
- Borrowers are limited to three.

HomeKeeper, like HECM, was designed to serve the cash needs of older

Homekeeper: Tearing down cash barriers to aging adults (62-plus years of age) with lower- to moderately-priced homes. There are customers with higher-priced homes, exceeding Fannie Mae's conforming national loan limit. We examine these jumbo reverse mortgages in Chapter 5.

Resources

- www.efanniemae.com/sf/mortgageproducts/products/reverse/homekeeper.jsp
- www.efanniemae.com/sf/guides/mtgprod/pdf/reversessg.pdf
- www.nrmlaonline.org

Part I: The new pillar of retirement security

Chapter Five
Jumbos in Reverseland

Chapter 5 objectives
After studying this chapter, the reader will be able to:
- Describe the Cash Account Advantage
- Explain the creditline, combo, and cash out options
- Define and explain equity choice feature
- Introduce The Independence Plan and Generation Plus
- Anticipate new-product development
- Explain how jumbos can be used as life-planning tools

My bias for market longevity
With other jumbo proprietary programs in the market since 2006, you may question my use of the Cash Account Advantage as a template for this chapter. Here is why.

The Cash Account Advantage is the granddaddy of proprietary jumbo reverse mortgages in the U.S. market. This product is more than a decade old and is available in more states than any other jumbo reverse mortgage product. It was the basis for the first U.S. reverse mortgage securitization in 1999. In short, it has market longevity. Note that Bank of America bought Reverse Mortgage of America (a Seattle Mortgage unit) in 2007, BNY Mortgage Company became Everbank Reverse Mortgage in 2007 and MetLife Bank acquired Everbank Reverse Mortgage in 2008.

Millionaires need cash too
The first person at a presentation I gave at a public library in a Twin Cities suburb was a very sharp 81-year-old woman who we'll call, Sally Anders.

Mrs. Anders has been a widow for a few years and, for her age, drove quite a distance from an old and affluent town to the library. As soon as she entered

Part I: The new pillar of retirement security

the room, she said she was expecting two family members, her nephew and his wife. About 10 minutes later, her middle-aged nephew and his wife joined us.

After my 35-min. presentation, Mrs. Anders and her relatives lingered to ask more questions about reverse mortgages. In course of our give and take, I learned a few things about Sally Anders. She lives in a lakefront house that, in December 2006, was valued at $1.9 million, "free and clear." Her late husband left her a good income, but escalating property taxes, homeowners insurance, home maintenance costs and the absence of a reasonable cash cushion for emergencies were becoming a source of worry. A friend mentioned reverse mortgage as a possible solution, so she drove more than 20 miles on a bitterly cold winter evening to find out.

The story's moral: People who live in million dollar homes need cash too.

While Fannie Mae's HomeKeeper has the highest loan limit for lower valued homes ($417,000 for 2007/2008, new temporary FHA loan limits in some markets can be as high as $700,000), affluent older adults like Mrs. Anders need other reverse mortgage programs. This is where jumbo reverse mortgage programs, such as Financial Freedom's Cash Account Advantage, Reverse Mortgage of America's The Independence Plan, Generation Mortgage's Generation Plus and EverBank's Reverse Select come in.

They are designed for homes valued at $450,000 and above. The Cash Account Advantage, the oldest jumbo reverse in the market, has even been done on a Beverly Hills, Calif. home valued at $10 million.[1] At closing, the well-heeled homeowner reportedly said, "Look, I just want to have the liquidity available, in case I had to quickly pay for some medical costs or in case I die and my wife needs some liquidity."

Cash Account Advantage, The Independence Plan, Generation Plus and Prime Advantage have the same essentials as HECM and HomeKeeper reverse mortgage loans: They are for customers who are 62-plus years of age; they must own their home and reside in it as primary residence (the Cash Account Advantage does not have "primary residence" restriction; it can be done on second homes); they must have enough equity in the home to allow a reverse mortgage in a first lien position; they do not have to repay the loan until they sell the home, move out or die; they cannot owe more than the home's value; there are no prepayment penalties (some jumbos have prepayment restrictions), and they must receive loan-related education.

Footnote
1-Interview with Jim Mahoney, co-founder and former chairman of Financial Freedom Senior Funding Corporation, The Mortgage Press, *August 2004.*

Cash Account Advantage property qualifications*
The following property types qualify:
- Detached single-family homes
- Manufactured homes
- Condominiums and PUDs
- One- to four-unit rentals with the owner occupying one unit as a principal residence
- Cooperative units (New York State only)
- "Gentleman" farms (non-professional, hubby-type farms)
- Second homes
- Excess acreage property

*This list is illustrative. Lender may adjust these qualifications at any time.

Cash Account Advantage program options
There are three program options as follows:
- ■ Creditline
- ■ Combo
- ■ Cash Out

Let's look at the elements of these options:

Creditline option*
- Origination fee is two percent of credit limit (minimum = $2,500)
- Standard closing costs apply
- No prepayment penalty
- No minimum draw at closing
- No restrictions on use of cash
- Minimum draw = $500
- Adjustable interest rate indexed linked to the six-month LIBOR plus a margin of 3.5 percent. The rate is adjusted twice annually and it has a six-percent lifetime rate cap. For example, (six-month LIBOR index on Nov. 19, 2006 was 5.38 percent) plus 3.5 percent (margin) plus six percent (cap) equals a 14.88 percent lifetime cap.
- No loan limits by home value, but better for homes $450,000 and over
- Open-ended revolving line of credit
- Unused creditline grows at five percent annually
- A loan officer must attend the closing
- Monthly servicing fee is $20
- Equity choice option available

*This list is illustrative. Lender may adjust these qualifications at any time.

Part I: The new pillar of retirement security

Combo option*
- No origination fees with 75 percent minimum draw (must be $200,000)
- Standard closing costs apply
- Partial repayment is not permitted for the first five years
- Full prepayment is allowed without penalty
- Adjustable interest rate same as Creditline option
- No loan limits
- Better for homes $450,000 and over
- An open-ended revolving line of credit
- Unused credit grows at five percent annually
- The loan originator must attend closing
- Monthly servicing fee is $20
- Equity Choice option available

Cash Out option*
- No origination fee and closing costs
- Borrower pays state required fees
- Minimum draw of 100 percent (must be $275,000)
- Interest rates, same as Standard and Zero point options
- No line of credit
- No prepayment penalties
- Partial prepayment not permitted in the first five years
- Full prepayment, fine at any time
- Same interest rate as creditline and combo options
- The loan originator must attend closing
- Monthly servicing fee is $20
- Equity Choice option available

About Equity Choice

Equity Choice is a feature in all Cash Account Advantage options. It allows a borrower to limit the percentage of home value used as collateral for the Cash Account Advantage reverse mortgage. Using Equity Choice, borrowers may shield a minimum of 10, and a maximum of 50 percent, of their home equity or value from use as security for the loan. The downside is that the borrower's line of credit may be less than what the borrower qualifies for. But the upside is greater flexibility and some assurance that leftover equity benefits borrower or her heirs at the loan's maturity.

*This list is illustrative. Lender may adjust these qualifications at any time.

Availability of the Cash Account Advantage program

The Cash Account Advantage reverse mortgage is available in the following states: Alabama, Arkansas, Arizona, California, Colorado, Connecticut, the District of Columbia, Delaware, Florida, Georgia, Hawaii, Idaho, Illinois, Indiana, Kansas, Kentucky, Massachusetts, Maryland, Maine, Michigan, Minnesota, Missouri, Mississippi, North Carolina, New Hampshire, Nevada, New Jersey, New Mexico, New York, Ohio, Oregon, Pennsylvania, Rhode Island, South Carolina, Texas, Utah, Virginia, Vermont, Washington, Wisconsin and Wyoming.

To find out whether your state is approved for the Cash Account Advantage program and updated program details, check the Financial Freedom Web site at www.financialfreedom.com.

The Independence Plan

For a decade, the Cash Account Advantage was the only jumbo program in Reverseland. That changed on Oct. 23, 2006 when Reserve Mortgage of America launched The Independence Plan (TIP). TIP is designed for higher-end homes, similar to Cash Account Advantage and Generation Plus. The DNA of TIP is similar to other reverse mortgage programs in the market. While it is an evolving product, it offers these features among others*:

- Loan amount based on youngest borrower, number of borrowers and home value
- Lien position: First
- Interest rate: Six-month LIBOR plus margin
- Lifetime cap: Six percent over the fully-indexed initial rate
- Home value: Minimum $100,000, no maximum
- Property type: SFR, one to four units (borrower must occupy one unit as principal residence), condo, PUD, no manufactured homes
- No credit or income requirements
- Mortgage insurance: none
- Monthly servicing fee: $33
- Minimum LOC draw: $100
- Cash advance option: Line of credit
- Unused credit grows at five percent annually
- Good for home purchase
- No prepayment penalty (one year partial prepayment restriction)

*This list is for illustrative purposes. Reverse Mortgage of America may modify features at any time.

Part I: The new pillar of retirement security

- Origination fee: Up to $4,000 if initial draw is $200,000 or less; no fee if first draw is over $200,000
- 90-day rate lock agreement with float down

Here is a lender compensation schedule for sample home values. It assumes initial loan advance of all available credit. If initial loan advance is zero, loan officer may charge an origination fee up to $4,000.

Appraised value	Age 72 single	Age 72 couple
$500,000	$4,340	$4,140
$1,000,000	$7,378	$7,038
$1,500,000	$10,416	$9,936
$2,000,000	$13,888	$13,248
LTV	43.4 %	41.4 %
Source: Reverse Mortgage of America		

Generation Plus

Generation Plus is a jumbo reverse mortgage which uses the one-month LIBOR index. It has the same DNA as other reverse mortgages; however, it has some distinct advantages for higher-end homeowners as do other jumbo products already in the market or expected to come into the market shortly. For more information, log on to www.generationmortgage.com.

Three scenarios: Jumbos as life-planning tools

The borrower who has a $4 million home may not consider FHA's HECM or Fannie Mae's HomeKeeper because of limits on home value. While both the HomeKeeper and HECM loans can be used for life-planning as well as for extra-cash, the $4 million home borrower whose primary need is life planning has to look to the jumbo reverse mortgages. The scenarios below should be of interest to financial planners, accountants, elder law attorneys, and other non-mortgage professionals and senior advisors who may be looking for ways to use a reverse mortgage for legitimate life-planning goals for their clients. The characters are fictional, the scenarios illustrative. Let's begin.

Scenario #1: Helping with estate planning

Hetta Heiress lives in a $12 million home in the Hollywood Hills. Her very creative financial planner knows that the full value of her home, owned outright, may be subject to significant estate tax, but a reverse mortgage against the property reduces the home's value, thus lowering any applicable estate taxes.

Ms. Heiress receives $4 million through her jumbo reverse. Her financial planner uses some of that money to buy a large life insurance policy. The life insurance policy is in place strictly to cover the estate taxes that her heirs will be required to pay. Because the estate has a lien on it (the reverse mortgage loan), the property may be taxed at a lower value. (Using reverse mortgage cash to buy insurance involves double-cost.)

Let's look a little closer:

- A reverse mortgage is a lien against property that must be repaid when borrower permanently leaves the property.
- At death, full value of the property would be included in estate valuation for tax purposes.
- However, the accumulated debt of the reverse mortgage would effectively reduce the property value and lower any applicable estate taxes.
- In addition, the accrued interest in the reverse mortgage repayment may be available as a tax deduction for the estate (consult a competent tax advisor).
- If a senior homeowner chooses to buy life insurance policy without the use of a reverse mortgage, she is likely using after-tax dollars or income to pay for premiums.
- However, if a senior uses reverse mortgage dollars to buy a life insurance policy, tax free dollars are used and her after-tax income stream is unaffected. Got it? Let's go on to the second scenario.

Scenario #2: Maximizing legacy asset transfer

Peter Patriarch has lived in his palatial Peoria estate for nearly 40 years. His children and grandchildren love visiting and have fond memories of growing up there, but it's not a practical place for them to live permanently.

Although the home holds immense emotional value for the family, upon Mr. Patriarch's death, the property will be sold. Mr. Patriarch's children know they will be forced to sell the property in a potentially sluggish real estate market with no assurance of market or value stability. They also realize that after the sale, which may drag out depending on market conditions, they will be faced with inheritance and/or capital gains taxes on the proceeds. Besides, net sales proceeds are often far less than the actual or perceived value of the home.

Mr. Patriarch's children talked with their father about the life-planning value of a jumbo reverse mortgage. They say it will provide him the comfort of having more control over his estate, assuring he leaves a higher legacy asset for his heirs.

Upon the sale of the palatial Peoria estate, any equity over the loan amount

Part I: The new pillar of retirement security

would be subject to taxes, but still revert to Mr. Patriarch's heirs. With the unknown nature of future real estate markets, this scenario provides for greater control of the legacy assets by the borrower. And finally, let's look at the third scenario.

Scenario #3: Leaving funds to charity
Filene Giver has planned to leave part of her estate to the Philadelphia Philharmonic. Seventy-eight-year-old Ms. Giver owns a home valued at $1.5 million.

With a jumbo reverse mortgage, she could receive $500,000-plus. Imagine the satisfaction she will feel being able to donate $500,000 to the Philadelphia Philharmonic while she is still living! She will no longer just be an attendee at a recital; she will actually have the joy of knowing she is a patron of the arts!

Many seniors have already planned to leave their estate to their Alma Mater, church, temple, mosque or favorite arts organization. Wouldn't it be fulfilling if they could see their financial gifts "at work" while they were still alive?

[The three scenarios in this chapter were written by Diane Byrnes of Financial Freedom and edited by Atare E. Agbamu]

Resources
- www.financialfreedom.com
- www.generationmortgage.com
- www.nrmlaonline.org

Jumbos in Reverseland

Part II: Marketing reverse mortgages: It's all about education

Part II
Marketing reverse mortgages: It's all about education

A different kind of customer: Chapter 6

Jason Miller needs help: Chapter 7

The marketing basket: Chapter 8

Become a rev-angelist: Chapter 9

Marketing postscripts: Chapter 10

Part II: Marketing reverse mortgages: It's all about education

Chapter Six
A different kind of customer

Opening quotes ...
"Without an understanding of aging and aging customers, how can a marketer be successful in marketing to the New Customer Majority?"
—**David B. Wolfe**

"Knowing something about your customer is just as important as knowing everything about your product."
—**Harvey Mackay**

"The marketing trend away from youth and toward age is irreversible."
—**Theodore Roszak**

Chapter 6 objectives
After studying this chapter, the reader will be able to:
- Cite some numbers that show the dominance of the senior market
- Describe the spring, summer, fall, and winter seasons of a customer's life
- Explain the human development tasks of each season
- Discuss some changes that mid-life can bring to a consumer's life
- Describe other behavioral evidence of aging
- Name at least six ways aging consumers are changing the market
- Explain the new "S" factor in marketing
- Know values that are most and least important to the 62-plus and the 45-61 age groups

"Son, been there, done that!"
In the book, *Ageless Marketing*, author David Wolfe, recounted a conversation between two men, one was 40-years-old, the other was 80. The younger man

Part II: Marketing reverse mortgages: It's all about education

was pushing his views too strongly when the older man stopped him with this reprimand: "I think I know a bit more about this than you do because you've never been 80, but I've been 40. You're talking like a 40-year-old, not like an 80-year-old."

As a father of two teenage sons who often express very strong views on almost every subject under Heaven, I have some understanding of the older man's rebuke of the younger. Depending on where you are on life's fascinating journey, intergenerational communication of any type, including marketing communications, can be a challenge.

If we are going to have any success marketing to those who are 62 and older, we must learn to do two things:

- Understand aging and how we (consumers) change and behave as we age; and
- Use our knowledge to improve our marketing communications.

The numbers have changed

From the 1960s to about 1989, youth [ages 18-39] ruled the American marketplace. By the early 1990s, maturity [40 years and older] became the new masters of the marketplace. Some very smart people have said that we are in a different market, with a different kind of customer. Before we go on to job one in any marketing [know your customer], let's review some interesting numbers:

- Overall, the median age in the U.S. is 37 years of age
- The median adult age is 45
- Adults 40 and older, at 132 million plus, make up the majority of the U.S. marketplace today
- There are approximately 86 million young adults between the ages of 18-39
- 40-60-year olds make up the largest 20-year age bracket in America today; they also control more of the nation's wealth
- By 2010, the 45 and older age group will spend approximately $2.630 trillion annually
- 25-44 age bracket will spend approximately $1.628 trillion annually
- Today, the 40-plus group is nearly 53 percent larger than the under-40 crowd; it is estimated to be 60 percent larger by 2010
- An AARP-funded study conducted by Roper ASW found that three out of four older consumers are unhappy with marketing directed at them (that's a 75 percent dissatisfaction rate with marketing as usual.). *(See Figure 6.1)* Source: Wolfe Resources Group

A different kind of customer

**Figure 6.1
First Half and Second Half Customers At A Glance**

[Bar chart showing: 2002 (40+) ≈ 123 million; 2002 (18-39) ≈ 84 million; 2002 (49+)* ≈ 138 million; 2010 (18-39) ≈ 88 million]

*60% Larger than 18-39 group
Source: Wolfe Resources Group

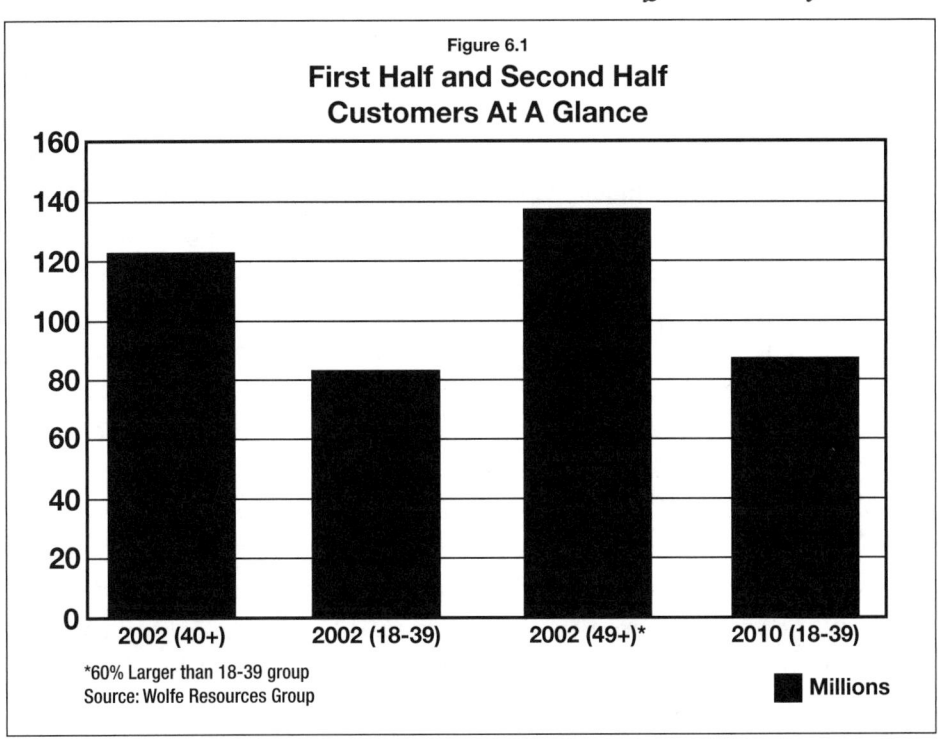

■ Millions

The numbers have changed. The youth who dominated our markets and our culture through the late 1980s have now become the new older adult majority in the marketplace. So, what's the difference? There is a lot. The level of older consumer unhappiness with marketing as usual suggests a huge "disconnect" between those who are writing marketing messages and those they think they are writing it for.

To every customer, there is a season

It turns out that human life and the four seasons are related. That is how David Wolfe and Robert Snyder see it in their book, *Ageless Marketing*. To understand people, they say we must know the season of life they are in. A 22-year-old sees life differently than a 42-year-old. The same is true between a 62-year-old and a 42-year-old. Here are four seasons into which customer's life is divided:

- From birth to age 22-plus = Spring
- From age 18-plus to 40-plus = Summer
- From age 38-plus to 60-plus = Fall
- From age 58-plus and over = Winter

Source: *Ageless Marketing*

Part II: Marketing reverse mortgages: It's all about education

At each season of life, there are human development goals, wired into our DNA. For example, in the spring of life, the urge to play is dominant. Through play, role-playing, and modeling, we learn much to prepare us for the next season. By the summer of life, our social growth is almost complete. We take our place in business and in society. Our primary goal in the first-half of life [spring and summer] is to be "somebody" in the eyes of others. Peer influences on our behavior and our buying preferences are usually very strong.

By the fall of life, we become more inner-focused and inner-directed, seeking balance, purpose, and meaning in life. The winter years usually take us deeper into the true meaning of life, where we yearn for peace and reconciliation with ourselves and with others.

Wolfe argues that it is vital to design marketing messages with the season of our target market's life in mind. In other words, it is not enough for us to know our target market's age, income, zip code, the type of car they drive and other numbers that dominate traditional marketing calculations. We must attempt to understand "the hearts and minds" of older consumers if we must, you guessed it: persuade them to take out a reverse mortgage.

It is fall and winter in reverse country

From the four seasons of consumer life, we can clearly locate a reverse mortgage marketing target market. Reverse mortgage borrowers are in the winter of life, but the reverse market includes those in the late summer and the fall of life too. These are the so-called trusted advisors, professional and non-professional, to the reverse mortgage decision-makers. The question is … what do we need to know about those in the fall and winter of life in order for us to connect with them effectively through our advertising and other marketing communications tactics?

To connect with customers in the fall and winter seasons of life, we need to know the general values, views, needs, and behaviors associated with these seasons of life. We are going to use the word "generally" a lot because there are always exceptions among people. However, seasons-of-life influence on consumer behavior is predictable, just as we can call snow in the winter, sunshine in the summer, or rain in the spring and fall.

Our society and our marketing mainstream know a great deal about youth and young adulthood because, until now, the spring and summer demographic [a.k.a. first-half markets] ruled the marketplace. So, what are the defining changes associated with the fall and the winter seasons of life?

A different kind of customer

Mid-course convulsions

Individuals go through both psychological and physical changes as they enter the second half of life. The physical changes are usually obvious:

- The mid-section expands (middle age begins in the middle)
- The hairline recedes and the hair begins to show a lot of gray where they are not hidden with hair color

Psychological changes may include feelings of restlessness and dissatisfaction with one's life, despite many professional and social achievements. Thoughts along these lines may cross the mind: "What is the purpose of my life?" and "Is this all there is to life?"

This season of personal daze and doubt has led to many drastic mid-life events, such as divorce, relocation, career change, spiritual conversions, a renewed passion for academic pursuits and other adventures. It is a time where the "pursuit of ambitions is being moderated by pursuit of balance," Wolfe says.

Also, during this mid-course convulsion, we generally begin to break free of peer influence in search of our "true selves." Let's review some second-half changes that make customers who are 40 years and older different from those who are below 40:

- Feelings of restlessness and dissatisfaction despite enviable personal professional and social achievements
- The search for meaning and purpose in life
- Drastic changes such as divorce, relocation, career change, renewed academic pursuits, spiritual pursuits and other adventures
- Breaking free of peer influence
- A quest for balance
- A search for the "real self"

The ways of maturity

Besides their expanding waistlines, thinning and graying hair, wrinkling skin, and weakening eyesight, there are other changes in people 40 years and older that make them different from the under-40 crowd. In a Web blog series, "How an Aging Population is Changing the Mind of the Market," David Wolfe outlines eight traits of older consumers:

- They are more realistic and more practical;

Part II: Marketing reverse mortgages: It's all about education

- Their perceptions are more dependent on context or background;
- They are more detached and more individuated or more their own person;
- Their resistance to persuasion [outside persuasion] is high;
- They are more emotional and more intuitive, i.e. "gut feelings" usually overrule logic;
- They are more focused on experiences than on products, that is, their desires are less materialistic, more experiential and pleasure sought in little things;
- They are more introspective or more self-informed, more trust in self; and
- They are more authentic.

These eight attributes of mature customers will change how we craft marketing messages. We will revisit the marketing implications of these and other older customers' traits in Chapter 7.

A Super Bowl "gut" call

Let me share a "gut feeling" family story during Super Bowl XXXVI. In 2002, as I sat down to watch the Super Bowl with my sons, Awesiri (then 11) and Akporefe (then nine), Akporefe said, "Daddy, the Rams are going to win! You want to bet me?" Awesiri promptly threw the same challenge at me.

Then I asked them, "Why do you think the Rams are going to win?"

They rattled off a torrent of statistics to support their forecast. They knew their football facts and National Football League history very well, and they communicated their knowledge with passion and confidence. No football or sports statistics guru myself, I was outgunned. But I was deeply impressed with their command of football history and facts.

I told them I would reserve my choice until the first few minutes of the game. Then the game started. The St. Louis Rams were introduced individually, with star quarterback Kurt Warner and other stronger team members getting extra applause. The New England Patriots chose to be introduced as a team. I was impressed. From pure gut feelings, from knowing that challengers tend to be a little hungrier than current champions, from real ignorance about football and the season's activities up to the Super Bowl, I made my choice known to my eager sons … the New England Patriots.

Second-half customers do pay attention to facts, but they then look at the facts and draw conclusions informed more by gut feelings or intuition. Combined, these seasonal changes in mature customers make for a different market, but there is more that separates first half from second half markets.

A different kind of customer

The new "S" Factor in marketing

It is as basic as the "S" word in youth-informed 20th century marketing. It is equally as powerful a motivator of maturing human behavior, but it is not sex. So, what is the new "S" Factor in a 21st century market dominated by aging customers? If you took Psychology 101, you have probably heard of it. It is an essential human need, like steak or vegetables. The great developmental psychologist, Abraham Maslow, drew a pyramid and placed this need at the very top. He said human beings usually grapple for this need after their need for food, shelter, security and love are met. If you plan to crack the expanding senior market with relevant marketing messages, you must understand "self-actualization." What is self-actualization? (Again, we will discuss its marketing implications in Chapter 7).

To understand self-actualization, we need to introduce another idea that David Wolfe called 'social-actualization.' Wolfe says the end game in the spring and summer of life is social-actualization. We want to be 'somebody' in the eyes of our peers. The drive is more materialistic, the big education, the big job, the big title, the big paycheck, the big suburban house, the beautiful family, the big cars, the list of our pursuits of social achievements continues.

Then comes mid-life, and with it, the big questions: What is the purpose of my life? Is this all there is? This is where the self-actualization need begins to push us more into becoming "more human." We begin to pay more attention to "giving back" much of the toys we have been accumulating in the first half of life. Those who don't have cash "give back" time by doing volunteer work for worthy community causes like Little Brothers—Friends of the Elderly, the Salvation Army, Doctors without Borders, etc. Those who have real money "give back" by donating millions to colleges, hospitals and the arts. CNN founder, Ted Turner, even gave $1 billion to the United Nations. We are not even talking about the billions Bill and Melinda Gates are pouring into health and education around the globe.

Now, giving money to causes or volunteering time does not mean self-actualization by itself. It is just one sign of a self-actualizing person. Some might be giving back for "I'm somebody" reasons. As David Wolfe has written, self-actualization is a journey, not a destination. The most important changes the self-actualization drive brings about are internal changes in the aging, self-actualizing person.

Self-actualization is about becoming the "real you" and being comfortable with the "real you." It is about rising above smallness and pettiness. It is about focusing on things that are bigger than you. It is about taking pleasure in the little things. It is about gaining a deeper and better understanding of life. It

Part II: Marketing reverse mortgages: It's all about education

is about growing into the person you were intended to be. It is the highest goal of human development. It is the "end game of life."

The drive to self-actualize is very powerful in consumers in the fall and winter seasons of life. The need to become the "real you" in mature customers is coded into our DNA, similar to the need for food, for play or for intimacy. It is the new "S" factor in marketing. Here is how Wolfe puts it:

Like gravity, the forces of self-actualization exert a constant tug on each of us, pulling us along the path of personal development until we become "fully human;" even though people differ in how far along that path they progress.[1]

It is all about values

You have heard the expression "we live and we learn" countless times. What we learn while living, we call experience. For better or for worse, our experiences shape our attitudes and values. Our attitudes and values, in turn, shape our behavior, including our economic behavior. Values consist of relationship principles, beliefs and ideas that we consider important. Our values influence our decision-making.

Our primary biological, or non-biological, relationship is with our family. It is important to us. Of equal importance are our relationships with other individuals or groups outside our families. We value principles or rules in our society that say, "A person is innocent until proven otherwise in a court of law." We value our laws and system of economic production. Love, equality, justice, responsibility, industry, freedom, God, country, peace, security, knowledge, fairness, simplicity, kindness, and community are ideas that we consider important (values) to varying degrees. We consider these values so important that often we are willing to die to preserve or advance them. David Wolfe and Robert Snyder say speaking to values is vital to connecting with mature customers.

"The key to capturing the hearts and minds of the mature audience lies in first understanding the values they find to be important and second to understand the values they hold which are least important."[2]

Wolfe and Snyder outlined 13 values that are held by mature Americans 62 and older, and 14 values that are significant to Americans that are between

---

Footnotes
1-Ageless Marketing, *page 47.*
2-Ageless Marketing, *page 163.*

A different kind of customer

the ages of 45 and 61. Let's look at the 62 and older list of values first (remember, the age of maturity for reverse mortgages is 62):

Values	Keywords
Self-respect	Integrity, perseverance, self-sufficiency, independence, dignity
Family ties	Family first, sacrifice for family, giving, caring
Faith and religion	God, church, temple, mosque, community of believers, divine purpose, heaven, hope
Warm relationships	Emotionally supportive, caring, loyalty
Kindness and compassion	Forgiveness, honesty, helping others, social justice, equality
Intellectual curiosity	New ideas, research, thinking, books
Health and well-being	Diet, exercise, meditation, yoga, massage
Fun and happiness	Life is a bowl of cherries!, cruise, travels, "Let the party begin!"
Conservative attitudes	Respect for tradition, authority, rules, social institutions, civility, politeness
Financial security	Savings, reserve, comfortable, security, insurance
Power and recognition	Community leadership, board member, chamber of commerce, candidate
Excitement	Climb mountains, sky dive, run marathons, thrills, adventure, spontaneous, rebellious
Material possessions[3]	Lexus, top brands, the right zip code, private island

Now, let's look at Baby Boomer values [the youngest Baby Boomers turned 40 in 2004].

Footnote
3-*Ageless Marketing, pages 166-167.*

Part II: Marketing reverse mortgages: It's all about education

Booming with values: The heart of the 45 to 61 age group

The 14 values Baby Boomers hold dear are not much different from those of the 62 and older cohort. While the choice of words may be different, the similarities are striking. As outlined in Wolfe and Snyder, the values that are important to those between age 45 and 61 are listed in order of importance.

Value	Keyword/Phrase
Altruism	Help those in need, a moral obligation to help, honesty is important
Family ties	Family is high priority, a source of satisfaction in life, makes sacrifices
Intellectual curiosity	Love mental challenges, problems, thinking and deep thought
Psychological well-being	A positive outlook on life, high self-respect, great personal achievement, independence
Spirituality	A higher purpose, part of God's plan, religion as a guide in life
Balance	A strong connection to nature, leisure, outdoors, exercise, meditation and yoga
Leadership	Initiative, self-motivation, persistence and action roles
Civility	Politeness, proper etiquette and manners, forgiveness, respect authority and conformity
Warm relationships	Close friends and community
Excitement	Indulge, enjoy activities, do something crazy, spontaneous, impulsive and daring
Regret	Financial insecurity, no savings, sadness, loneliness and anxiety
Conservatism	Respect for tradition and culture, compassionate conservatism, social justice and equity
Recognition	Social recognition, praise, status symbols, top brands
National security	Terrorism and money for national defense

A different kind of customer

In using these values as road maps into the hearts and minds of the mature market, it is critical to recognize that these values are universal. They are present in various groups in varying "degrees of intensity depending on how individual experiences have shaped individual beliefs."[4] It is important to repeat this qualification in the words of Wolfe and Snyder:

"While the human values are constant, what varies from one individual to the next is the relative importance one places on different values, depending on one's background and life circumstances."[5]

To craft marketing messages that resonate with mature customers, it is vital that we know the values that are most important as well as those that are least significant to them.

Let's review what we have learned in this chapter. Using some numbers, we saw that the senior market is the majority and the richest market today. We looked at aging and aging customers from a seasons-of-life perspective, and have concluded that it is fall and winter in reverse country. We also describe the human development objectives of each season of life. We discussed the behavioral changes that aging brings about in aging consumers. We looked at eight ways that aging consumers are influencing the market. We introduced and described the new "S" (self-actualization) factor in marketing. And finally, we concluded by outlining the values that are most and least important to the 62 and older market and the 45-61 age group. In Chapter 7, we will examine the marketing consequences of these changes in the marketplace.

Footnotes
4-Ageless Marketing, *page 169.*
5-Ageless Marketing, *page 169.*

Part II: Marketing reverse mortgages: It's all about education

Chapter Seven
Jason Miller needs help

Chapter 7 objectives
After studying this chapter, the reader will be able to:
- Know the marketing meaning of some of the key values outlined in Chapter 6
- "Craft" reverse mortgage marketing messages based on key values
- Appreciate the role of stories in reverse mortgage marketing
- Know how to find and use stories in reverse mortgage marketing
- Understand the marketing meaning of the eight ways aging customers are changing the market's mind

Family values matter
Patrick Miller, 85, is a frail but sharp-minded retired 3M engineer in St. Paul, Minn. His income was not typical of reverse mortgage customers I had served in the last couple of years. He had a strong income and his house was paid for. He even had nearly $40,000 in the bank. A widower since 1999, he came to the application interview with his grandson, Jason Miller. Jason is in his late 20s. When the older Miller's accountant arranged our initial meeting three months prior to the interview, Jason was present. It was Jason who called me almost three months after our initial meeting to say his grandfather had completed the required counseling and was ready to go through with the application.

Because Mr. Miller's income and savings were unusually robust, I started wondering what the goal of the reverse mortgage was. I asked him whether the property needed some major repairs; he said no. I asked whether there was a major health expense on the way; again, he said no.

Then, we got to the "Declarations" section of the reverse mortgage application form (Fannie Mae's Form 1009). I asked him if he had "any outstanding judgments" against him, any "bankruptcy that had yet to be resolved,"

Part II: Marketing reverse mortgages: It's all about education

any "lawsuit" to which he was a party, or any "presently delinquent federal debt." He answered a resounding "no" to all four "Declarations" questions. And I asked, "Are you a co-maker or endorser on a note," an optional question for the FHA HECM he was applying for. He said, "Yes."

Out of curiosity, I asked whom he had co-signed for and for what amount. Before he could answer, his dutiful grandson answered that it was for him, and that he intends to seek Chapter 13 bankruptcy protection in a month. I didn't probe any further. It was obvious that Mr. Miller was taking out the reverse mortgage to help his grandson Jason.

Family ties, the second highest value for the 62 and older age group, triggered this reverse mortgage origination. There are no industry statistics that I am aware of in this area, but anecdotal evidence suggests there are customers like Patrick Miller who would take out a reverse mortgage to help a relative through financial storms because of the premium they place on family ties. Recently, a parent on Long Island, N.Y. consulted me about taking out a reverse mortgage to help their son, who is fighting cancer and contending with foreclosure at the same time. With family ties in mind, a powerful marketing message can be crafted to reinforce this potent value among mature borrowers and persuade them to action.

The story is the message

You don't have to craft any "powerful marketing message." Your marketing message will fall on deaf ears. Remember, the older mind is more resistant to outside "persuasion." They have survived a lifetime of bogus marketing claims. Recall the Roper ASW survey mentioned in Chapter 6, where three out of four older adults feel marketing, as usual, is not speaking to them. What you need to do is tell real life stories similar to the Patrick Miller story.

The story you choose should be woven around key values of consumers in the winter of their life. The Patrick Miller story stressed the "family ties" value. It's what I call a "values added story" or "VAS." Look for a story that discusses self-respect, about how reverse-mortgage-generated cash can enhance self-respect, the number one value. Seek a story that addresses "faith and religion," the number three value. Find good, authentic stories. Why stories? Well, the story is the marketing message. Here is what Rolf Jensen, author of *The Dream Society*, says about storytelling:

"Storytelling has become an important part of market strategy; whoever tells the best story and whoever tells it best will win."

In a July 2005 blog posting titled, "Story: The natural way to talk to people," author and marketing guru David Wolfe writes:

"Emotionally barren claims about product features and benefits are out. Rich narratives connecting products [and services] to real life scenarios are in."

For reverse mortgage marketing, we might add that good stories linking reverse mortgages with key values of consumers 62 years and older are the way to go.

In his book *All Marketers Are Liars*, Seth Godin states:

"Stories make it easier to understand the world. Stories are the only way we know to spread an idea."

A reverse mortgage is a simple but complex idea. What better way to spread this beneficial idea than through "rich narratives" linking reverse mortgages with real life situations?

Feelings over facts

Stories are the way we process our lives. We mortgage financiers have a strong bias toward numbers or "facts." We look at the numbers … income, credit score, ratios, appraised value … and we make a decision. Our marketing tends to be mostly about features, benefits, and price. Following the lead of traditional forward mortgages, most reverse mortgage marketing have a similar bias:

- Borrower must be 62 years of age and older
- Get tax-free cash
- Pay off other debt
- Receive a monthly income
- Purchase a new home
- No mortgage payments—ever again
- Non-recourse loan
- Government-insured loan

But stories are a stronger means of spreading the reverse mortgage message. Unlike the benefits and features marketing, stories trigger emotions. Emotions make stories relevant to older consumers who are more "right-brained" as a result of the aging process. Again, marketing expert David Wolfe:

"A little recognized fact in marketing is that as we move through the second half of life, we rely more on emotions and less on reason in sorting things out. The corollary is we rely more on stories (which arouse emotions), and less on expository (which dulls the emotions)."

Think of the matter this way. Around the onset of midlife, our cognitive operations increasingly take on characteristics that draw from the emotional, creative right brain. Thus, marketing messages to the middle-aged and older people should follow the Hemispheric Principle of Communications:

Lead with the right,
Follow with the left.

In that way, you'll be delivering your message to customers' brains in the way their brains naturally process information. So, don't start with facts, start with feelings.

Begin with emotions. Wrapping short, but engaging, stories around the key values of the 62 and older group is a winning strategy. Each of the 13 values is loaded with emotions, from self-respect (the most important), to material possessions (the least significant), feelings run deep. Values added stories are the most effective ways to market reverse mortgages to older adults.

Why stories succeed

From the beginning of time, we humans told stories. We told stories to each other. We told stories to ourselves and to our children. Our children told stories to their children. On and on, the stories spread from one generation to the next. In addition to the stories handed down from previous generations, every new generation invents and tells its own stories. As Seth Godin has written, "Stories (not ideas, not features, not benefits), are what spread from person to person." True stories succeed as marketing vehicles because, among others, they:

- Arouse human emotions
- Capture the imagination of many
- Induce belief and trust

Jason Miller needs help

- Make subtle promises
- Have a ring of authenticity

Let's take the story of my customer who was featured on NBC's Today Show in May 2005. She's a retired personal banker, widow, mother of four children, and a grandmother of six. When her husband died in 2002, an experienced financial planner took a look at her finances (oblivious to the potential of reverse mortgages in retirement finance), and concluded that there was no way she could live in her suburban St. Paul, Minn. home. Yet, the beautiful, wooded home overlooking the Mississippi is where she knew she wanted to remain. Thanks to reverse-mortgage-generated cash, she is living in her home today, free of financial worries. Reprint a story like hers in your local newspaper, add your name and phone number, and invite readers to call you for more information. That's all the advertising you need to do.

Besides reprinting, you can retell her story and others in conversations with your target audiences before or after formal presentations. Even left-brained-dominant, analytic types, such as accountants and financial planners, can respond to your stories. They are human beings first. Of course, with dominant left-brained audiences, you must be ready to show numbers after your stories. Stories are powerful.

How to find stories

We know the values that are most and least important to the 62 and older group. We know that the best way to market reverse mortgages is tell authentic stories that bring reverse mortgages and these values together similar to the Patrick Miller story or the story of my customer featured on NBC's Today Show. Now, how do we go about finding these stories? Here is how:

- Log on to Google, Yahoo!, or do an MSN Web search
- Type in "reverse mortgage stories"
- Click on the links
- With one value as a reading guide (i.e. family ties), select a story that reinforces that value
- Make it a short story (one page maximum)
- Print or download the story
- Locate the names and phone numbers of the author and publisher
- Call the author, editor and publisher, and request permission to use the story

Part II: Marketing reverse mortgages: It's all about education

A few tips are in order here:

- Not all links will turn out to be reverse mortgage story links. Some are marketing links to forward mortgage lenders;
- A consistent source of reverse mortgage borrower stories are borrower profiles in *Reverse Mortgage Advisor (RMA)*, a quarterly publication of the National Reverse Mortgage Lenders Association (NRMLA). Membership in NRMLA gives you access to these stories. *RMA* has been reborn as *Reverse Mortgage*, a magazine with ads.
- Post-closing interviews with customers are the surest source of good human interest stories.

Tips for interviewing customers
- Get to know your borrower and their story from day one
- Ask for permission to record and use their story well before closing
- If they agree, set up a date after closing, preferably a month or two after closing (there's a 99.9 percent chance that they would agree)
- If they disagree, drop the idea completely
- Tape the interview and record their consent
- Disclose that you would use their story for marketing (education) without their name
- Write down some questions (for example, "Where were you born?" "Where did you grow up?" "What do you plan to do with your reverse mortgage cash?" etc.)
- Be alert to values statements

During the taped interview, other questions will naturally come up. The goal is to mine a rich personal story, complete with colorful quotes that reflect your customer's personality and values. In my experience, customers and their relatives are usually willing to talk about their lives and the impact of the cash from reverse mortgage in their lives.

What to do with the story?
We want to share the story (one at a time) in our local market. We should talk about it with everyone we interact with. We should ask the editor of our local newspaper or local senior newspaper to reprint it. Or, we should reprint it in our company newsletter, hard copy or electronic version. Always acknowledge the source. At the end of the story, add this phrase **"For more information, call …, reverse mortgage specialist."**

We have a choice in our reverse mortgage marketing: We can find and share authentic stories or we can buy commercials.

The new mind of the market

The new ruling minds of the market are aging minds. Because the marketing battlefield is in the minds of consumers, we must know how aging minds work if we expect to be successful in marketing reverse mortgages to second-half customers. As David Wolfe has noted, most "Everything we know about marketing was learned and developed when youth ruled the market and the culture." We need new insights into the aging mind. In Chapter 6, we listed eight traits of the older mind. Let's revisit Wolfe's eight traits and examine their marketing impact for reverse mortgage marketers.

More realistic, practical
Marketing impact: Your advertising should avoid shock as a way to grab an older adults' attention. Those tactics, which worked with youth, might well turn off your intended audience. Do the reverse, use simple and familiar attention-grabbing tactics, such as a flower, a baby's picture, and a lake.

Perceptions more dependent on context or background
Marketing impact: If you are doing marketing research among older adults, "black-and-white" type questions won't yield you any useful data. Their responses will take many background factors into consideration. Predicting their behavior is more challenging.

Detached, more individuated
Marketing impact: Give senior customers individual attention. One-size-fits-all marketing won't yield much with this group.

Increased resistance to persuasion
Marketing impact: An outside attempt at persuasion through advertising is likely to be resisted. Hyped claims about product features and benefits may be ignored because they have "being there, done that." Recall the Roper ASW study we mentioned in Chapter 6: Three out of four older consumers is unhappy with marketing directed at them.

More emotional, intuitive
Marketing impact: The older mind is more right-brained; while reason will

Part II: Marketing reverse mortgages: It's all about education

be present in decision-making, gut feelings often win. They have years of worldly wisdom to draw on.

More focused on experiences than on products
Marketing impact: Senior customers tend to want less stuff and want more experiences. A marketing plan designed to induce desire in stuff may fail, but one created to enhance an experience will succeed. With the senior market "experience is the marketing."

More introspective
Marketing impact: Unlike younger consumers whose orientation is more outward and social, the older adult consumer looks more to the "self" for guidance. They are more self-directed and self-taught. They have more trust in their own judgment. So, a marketing message that says "Get a reverse mortgage because your friends are getting one" will not work with this group of customers.

More authentic
Marketing impact: Consumers 62 and older prefer what is real over the ideal. In other words, they know that the perfect cover girl or the GQ man or woman is not real. Hype and mindless self-promotion will not help you with this group of consumers. Be humble, vulnerable, and be real.

Let's review what we have covered about reverse mortgage marketing in this chapter:

- We learned that values that are important to customers 62 and older, such as family ties, self-respect and financial security, can trigger reverse mortgage decisions.
- As reverse mortgage marketers, we should recognize, reinforce, and link reverse mortgages with these values through stories. The story is the marketing message.
- As a marketing vehicle, stories are effective because they arouse human emotions, capture the imagination, induce belief and trust, make subtle promises, and have rings of authenticity.
- We learned how to find reverse mortgage stories on the Internet and what to do with them.
- Finally, we reviewed the eight traits of the aging mind and how these traits can impact marketing to older adults.

Experienced reverse mortgage marketers agree that a "marketing basket" approach is the best way to market reverse mortgages. In Chapter 8, we will sample the marketing treats in a typical reverse mortgage "marketing basket."

Resources

- www.agelessmarketing.com

Part II: Marketing reverse mortgages: It's all about education

Chapter Eight
The marketing basket

Chapter 8 objectives
After studying this chapter, the reader will be able to:
- Appreciate the marketing basket approach to reverse mortgage marketing
- Know the do's and don'ts in crafting reverse mortgage advertisements
- Understand the role of public relations (PR) in reverse mortgage marketing
- Know how to plan and execute a PR program
- Know how to plan and carry out networking for reverse mortgage marketing
- Appreciate the Aging in Place coalition as a networking forum

No matter where your reverse mortgage business is located, veteran reverse mortgage lenders agree that a "marketing basket" approach consisting of advertising, public relations, networking, and even some "educate and link" lead generation works better than reliance on simply one marketing tactics.

Advertising
If you are just starting your business or have some experience in reverse mortgage lending, you may be able to use advertising to drive business in the short-term. Depending on your advertising budget, targeted print, radio, television and cable ads could get your phones to ring.

Some lenders limit their advertising to print ads in "free" older-adult publications, where ad rates are lower and the readership is pre-defined. Some place ads in publications for professional such as CPAs, CFPs, elder law attorneys, healthcare providers and others who have frequent access to older adults.

Some have used a combination of print, radio, television or cable advertising. Internet advertising will bring in leads generally from children or grandchildren searching the Web for reverse mortgage information for their

Part II: Marketing reverse mortgages: It's all about education

parents or grandparents. Some older adults use the Web to get information about reverse mortgages. Depending on the quality of the mailing list, direct mail has worked for some, while others consider it a waste of resources.

Needless to say, advertising is expensive, its value is dubious, but it may be a practical option for bringing in business to sustain operations for someone just starting out in the reverse mortgage world.

"Educate and link" lead generation

Another option for jump-starting your business that could be more cost-effective than advertising is what I call "educate and link" lead generation. Senior Lending Network (SLN), a Long Island, N.Y.-based division of World Alliance Financial, a top-10 reverse mortgage lender, takes a novel approach. In a nutshell, here is how the program works:

- SLN advertises nationally or locally via television, mail or print.
- A senior calls SLN's call center to request the SLN-produced reverse mortgage educational video featuring actor Robert Wagner.
- The caller goes through SLN's 15-question process before SLN takes the video order.
- SLN processes the customer's information and downloads it into their system.
- SLN's system matches and links the senior to a reverse mortgage lender in the senior's area. The system generates a letter from a local lender that goes out with the video introducing the lender to the senior, asking the senior to call the local reverse mortgage lender if they have any questions arising from the video.
- The contact information is uploaded into lender's Web site; the lender receives that lead; and the manager can either assign the lead to a loan officer or take it themselves.
- The manager can track all leads that come in, while the loan officer can only view their own leads.

SLN says they train lenders' loan officers and managers on how to use their exclusive leads and provide lenders with the ability to grow their reverse mortgage businesses. The educational video they give seniors is well-produced. The education part sets SLN apart. For more information, visit them at www.seniorlendingnetwork.com.

Basic ad tips (BATs)

The following basic ad tips (BATs) should be helpful in crafting and execut-

The marketing basket

ing your reverse mortgage advertising plan:

1. Know the older adult community in your market.
The effectiveness of your ad messaging, design and execution will depend on a correct knowledge of your demographics. You find out through old-fashioned research. Read local history; read the publications that the older adult community reads; visit and listen to them. Talk with them, but do more listening. Know the words, symbols, icons, etc. that move them. All of this is time-consuming, but it will pay off. Understand your local culture. Traditional tools such as age, income, zip code and purchasing habits won't do much good.

2. Know how newspapers, magazines, newsletters and flyers are distributed.
If you are using print ads, you want to know how the medium is distributed. Is it distributed door-to-door, or is it circulated through newsstands or at a senior center, doctor offices, supermarket entrances, or other places frequented by older adults? A door-to-door delivery is more likely to be read than a newsstand publication.

3. Shelf life is important.
A monthly is more likely to be kept than a daily.[1]

4. Craft your message carefully and test your ad before launching your campaign.
The meaning you ascribe to a word or symbol may often be different from that of a 62-year-old.

5. Advertise in mature publications and in the personal finance sections of major newspapers.
Due to cost, network, cable or satellite television time may not be cost-effective options for you. You may get the benefits of national television advertising by joining the Senior Lending Network program of Lender Lead Solutions (See the "Educate and Link" lead generation sub-section).

6. Customers and their needs and values should be the focus of your ad copy, not program features and benefits.
Program features and benefits have no emotional hook for seniors or for anyone else.

Footnote
1-Interview with Sarah Hulbert.

Part II: Marketing reverse mortgages: It's all about education

7. Use common words and images ... avoid shock and novelty.
There is too much of that in our mainstream advertising already so it is less effective, especially with customers in the second half of life.

8. Your message should have relevance and emotions.
Your message should speak to the core values of the older adults in your community.

9. Project the experience that cash from reverse mortgages can bring for the senior, not reverse mortgages itself.
In crafting your copy, ask yourself these questions: What experiences can cash from reverse mortgages give the older adults in my community? What experiences have the extra cash from reverse mortgages given other older adults in the community? *(See Figures 8.1 and 8.2).*

10. Get your pictures off your ads!
You have been told from forward mortgage advertising to sell yourself, right? Well, do the opposite with reverse mortgage advertising. Let your ads show pictures or images of seniors and kids, grandparents and grandchildren. In other words, your ad symbols or pictures should be intergenerational.

11. Avoid age segregation or symbols of age segregation.
Older people want to connect with people of all ages.

12. Make sure every detail of your ad copy project a positive meaning.
Again, this is why "testing before launching" is so critical.

13. Project universal values like love, peace, family, justice, etc

14. Avoid negative symbols.

15. Represent aging honestly in ads.

16. Avoid ads that speak to the left brain (i.e., statistics, charts, details, etc.).

17. Emphasize the virtues of aging, (e.g. more temperate, wiser, more caring, less judgmental, more refreshing and interesting because age has more stories to tell).

The marketing basket

Figure 8.1

Receive Income From Your Home!
Consider a Reverse Mortgage

If you are 62 or older, you can use a **Reverse Mortgage** to:
- Pay off existing mortgage
- Pay off other debt
- Get cash from your home
- Fund home improvements or repairs
- Receive monthly income and/or lump sum
- Purchase a new home
- Receive a tenure, term, or creditline payments

No Mortgage payments ever again!
Call today for determining if a Reverse Mortgage
Is right for you.

555-555-5555

Your home…a valuable source of income

Figure 8.2

"My parents are so much happier now that their bathrooms and kitchen look brand new."

"It really turned Daddy on to know he could get all this money without having a monthly payment to worry about."

--**Jane Doe**, James Island, South Carolina, speaking of her parents after they got a reverse mortgage

Call me for information about reverse mortgages today

John Tenure
Reverse Mortgage Specialist

555-555-5555

111

Part II: Marketing reverse mortgages: It's all about education

18. Let your ads tell very short stories.
A reverse mortgage lender in Granger, Indiana says his story ads generate more calls and leads than regular product/benefits ads. This lender says at least 40 percent of his business comes from ads. In scores of interviews with lenders across the country on their marketing methods, this was the most intriguing of the possibilities of print ads in reverse mortgage marketing. Why do "story ads" connect with older adult customers? They arouse emotions and capture the imagination of readers. A story ad tells the experience of others in capsule. Customers in the second-half of life tend to value "experience over things."[2] Again, "the experience is the marketing."[3] Let me repeat the words of Wolfe and Snyder on the importance of experience to mature customers:

"If you get the experience right, you've done all the marketing you need to do."[4]

19. Get a positive first impression advantage.
In crafting and designing your ads, make sure they generate a positive first impression with mature customers. Your best shot at this is to use universal symbols and words with positive emotions.

20. Teach don't preach.
It has been said, "Never preach to people over 40." This is especially true for people over 60. Mature customers' heightened sense of autonomy makes them resistant to marketing communication that tells them what is in their best interest. So your ads should not be preachy.

Public relations
"Public sentiment is everything ... With public sentiment nothing can fail. Without it, nothing can succeed. He who molds public sentiments goes deeper than he who executes statutes or pronounces decisions. He makes statutes or decisions possible or impossible to execute."
—**Abraham Lincoln, 1860**

Ray Peters came to you for a reverse mortgage. From application to closing,

---

Footnotes
2-Ageless Marketing, *page 250.*
3-Attributed to Joseph Pine and James Gilmore *(authors of* The Experience Economy*) in* Ageless Marketing, *page 262.*
4-Ageless Marketing, *page 262.*

his experience with your staff and your company was outstanding. That is good PR. Your feature article on reverse mortgages in your local newspaper made a solid impression in your community because of the depth of your knowledge. That is good PR. You and your staff routinely give time to Little Brothers—Friends of the Elderly, Meals on Wheels, Big Brothers, Salvation Army and other worthy causes in your community. That too is good PR. We need a working definition of PR, and here is a very good one:

"Public relations is the total communication effort of a person, a company, an agency, a group, a government, or any organization to its various publics."[5]

"Total communication effort" means you should pay as much attention to what the appearance of your reception area and your restrooms are telling customers about your company as you should to your employee, customer or community relations. Every business impacts many communities or "publics" as they call them in PR. Your PR program should begin with a clear idea of the communities you need to communicate with for you to remain (and thrive) in the reverse mortgage business. That list should include the following:

- Older adults 62 and older
- Older adult advisors (professional and personal such as accountants, attorneys, bankers, mortgage brokers, insurance agents, children, other relatives, etc.)
- Anyone over the age of 40
- Reverse mortgage counselors
- Government agencies (HUD/FHA, if you are FHA-approved, local regulatory agencies)
- Fannie Mae
- Business and civic organizations (Chamber of Commerce, Rotary, United Way, etc.)
- Media (electronic and print in your operating communities)
- Thought leaders in the community

This is not a compete list. You can come up with more. The idea is to identify and study the ways of your publics before you can craft your PR program.

Footnote
5-Culligan and Greene, page 1.

Part II: Marketing reverse mortgages: It's all about education

After you decide on the communities you want to "touch," the next step is to clarify your objectives. What do you want to achieve with your PR program. Your PR objectives could include the following:

- Position yourself or your company as a reverse mortgage resource.
- Increase reverse mortgage leads/origination.
- Increase earnings (basis of business survival).
- Build the products and your company's credibility.
- Create a respected place for your company in your industry.

The list continues, but the important thing, again, is to be clear about your objectives.

We have identified the communities or publics you must communicate with in order to remain in business. We have also outlined your PR objectives. The next step is to decide on the best way to execute your PR program. In order to achieve the outcome you want, you must deliver a predetermined message to selected publics or audience. The media are of central importance to your PR program execution.

Our basic story is reverse mortgages. You want to tell your many communities about how these unique loans are helping seniors and the community; how they can help seniors and their families; how they are structured. In all these reverse mortgage stories, you want your audiences to see you and our company as a resource, as experts.

The essentials of an effective PR program

There are at least two critical elements to any PR program: The media and the community.

The media

Newspapers, magazines, newsletters, television, radio, hundreds of cable channels, satellite television, Web sites, TiVo, iPods, blogging and podcasting are important to telling your story. The press conference is also a useful PR tool, but we'll not dwell on it.

Advertising

Although advertising is not PR, PR frequently uses advertising as a tool. The advantages are obvious. The advertiser has complete control of the message, within legal and ethical limits. It decides whether to use a newspaper, magazine, TV channel, cable, etc. It also dictates the time it wants its message to appear.

The disadvantages of advertising are equally known. It is very expensive and it carries the odor of vested interest. It is easy to dismiss advertising. The most serious disadvantage of advertising today is that is not effective in part because of the fragmentation of media and failure of advertising to speak the language of aging consumers. As the Roper survey mentioned in Chapter 6 says, 75 percent of seniors are dissatisfied with advertising aimed at them.

Publicity and media relations

Publicity is all about building bridges to your local media, print and electronic. The foundation of lasting media relations are the qualities of truthfulness and reliability. Just because you are a nice guy will not bring you publicity. There are many nice guys and gals out there. Publicity will not happen because you know the reporters and editors in your community. You must be a truthful, reliable resource in addition to doing deliberate bridge-building work.

Smell news everywhere

A good nose for news and the capability to get that news to the right media contact at the right time are essential skills on which much of PR is built. So, what is news? News is anything that is outside the ordinary. For example, when a dog bites a woman, it is not news; however, when a woman bites a dog, it is classic news!

Reverse mortgages have some newsworthy attributes that merit focus in a news story or a news feature. For example, Article 3 of the HECM loan agreement obligates a lender to pay a penalty to a borrower if the lender is late in its obligation to make timely cash advances to a HECM borrower. Friends, this is not the natural order in lending! The common rule is that borrower makes payments to lender. If borrower is late, lender is entitled to collect a late fee or penalty.

A normal forward mortgage deal consists of a promissory note and a mortgage or deed of trust. With the FHA reverse mortgage, we have two notes, two mortgages and a loan agreement. The growth feature in the FHA's HECM and jumbo reverse mortgages are unique attributes. These are the stuff of news.

Besides reverse mortgage programs, there are news items in several parts of reverse country. Sniff around, write a good news story or feature and pass it on to the right media contact.

Writing a letter to the editor of your local newspaper in reaction to reverse mortgage news stories or features is a good PR technique. You should not

Part II: Marketing reverse mortgages: It's all about education

limit your letters to the editor to reverse mortgage stories. Any event or story that affects the welfare of older adults should draw a reaction from you. A letter to the editor of a Seattle newspaper by a reverse mortgage lender brought in 350 inquires.[6] Imagine that! One letter generates 350 leads!!

Well, it is not every day you will have reverse mortgage news stories to react to. You can react to other aging-related issues. *(See Figure 8.3)*

Figure 8.3
Letter to the Editor

To the editor:

Your story on the new Medicare prescription drugs benefit program [*The Recorder*, Saturday, June 15] was very helpful, except it failed to mention how complicated the program is with monthly premiums and annual deductibles. For example, there was no mention that seniors cannot have both Part D and Medigap drug coverage. Also, key concepts such as "coverage gap" and "creditable coverage" need to be clearly explained. In my frequent interactions with seniors as a reverse mortgage specialist, it is clear that more attention and resources should be devoted to educating seniors about the new Medicare drug prescription program in our town.

Atare E. Agbamu, CRMS, Reverse Mortgage Specialist
Credo Mortgage, Inver Grove Heights, Minnesota

Let's examine the "Letter to the Editor" in Figure 8.3. The letter shows that the writer:

- Cares about issues affecting seniors enough to comment.
- Knows the intricacies of a new and fairly complicated senior program.
- Has a background dealing with seniors as a reverse mortgage specialist.

The point is that the writer cares enough to write. This letter will not only make a positive impression on readers, it will also impress the editor … "Hey! Here is a fellow who knows complicated senior programs. May be I should ask him to explain reverse mortgages to our readers."

Footnote
6-Interview with Sarah Hulbert.

News releases

A news release and a press release are the same thing. It is a time-honored PR technique. Like a new story, a news release can be sent out as an introduction of new reverse mortgage products, new features of the same products, new regulation or new development in your company (for example, personnel changes, promotion, new CEO or CFO, corporate social concern, general marketing activity, mergers, acquisitions, "growth" stories, any news, positive or negative) or in the reverse mortgage industry. Remember, the reverse mortgage industry is relatively new. It seems mysterious to the media and consumers alike.

A news release should answer the following questions in a very concise language:

- **Who** did it happen to or who caused it to happen?
- **What** happened or what is going to happen?
- **Where** did it happen?
- **When** did it happen?
- **Why** did it happen?
- And **how** did it happen?

Your news releases should contain the following elements:

- Timeliness
- Human interest
- Public interest
- A well-known personality
- Conflict
- Tragedy
- Mystery
- Romance
- Meaningful predictions
- Money
- Exclusivity
- Sex
- Novelty
- Humor[7]

Footnote
7-Culligan and Greene, page 27.

Part II: Marketing reverse mortgages: It's all about education

Notes to NRMLA's News Release of April 14, 2004
(See Figure 8.4)

1. When you send out a new release on company stationery, make sure you indicate it's a news release. Use company letterhead for the first page only.
2. Always date your news releases.
3. Plaster "For Immediate Release" on all stories you send out and name a company contact person. This is the person who has authority to speak to the media when they call for more information or clarification.
4. Story headline should be both informative and dramatic. How can you improve on this very good headline?
5. Your company location (the city of origin, in this case, Washington, D.C.) should appear at the beginning of your news release. Also, the first paragraph should tell your story. If the editor decides to use it alone, you have achieved your objective.
6. This paragraph builds on the first by providing possible reasons (or why's) for the volume surge.
7. This is an expansion on the story and a deft way to highlight senior needs and suggest reverse mortgages as a solution. Loaded with the right emotions for maximum connection with editors.
8. Citing authoritative federal numbers, this paragraph adds more punch to the story.
9. Builds on point number eight.
10. States a common fact about HECMs and shows its link to the federal government, builds credibility.
11. More specific details about HECM volume in top 10 markets, comparing fiscal 2004/2003 numbers. Remember, these are interim numbers. What is important here is the unmistakable growth trend.
12. Reverse mortgages are defined. Always include a definition because the editors may not know. Even if they know, your definition carries more weight because you are an industry expert.
13. Takes aim at a common misconception that well-meaning product literature from HUD and Fannie Mae has unintentionally helped create.
14. Tells editors that NRMLA is a reverse mortgage resource. In your local market, you want to tell your editors that you are the local revere mortgage guru.
15. Identify NRMLA. Make sure you identify your company as a local reverse mortgage company. Mention any professional affiliation with relevant national organizations. An affiliation with NRMLA will give your

The marketing basket

Figure 8.4
NRMLA's News Release of April 14, 2004

NATIONAL REVERSE MORTGAGE LENDERS ASSOCIATION
1625 Massachusetts Ave., NW, Suite 601
Washington, DC 20036

1. NEWS RELEASE

2. April 14, 2004
3. FOR IMMEDIATE RELEASE

Contact: Glenn Petherick, Director of Communications, NRMLA
202-939-1753, gpetherick@dworbell.com
Peter Bell, President, NRMLA
202-939-1741, pbell@dworbell.com

4. Reverse Mortgage Volume Up 112% from Year Ago, Group Says
Top 10 Markets All Show Increase in Originations.

5. WASHINGTON, DC — The volume of federally insured reverse mortgages taken out by older homeowners in recent months has increased by 112% from a year ago, as a blistering record pace of originations continues, according to the National Reverse Mortgage Lenders Association.

6. NRMLA attributed the surging popularity of reverse mortgages to several factors, including greater consumer awareness of and comfort with the product, and the increasingly tighter budgets of America's seniors.

7. "While some signs suggest a recovering economy, many retirees are still struggling day-to-day to live comfortably or make ends meet," said NRMLA President Peter Bell. "As a result of this, more and more older Americans are turning to reverse mortgages as the solution to their financial needs. With the help of a reverse mortgage," he continued, "these seniors find they can cope with the myriad of financial pressures that include rising out-pockets-costs for medical care and prescription drugs, increasing property taxes on their homes, eroding Social Security checks, and meager rates of return from CDs and money market funds due to low interest rates."

8. According to NRMLA, federal statistics show that the volume of federally insured reverse mortgages — called Home Equity Conversion Mortgages (HECMs) — made nationwide in the five-month period from October 2003 through February 2004 (12,848 loans) was 112% higher than the level during the five-month period ending February 2003 (6,061). HECM volume in February 2004 alone (4,148) was a new monthly record, and was 273% higher than the level of February 2003 (1,113).

9. The figures illustrate the growing, record popularity of reverse mortgages among older homeowners. In the federal fiscal year (FY 2003) that ended September 30, 2003, there were 18,097 HECMs made nationwide, an increase of 39% from the previous fiscal year.

10. HECMs are the most popular of the three reverse mortgage products currently available. Accounting for about 90% of all reverse mortgages made today, and available in every state, HECMs are insured by the Federal Housing Administration (FHA), a part of the U.S. Department of Housing and Urban Development, which compiles the statistics on HECM volume.

Figure 8.4 continued on page 120

Part II: Marketing reverse mortgages: It's all about education

---

Figure 8.4
NRMLA's News Release of April 14, 2004

11. HECM volume for the five-month period ending February 29, 2004 was up from a year ago in each of the top 10 markets in the country. According to HUD's statistics, the top 10 HUD field offices reporting the greatest HECM volume in the five-month period ending February 29, 2004, were: (1) Los Angeles, 891 HECM loans made (compared with 298 in the five-month period ending February 28, 2003); (2) Santa Ana, CA, 620 (234); (3) New York, 533 (330); (4) San Francisco, 457 (197); (5) San Diego, 453 (138); (6) Denver, 445 (325); (7) Detroit, 395 (267); (8) Boston, 381 (110); (9) Minneapolis-St. Paul, MN, 342 (145); and (10) Coral Gables, FL, 341 (177).

12. A reverse mortgage is a loan that enables homeowners 62 or older to borrow against the equity in their home, without having to sell their home, give up title, or take on a new monthly mortgage payment. The loan proceeds can be used for any purpose, and taken out as a lump sum payment, fixed monthly payment, line of credit (except in Texas), or a combination. The loan amount depends on the borrower's age, current interest rates, and the value and location of their home. A reverse mortgage isn't repaid until the borrower moves out of the home permanently, and the repayment amount can't exceed the value of the home. After the loan is repaid, any remaining equity is distributed to the borrower or borrower's heirs/estate.

13. A senior's home doesn't have to be owned free and clear to qualify for a reverse mortgage.

14. NRMLA distributes a free information booklet on reverse mortgages, called *Just the FAQs: Answers to Common Questions About Reverse Mortgages*. Consumers can order it by telephone (1-866-264-4466, toll-free) or at NRMLA's Web site, http://www.reversemortgage.org. The Web site has extensive information on reversre mortgages, a state-by-state list of lenders, and a reverse mortgage calculator.

15. NRMLA is a nonprofit trade association, based in Washington, DC, whose members make and service reverse mortgages throughout the U.S. and Canada. Members sign a Code of Conduct pledging to abide by guidelines that assure fair, ethical, and respectful practices in offering and making reverse mortgages to seniors.

16. *[Note to Reporters and Editors: NRMLA can provide statistics and comment on reverse mortgages, and help find reverse mortgage borrowers and lenders in your area for interviews.]*

17.   # # #

Source: National Reverse Mortgage Lenders Association

---

company credibility. We will say more about the marketing value of NRMLA later in Chapter 10.

16. Again, let the editors and reporters know that not only are you a resource on reverse mortgages, you can also help them find other sources of reverse mortgage information.

17. The three number symbols mean end of story.

The marketing basket

Notes to NRMLA's Imaginative Release of November 20, 2003

(See Figure 8.5 on page 123)

Figure 8.5 is not your typical news release, although it is labeled as one. It's an ad brilliantly crafted and targeted at a very powerful reverse mortgage public: Children and grandchildren of potential reverse mortgage borrowers. I suggest that you read and re-read this truly imaginative release. Using Figure 8.5 as a model, you can design a similar targeted imaginative release at other reverse mortgage audiences or publics: certified public accountants (CPAs), certified financial planners (CFPs), small community banks, long-term care insurance agents, geriatric care professionals, etc. The creative possibilities that Figure 8.5 can inspire are endless. I just couldn't resist this brilliant illustration of reverse mortgage marketing from NRMLA.

Editorial conversation

As part of your public relations program, you should be setting up editorial conversations or interviews with local newspapers, magazine, radios, televisions, cable or financial wires. Obviously, before you get to this stage of your public relations work, you have established some credibility in your community as a reverse mortgage resource. Actually, one indication that you are perceived as a reverse mortgage expert will be calls from reporters, editors, or program producers asking to interview you on reverse mortgage-related issues. You should also take the initiative and suggest interviews to reporters, editors and producers that you have developed some relationship with. Newspapers, magazines, radios, television, and cable outlets are always looking for fresh angles on old materials to use.

Whether the reporter, editor or producer call you or you initiate the call for interview, you should establish some ground rules at the time you schedule the interview. Essentially, there should be agreement on the topics to be covered, and you should resist the temptation to go outside the boundaries, especially if you lack the expertise to address outside topics. Assuming you are the interviewee, you will find the following guidelines useful:

1. Be prepared.

Familiarize yourself with the publication and the writings of the reporter or editor who will be interviewing you. Arm yourself with facts to support your statements. Do the same homework for radio, television or cable interviews.

2. Be yourself, be friendly and be candid.

Part II: Marketing reverse mortgages: It's all about education

3. Focus on the subject of the interview and get to the point.
Never push or promote your company unless the interview is about your company.

4. Expect questions that may seem childlike.
The interviewer may be playing the role of a simple reader, listener or viewer who is finding out about reverse mortgages for the first time and are not well-versed in reverse subject matter.

5. Admit ignorance when you do not know the answer to a questions, offer to find out answers and call the interviewer with the answer.

6. Know the interviewer's area of interest and know their deadline.

7. When you have covered the topic, thank the interviewer.
Let them know you are always available for more information and stop talking.

8. Asking an interviewer whether your story will be used and requesting to see a story before publication should be avoided.
The interviewer may not be the person to decide what story will be used, and the media fiercely guards its independence.

9. Never make "off the record" comments to a media person.[8]

The community: Do good to do well
In addition to the media, an effective PR program should include the community or communities where your reverse mortgage business operates. Let's define the community:

"The community includes all people and organizations affected by, or who can affect, your company because of its geographic location. Your community may include employees, shareholders, customers, suppliers and others with whom you have some direct relationship. But it includes also a great many more people with whom you have no direct involvement."[9]

Footnotes
8-Culligan and Greene, pages 16-17.
9-Culligan and Greene, page 41.

The marketing basket

Figure 8.5
NRMLA's News Release of November 20, 2003

NATIONAL REVERSE MORTGAGE LENDERS ASSOCIATION
1625 Massachusetts Ave., NW, Suite 601
Washington, DC 20036

NEWS RELEASE

November 20, 2003

FOR IMMEDIATE RELEASE
Contact: Glenn Petherick, Director of Communications, NRMLA
            202-939-1753, gpetherick@dworbell.com
            Peter Bell, President, NRMLA
            202-939-1741, pbell@dworbell.com

Holiday Checkup: Are Mom & Dad Financially Secure?
A Reverse Mortgage May Be the Cure for Financial Peace of Mind

The holidays are a time for family get-togethers and catching up.

But for adult children of seniors, holiday visits can bring awareness that Mom and Dad — as a couple, widow, or widower — are struggling to make ends meet.

They may not tell you outright — in fact, they probably won't. But the signs are probably there in your paraent's house and lifestyle. Ask yourself:

- *Is Mom & Dad's house in need or repairs or "dressing up"?*
- *Do prescription drugs appear to be a major part of your parents' daily life?* If so, out-of-pocket costs for prescriptions and medical insurance premiums could be taking a big bite out of Mom & Dad's budget, forcing them to give up other necessities and small pleasures.
- *Are there some physical changes — grab bars in the bathrooms, better lighting, wider doorways — that would help Mom & Dad live more safely, comfortably, and avoid accidents?*
- *Have home prices around Mom & Dad jumped considerably the past few years?* If so, Mom & Dad's bills for property taxes and homeowners' insurance likely have risen as well.

A growing number of seniors are taking care of these financial needs and others with a reverse mortgage — making their retirement a period of enjoyment instead of worry, and allowing their "kids" to stop fretting about Mom & Dad's finances as well.

"For too many older homeowners, the holidays can be a time of want and worry with the bills piling up, work needed on the house — but not enough money to pay for it," says Peter Bell, president of the National Reverse Mortgage Lenders Association. "Fortunately, many seniors are sitting on the answer to their problems — their home. By getting a reverse mortgage, where appropriate, seniors can take care of their own needs and live more comfortably, and ease their kids' concerns as well."

Figure 8.5 continued on page 124

123

Part II: Marketing reverse mortgages: It's all about education

Figure 8.5

NRMLA's News Release of November 20, 2003

Reverse mortgages are booming in popularity. For the 12-month period ending September 30, 2003, the volume of federally insured reverse mortgages rose 39% from the previous year, which was 68% higher than the year before. The federally insured reverse mortgage insurance product is called the Home Equity Conversion Mortgage (HECM).

"We've seen an increase in the number of reverse mortgages originated for the last few years," says Bell. "But unfortunately there are many seniors — and their adult children — who still aren't aware of this product and its potential benefits. Reverse mortgages can have a dramatic impact on seniors' quality of life by increasing their income, enhancing their financial security, and letting them fully enjoy their retirement."

A reverse mortgage is a loan available to homeowners 62 or older that enables them to borrow against the equity in their home, without having to sell their home, give up title, or take on a new monthly mortgage payment.

The loan proceeds can be used for any purpose, and taken out as a lump sum payment, fixed monthly payment, line of credit (except in Texas), or a combination. The loan amount depends on the borrower's age, value and location of their home, and current interst rates. A reverse mortage isn't repaid until the borrower moves out of the home permanently, and the repayment amount can't exceed the value of the home. After the loan is repaid, any remaining equity is distributed to the borrower or borrower's heirs/estate.

A senior's home doesn't have to be owned free and clear to qualify for a reverse mortgage.

NRMLA distributes a free consumer booklet, called Just the FAQs: Answers to Common Questions About Reverse Mortgages. Consumers can order it by telephone (1-866-264-4466, toll-free) or at NRMLA's Web site, http://www.reversemortgage.org. The Web site also has a state-by-state list of reverse mortgages throughout the U.S. and Canada. Members sign a Code of Conduct pledging to abide by guidelines that assure fair, ethical, and respectful practices in offering and making reverse mortgages to seniors.

[Note to Reporters and Editors: You can view the Just the FAQs *consumer guide at http://www.reversemortgage.org/justfaqs.pdf. NRMLA can provide you with statitics and comment on reverse mortgages and help find local reverse mortgage borrowers and lenders to interview.]*

# # #

Source: National Reverse Mortgage Lenders Association

The marketing basket

The first task then for a reverse mortgage total community relations program is to clearly define its community or communities. For reverse mortgages, your community may include the following:

- Mortgage brokers
- Mortgage lenders
- Certified financial planners (CFPs)
- Accountants
- Bankers (small community banks)
- Estate planners
- Conservators
- Guardians
- Long-term care agents
- Credit unions
- Elder law attorneys
- Life insurance agents
- Sons and daughters
- Neighbors
- Relatives
- Grandchildren
- Clients
- Prospects
- Clergy
- Pharmacists
- Doctors
- Healthcare providers
- Senior centers
- Undertakers
- Area agency on aging
- Local HUD office
- Real estate agents
- Cultural institutions
- The media
- Civic and fraternal organizations
- Churches, synagogues, mosques, etc.
- Aging in Place network in your market
- Local Chamber of Commerce
- All levels of government

After developing a list of reverse mortgage communities, the next step is to draw up a plan for community involvement. Obviously, you cannot be involved in all communities at the same time. You want to identify a few organizations or communities you want to become involved with. Encourage your staff to pick up from the list you have jointly developed. Depending on the size of your staff, you can pick three or four organizations each, provided there is no overlap. If one of your staff members is already involved with senior centers, doctors and clergy, for example, the other should work with pharmacists, an area agency on aging and churches. Spread your staff (your community capital) out so that you can have a greater impact in the reverse mortgage communities.

If your reverse mortgage operations take place in more than one state or location, you should prepare a similar list for each region. The local staff should be persuaded to engage actively in the community. In fact, key criteria for hiring a reverse mortgage specialist should be a capacity or passions for community involvement. The catchwords of your community relation effort should be: "Do good to do well."

Part II: Marketing reverse mortgages: It's all about education

For the health of your reverse mortgage business is inextricably linked with the health of the community in which you operate. The following are some guidelines for good community relations:

- Know how the community in which you operate is wired politically, economically, socially, and culturally.
- Familiarize yourself with the specific problems that confront the community, as well as the opportunities and interests.
- In concert with other community groups, position your company as part of the solution to the problems.
- Communicate your community involvement consistently to all without fanfare. Your news release should go to all contacts on your community list.
- The physical appearance of your company should be attractive, clean and it should blend into the surrounding area in a pleasant way.
- Any complaints against your company should be addressed courteously and quickly, even if it is unfair in your opinion.
- Treat your employees well, for they are a part of the community.
- Treat your customers better, your survival depends on them.
- Always use local vendors or suppliers.
- The media is the mirror of the community, so enlist the media in your community effort.[10]
- Be a caring individual and hire truly caring loan officers for your reverse mortgage business.
- Do what is right by the customer … always!
- Develop the capacity to work in other people's shoes (or empathy).
- Be knowledgeable about the issues that are important to older adults, such as Medicare and Medicaid, Social Security benefits, prescription drugs, etc. It is not enough to know just reverse mortgage products features and benefits.[11]

Standing on the shoulders of others

Almost every reverse mortgage veteran I interviewed on the subject of marketing reverse mortgages agreed with this statement:

Networking is the key to your long-term success in reverse mortgage marketing.

Footnotes
10-Culligan and Greene, pages 42-44.
11-Interview with NRMLA President Peter Bell.

The marketing basket

So, what is networking? *Merriam Webster's Collegiate Dictionary (10th Edition)* defines networking as "The exchange of information or services among individuals, groups or institutions."[12] *Webster's New World Dictionary* defines it as "The developing of contacts or exchanging of information, as to further a career."[13]

Considered a networking virtuoso, author and speaker Liz Carpenter of Texas defined networking as "standing on the shoulders of others to help you get where you want to go. It's people helping each other."[14]

As a reverse mortgage specialist or lender, your goal is to grow your business. While you can exchange contacts, information and services with individuals, it is clear from all three definitions that you will be more effective networking within groups or organizations. That way, you simply multiply the number of shoulders on which you stand and increase your chances for success.

How to stand on shoulders

How do you go about networking? Again:

- Start by writing down your networking goals.
- Make a list of local businesses and civic organizations, such as the Chamber of Commerce, Rotary, Boy Scouts, Girl Scouts, United Way, Mason's, Knights of Columbus, Catholic Charities, the Urban League, United Negro Fund, Federation of Jewish Philanthropies, Little Brothers—Friends of the Elderly, etc.
- Call a few of these groups and ask them to send you some literature about their mission and work.
- Select a few with mission statements that you feel strongly about.

Although your ultimate goal in networking is to grow your business, the nature of networking is give and take. You give first. You invest your time and resources to advance the group's mission. Over time, you will gain trust and credibility within the group and you will begin to take in the form of leads, referrals, and other contacts with individuals and groups. Because networking is give and take for the long haul, you should believe in the mission of the group or groups you choose as your networking vehicles. It is your belief in the mis-

---

Footnotes
12-Merriam Webster's Collegiate Dictionary (10th Edition), *page 780.*
13-Webster's New World Dictionary, *page 395.*
14-Dilen-Schneider, *page 78.*

Part II: Marketing reverse mortgages: It's all about education

sion or missions of these organizations that will keep you focused. It is your belief that will sustain you through the usual frustrations that come with any group effort. And it is your belief in (and your commitment to) the mission of the group that will help persuade others that you are referable.

Some tips for standing on shoulders

As you move to implement the networking aspect of your reverse mortgage marketing plan, keep the following in mind:

- Networking is critical to your long-term reverse mortgage marketing success.
- Networking is give and take, and you must give first.
- Networking will demand both your time and resources.
- Join groups whose mission you believe in.
- Actively encourage your staff to join organization they believe in and network.
- Volunteer for committee and subcommittee assignments within organizations. That is where the real work of organizations gets done. That is how people get to know you and where you start to develop credibility, and also where you meet the key people.
- Position yourself as the reverse mortgage specialist within the group
- Do favors for other members of the group. If you find that a member of a committee you are serving on is a financial planner, send her some customers who need financial planning work. Favors tend to lead to favors.
- Be referable. A reputation for reliability within the group will enhance your credibility and give access to key people and their networks outside the group. An important question you must ask yourself before embarking on the networking track is, "Am I referable?" In other words, do you do what you say you are going to do? Some seasoned networkers believe you shouldn't even consider networking unless you are "referable."[15]

The "ultimate" in reverse mortgage networking

The National Aging in Place Council (NAIPC) is made up of professionals including reverse mortgage lenders, mortgage bankers, elder law attorneys, insurance agents, home modification contractors, nurses, home healthcare providers, geriatric care managers, etc. with one goal: To help older adults age at home or age in place. The council was formed in 2003 with NRMLA's help.

Barbara Franklin, a long-term care planning and financing expert from

---

Footnote
15-Interview with Paul and Barbara Franklin of Franklin Funding, Charleston, S.C.

The marketing basket

Charleston, S.C., has called the council the "ultimate" in reverse mortgage networking because participation in the coalition gives the reverse mortgage lender an opportunity to "stand on the shoulders" of many aging-focused professionals with one membership. For more information on the NAIPC, visit www.naipc.org.

In Chapter 9, we look at some reverse mortgage marketing rules from the trenches. I gleaned these principles from hours of interviews with active reverse mortgage lenders and thought leaders across America. My own field experience since 2001 confirms these guidelines. They apply in any reverse mortgage marketing environment.

Part II: Marketing reverse mortgages: It's all about education

Chapter Nine
Become a rev-angelist

Chapter 9 objectives
After studying this chapter, the reader will be able to:
- Identify eight lessons of reverse mortgage marketing
- Explain the reverse mortgage marketing lessons
- Know how to apply the lessons to educate older adults and their advisors

"What is it?"
A few months ago, I called the coordinator of a community education program in the Twin Cities. After introducing myself, I said I would like to teach a reverse mortgage course. This seasoned community educator paused for a minute before asking me, "What is it?"

Before I answered her question, I asked whether she had run mortgage courses in the past; she said she had. Since almost everyone in America "knows" what a mortgage is, I said, "It is the other side of a mortgage. A lender makes payments to you, the homeowner." I got her attention.

What have we learned about reverse mortgage marketing after almost 20 years of active marketing and origination? The following are some lessons from the field:

Lesson #1: Educate older adults and their advisors
As my conversation with the Twin Cities-based community educator shows, education of older adults and their advisors is *essential* to marketing reverse mortgages. Many older adults and their advisors are gaining awareness of reverse mortgages, but they have misconceptions that often keep them from looking into reverse mortgages as vehicles for their retirement cash needs. These misconceptions could have potentially tragic results as a story one of my customers, Patrika Olson of Cottage Grove, Minn. told me illustrates. I

Part II: Marketing reverse mortgages: It's all about education

shared the story with readers of my column in June 2005. Let's revisit the story here in her words:

"Unfortunately, this lady passed away a couple of months ago. She had lived in Greenwich, Conn. in a $3 million-plus home [paid for]. She was getting to the point where she could not pay her insurance and her taxes. She and her friends seemed to have the same concept that I had [and so many people have] about reverse mortgages. I mentioned the possibility of a reverse mortgage and it was like I was telling her to jump off the Brooklyn Bridge or something.

"But, unfortunately, like I said, she passed away. She was only 72-years old, and I don't think that's very old anymore. There she was, living on a piece of property that is worth millions of dollars, and yet she was stressed because her monthly income wasn't allowing her to pay the taxes and insurance."

When I suggested financial worries may have contributed to the Greenwich millionaire's untimely death, she replied, "In this case, I absolutely believe that could have been a factor."

Now, ask yourself: How many Greenwich millionaires [or thousand-aires] are there in America? Needless to say, reverse mortgage marketing (education) is serious business.

So, we must answer the question: "What is it?" for every older adult and for their advisors. For those who know what reverse mortgages are, we must make sure that what they know is correct by asking questions and listening carefully to their responses. Some common misconceptions about reverse mortgages include the following:

- My home must be "free and clear" for me to qualify for a reverse mortgage.
- Only people in extreme financial situations need a reverse mortgage.
- On my death, the lender will push my heirs aside and sell my home.
- A reverse mortgage is too costly compared to home equity loans or lines of credit.
- There will be nothing left for my heirs if I take out a reverse mortgage.
- My heirs will be liable for whatever I owe beyond the value of my home.

There are other misconceptions about reverse mortgages "out there." And to market reverse mortgages, we must identify and replace them with correct information. How do we identify them? Again, we identify reverse mortgage misconceptions by asking questions and listening carefully and actively. As the Greenwich millionaire's story shows, ignorance of reverse mortgages as means to financial security can be very costly.

Lesson #2: Become a solution-supplier
A reverse mortgage, says Barbara Franklin of Franklin & Associates (Charleston, S.C.), is not "a product to be sold, but a solution to meet a life-planning need."[1] It follows that you should not come across as a salesperson. Your focus should not be on the product, but on how reverse mortgages can meet the customer's need.

NRMLA President Peter Bell knows something about marketing reverse mortgages on a national scale. He has helped to put the reverse mortgage industry on the map in America. Here is what he said about focusing on the needs of older adults:

"Nobody is going to get a reverse mortgage for the sake of a reverse mortgage; it is all about needs."[2]

Among others, extra cash via reverse mortgages can help address four core needs of older adults:

- Sustenance
- Security
- Lifestyle
- Life-planning

When an older-adult's total monthly income is $550 and her expenses are $950 due to inflation, the choice is often unpleasant: to buy food or to buy medicine. For this older adult, the need is sustenance or survival. The solution we offer is extra cash (through reverse mortgages) to make up the $400 monthly budget shortfall.

There are older adults who have bread, butter, steak, fish and medicine, but they worry about cash for a new roof, a new kitchen, or a new car. These older adults have security needs, a pot of cash they can reach into as needed to pay for potential leaky roofs, new kitchens, or new cars should calm their

---
Footnotes
1-Interview with Barbara Franklin of Franklin & Associates, Charleston, S.C.
2-Interview with NRMLA President Peter Bell.

minds. Solution: Tax-free cash through a reverse mortgage.

Some older adults want to see the Acropolis in Greece, touch the majestic Mount Kilimanjaro in Africa, walk along the Great Wall of China with their grandchildren, take a college course in Quantum Mechanics to challenge their minds and pay the college tuition for their grandchildren. They have a lifestyle need. Solution: Cash via a reverse mortgage.

And there are older adults who want to give efficiently to their favorite charities, as well as manage the tax consequences of their estates. Solution: Tax-free cash and debt through a reverse mortgage. Gifting tax-free cash may meet their efficient-giving test. Debt [a reverse mortgage debt] reduces their estate's value and lowers taxes for their heirs.

So, find out what the core needs of the older adults in your markets are first. Some may need to keep body and soul together. Some may want peace of mind, and others desire experiences they could only now imagine. Finally, some want to give prudently and reduce the taxman's cut of their estate. Whatever the needs are, reverse mortgages may supply solutions. Therefore, position yourself or your company as solution-supplier for older adults' needs.

Lesson #3: Build credibility

Credibility means your target market believes you when you speak about reverse mortgages. They view you as an expert. They hear others refer to you as an expert. How do you build credibility? You do it the same way all experts are made: Know your subject as thoroughly as you can. Share your knowledge with others in the mortgage community and in your market through presentations, seminars, newsletters and articles in industry and non-industry publications. Why the mortgage community first? When your industry colleagues recognize your expertise and refer to you as an expert, it gives your credibility a tremendous boost with others. If your industry associates do not know you as an expert, your standing or credibility with the public will be nil. Why share your reverse mortgage expertise? That's how you establish your credibility.

If you have expert knowledge and cannot communicate that know-how to your target audience, then you have a credibility problem. Again, the means for sharing your special knowledge are presentations, seminars, radio or TV talk shows, newsletter, and articles in publications. When people read your articles about reverse mortgages consistently over a period of time, when they hear others in your industry refer to you as a reverse mortgage expert, when they read about your reverse mortgage seminars and presentations, you have established credibility.

Become a rev-angelist

As a reverse mortgage educator (marketer), your credibility is your most important asset. It will not be built overnight. It will require focus, hard work, time, and commitment. And remember that without credibility in you as an expert, you cannot be effective in educating older adults and their advisors. As Paul Franklin of Franklin Funding in Charleston, S.C. said, "There has to be confidence and credibility in the messenger."[3] Let's look at it this way: If you get a flyer in the mail about Michael Jordan giving a talk on basketball, you will likely attend and hang on to every word from his lips. However, if the flyer says His Air-ness is giving a lecture on brain surgery, well, that's another story.

Lesson #4: Become a focused specialist
A specialist is someone who has developed specialized skills in one area. All reverse mortgage veterans I interviewed agreed that becoming a committed specialist in reverse mortgages will give your presentation an edge reserved only for those who are focused on one thing. This singular focus will enhance the passion for the subject (Rule #5). Besides supporting your passion, becoming a specialist builds your credibility (Rule #3).

Jack Trout, one of the leading marketing minds in the world, has said that in a world of mind-boggling choice, the specialist in any field gets special attention:

"People are impressed with those who concentrate on a specific activity or product. They perceive them as experts. And as experts, people tend to give them credit for more knowledge and experience than they sometimes deserve."[4]

Reverse mortgages are relatively new, unique, complex, and specialized mortgage lending products. To enhance your credibility and give intensity to your passion during marketing presentations, it is vital to focus completely on reverse mortgages. As Jack Trout has said, "We are in the age of the specialist."[5]

There are many advantages to becoming a dedicated specialist. As a specialist, your knowledge and insights into reverse mortgages will be deeper. This deeper knowledge will enhance your passion and increase your confidence. Specialization and focus will position you as an expert in the minds of your professional colleagues and in the public's mind. This special status

---

Footnotes
3-Interview with Paul and Barbara Franklin of Franklin Funding in Charleston, S.C.
4-Trout on Strategy, McGraw-Hill, New York, 2004, page 77.
5-Trout on Strategy, McGraw-Hill, New York, 2004, page 81.

Part II: Marketing reverse mortgages: It's all about education

as an expert will enable you to become a resource in any group to which you belong. As a resource, people will come to you for answers and solutions to reverse mortgages problems or needs. As a dedicated reverse mortgage resource, you can develop better referral relationships with other non-reverse-mortgage professionals. Your professional referral partners will have confidence in you because you will not be in competition with them.

There are some disadvantages as well. As a single-product specialist, you do not have the protection that product-diversification affords in case reverse mortgages hit a slump. Although a reverse mortgage slump is a remote probability, there are no guarantees in any business. As one reverse mortgage lender in New Mexico who does not believe in specialization said, "To specialize is to cut your income."[6]

Lesson #5: Become a rev-angelist

A rev-angelist is a reverse mortgage specialist who *passionately believes* in the good a reverse mortgage can do. As you go about educating older adults and their advisors, your presentations must show that you passionately believe in the value of reverse mortgages for you to make an impression on your audience. Coldly and objectively going over program features and benefits will not do the job. Passion for the good reverse mortgages can do, coupled with credibility and confidence, will give your presentations and other marketing communications critical emotional power to connect with your audience. Of course, you do not want your passion to overflow and cause damage. The key, as in all things, is moderation.

Lesson #6: Be visible in the community

"Visibility matters," said Jack Welch. Another essential principle of marketing reverse mortgages is to be visible in the community where you operate your reverse mortgage business through "good works." In other words, do good and your reverse mortgage business will do well. Can you do well and become visible without doing good works? Of course, you can in the short term. A value that is very important to people in the second half of life is altruism or doing good for good's sake.

How do you become visible in your community? Become a volunteer and encourage all your team members to become volunteers. Do you just volun-

---

Footnote
6- Interview with Alfred Sanchez of ADS Mortgage Corporation, Albuquerque, N.M., Sept. 3, 2004.

Become a rev-angelist

teer for any non-profit project? No! Look inside yourself and ask: What do I believe in? What are the social causes that are important to me as a member of my community? In addition:

- Research the not-for-profit sector of your community
- Identify a few organizations serving causes that are important to you
- Visit these organizations
- Get some literature on them
- Read their mission statements
- Decide on one or two
- Volunteer your time and other resources
- Encourage your team members or employees to do the same
- Preferably, disperse the volunteer or civic capital of your company
- Let your employees volunteer for causes that are important to them, not to you because you are the boss
- Let those who are interested in abandoned children give time to that cause
- Let those who are concerned about lonely and isolated elders, about hunger and poverty follow their passion

As the team leader in your company, the important thing is to nurture a culture of civic engagement by your example. If you have a lot of money for newspaper, cable, television, billboard or other forms of advertising, you can achieve visibility in your community for your reverse mortgage business for a while. It is not clear that you can sustain that level of spending for visibility over the long-term. However, deploying the full civic capital of your company by volunteering a few hours of your time and some cash and encouraging your employees to do the same, you will, over time, gain visibility in the community. You will gain something more: Goodwill for your business.

Lesson #7: Humanize the customer experience
In contrast with the rampant automation of the customer experience in most industries today [i.e., "your call is very important to us …"], you should humanize the customer service experience for the reverse mortgage customer as much as possible. Mature customers want to chat with a person, not talk into a machine. By giving customers warm human contact and time, you humanize and strengthen their relationship with your company. This should be common sense, but we know common sense is uncommon, especially when we buy into the idea that "automated" customer service is "efficient."

Part II: Marketing reverse mortgages: It's all about education

A first quarter 2005 financial industry study by J.D. Power and Associates underscores this point. The study says a majority of consumers, a huge 64 percent, prefer human contact throughout the mortgage loan process. Telephone contact came in second at 21 percent. Our regular snail mail was third at 18 percent. Vying for last place were Web and e-mail interactions at two percent each. Although the study looked at the mortgage loan process through the eyes and experiences of traditional forward mortgage customers who may be younger than reverse mortgage customers, the lesson applies even more directly to reverse mortgage customers: Older customers strongly prefer human interaction. Therefore, make sure they get it from your company or they will look elsewhere. *(See Figure 9.1)*

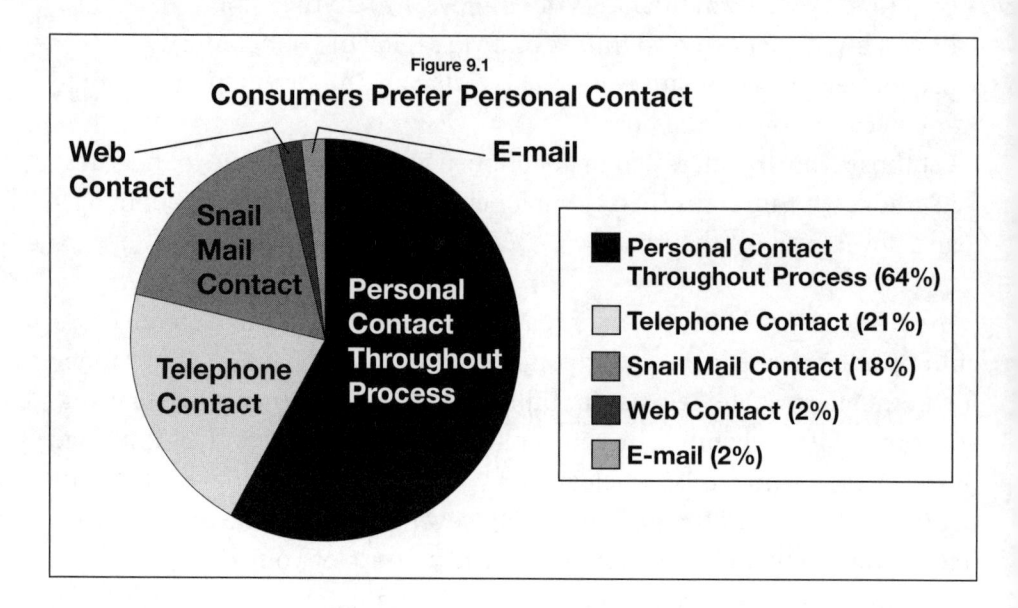

Figure 9.1
Consumers Prefer Personal Contact

- Personal Contact Throughout Process (64%)
- Telephone Contact (21%)
- Snail Mail Contact (18%)
- Web Contact (2%)
- E-mail (2%)

Lesson #8: Talk to everyone

For a program with a pre-selected demographic (62 and older), the temptation is to target only that demographic, and those who advise them: Bankers (especially small community bankers), credit unions, financial planners, mortgage brokers, insurance brokers, real estate agents, long-term care providers, geriatric workers, lawyers, accountants, doctors, estate planners, conservators, sons, daughters, neighbors, relatives, grandchildren, clergy, pharmacists, and undertakers, etc. However, *there is a reverse mortgage in the future of every homeowner.*

Therefore, talk to anyone who would listen about reverse mortgages. Your 25-year-old first-time homebuyer may have grandparents with sustenance needs that cash from a reverse mortgage can address. Your barber or hairstylist may have a parent with security needs that cash from a reverse mortgage can solve. Your golf buddy may have an uncle with insufficient cash to meet some lifestyle needs and a reverse mortgage can help. And your seatmate on a flight may be a small, successful businessman, contemplating an efficient way to give and manage his estate liabilities.

For traditional forward mortgage professionals, there are many daily cross-selling opportunities at application and on the closing table: "Who can we help beside you?" A very successful reverse mortgage lender in Florida believes that the best way to get attention and start a conversation with anyone is to plaster "Reverse Mortgages," in eye-catching colors on t-shirts, cars, trucks, etc. He says the words "Reverse Mortgages" always invite questions from people on the streets, at the supermarket, and at the gas station. Questions soon lead to conversation and to reverse mortgage teaching moments. His success suggests that his method is working.

Wearing a *"Got Reverse?"*[7] button or t-shirt may also help to stimulate questions about reverse mortgages from people you interact in the course of your daily activities. Let us review the eight basic lessons of reverse mortgage marketing:

- Educate older adults and their advisors
- Become a solutions-supplier
- Build credibility
- Become a dedicated specialist
- Become a rev-angelist
- Be visible in the community
- Humanize the customer experience
- Talk to everyone

The important thing is to recognize that everyone needs a reverse mortgage education, not just those who are 62 and older. There is a reverse mortgage in your future!

Reverse mortgage marketing rules, such as talking to everyone about reverse mortgages, being visible in the community, providing solutions to older adults needs, becoming a dedicated specialist, becoming a passionate believer, and building credibility reinforce the first principle: Educate older adults and their advisors.

Footnote
7- My friend and editor, Eric C. Peck of The Mortgage Press, *is the originator of the "Got Reverse?" idea.*

Part II: Marketing reverse mortgages: It's all about education

Applying the education principle

With education of older adults and their advisors as our strategy, we move into our communities as reverse mortgage educators, not salesmen or saleswomen.

What to teach

Our first task as reverse mortgage educators is to decide what to teach. I suggest starting with clearing up misconceptions about reverse mortgages (a list of common misconceptions can be found under Rule #1 and in Chapter 1), and moving on to "How Reverse Mortgages Can Meet Older Adult Needs." Remember to find stories to deliver your lessons. I believe in retelling the "Greenwich Millionaire and Other Reverse Stories" [*The Mortgage Press*, June 2005]. It shows how costly misconceptions can be if they stop older adults from taking action.

Where to teach

Anywhere older adults or their advisors meet as a group should be useful. Community centers, retirement communities, public libraries, churches, temples, synagogues, and mosques are possible venues. Community education programs are always looking for fresh and interesting subjects to put on their schedules. Most professional associations make the education of their members a priority. So look up your local elder law attorneys, certified financial planners (CFPs), certified public accountants (CPAs), enrolled agents (those who prepare taxes), healthcare providers, insurance agents, etc. Talk to the people who chair the education committees in these groups and ask to be placed on their schedules.

How to teach

How you share your reverse mortgage knowledge will depend on the group you are addressing:

- With older adult groups, informal, conversational, questions and answers methods may be useful.
- With CPAs, CFPs and elder law attorneys, for example, formal presentations with charts, numbers, and scenarios may be more effective. Even with analytical types, begin with human interest stories that lead into your presentation.
- Do your homework on any group you are scheduled to speak to.
- Find out the average age of the group, their education, history, and culture. You can find this information by going to their Web sites, reading their pub-

lications, their mission statements, and talking with their members individually.
- Find out who spoke to the group last and talk with that person. You will learn some useful things about the group. With these insights, design your presentation.
- Design flexible presentations around clearing up reverse mortgage misconceptions and what reverse mortages can do for seniors.
- Keep it simple and lively.

You will find my 7-Point ReverseTalk™ (See Appendix 2 [a]/[b] useful in talking with older adult groups about reverse mortgages because it helps audience and presenter focus on experiences extra-cash can make possible. It simplifies presentation to older adults by zeroing in on what they want and what reverse mortgages are about.

In Chapter 10, we will review more lessons and the marketing value of NRMLA's membership.

Part II: Marketing reverse mortgages: It's all about education

Chapter Ten
Marketing postscripts

Chapter 10 objectives
After studying this chapter, the reader will be able to:
- Review key lessons in the marketing chapters
- Know marketing value of NRMLA's membership

Virgin territory
With reverse mortgage marketing, we are in virgin territory, a new frontier in residential mortgage lending. The rules of the game are still being written in the field of real-time reverse mortgage marketing and lending across America. The following reverse marketing postscripts will help you grasp the essence of reverse mortgage marketing in bite-size form. You may begin studying the marketing chapters from these postscripts and learn much, but getting full value will require studying the chapters.

PS #1: Key is education
The primary marketing task with reverse mortgages is the education of older adults and their advisors or "centers of influence." Once they understand, the value of reverse mortgages becomes self-evident. Start with reverse mortgage basics. Use stories. Ask questions. Listen.

PS #2: Put customers' interest first
Care deeply about older adults and put their interests first. An African proverb says: "When we honor our elders, we honor ourselves." Honor your business by caring about older adults and their issues. They are your issues as well. We are the elders.

PS #3: Establish credibility in your community
You establish credibility over time through specialty knowledge, presenta-

tions, seminars, doing good works in the community and other PR activities. You should also join NRMLA (see below).

PS #4: Diversify your marketing
Your marketing should include advertising, PR and publicity and networking. Advertising could help jump-start your business. PR, publicity and networking will sustain your business over the long haul.

PS #5: Specialize to win
Put your reverse and your forward mortgage eggs in separate baskets, if you are not comfortable putting all of your eggs in the reverse mortgage basket. Specialization and focus are sources of strength with reverse mortgages.

PS #6: Become a consultant
Listen to reverse mortgage customers with empathy. Try to walk in their shoes. Let them know when a reverse mortgage is inappropriate for them. Refer them to other professionals who can meet their needs better.

PS #7: Avoid pushy sales tactics
Reverse mortgage marketing is not a sales process, it's an educational process. Fancy marketing gimmicks won't work. You should be willing to meet with a customer and end the meeting without taking an application. Do not force a loan application. Pushy sales methods will push you out of the reverse mortgage business.

PS #8: It's all about needs
Focus on older adults' total life-planning needs (sustenance, security, lifestyle, estate management). Recognize that a reverse mortgage is a solution, not the only solution.

PS #9: Simplify complex ideas
Develop the ability to break down complex ideas. Help people understand what reverse mortgages can do for them. Avoid industry jargon. Use metaphors generously.

PS #10: Patience, patience, patience
Where a forward mortgage is a sprint; a reverse mortgage is a marathon. Patience is essential.

PS #11: Play Uncle Sam's connection
Although there are other programs, FHA's Home Equity Conversion Mort-

Marketing postscripts

gage (HECM) is the flagship reverse mortgage program in part because the U.S. government is behind it. Play this connection. If you find the prospect or the local culture is anti-big government, hold your peace.

PS #12: Use targeted ads, PR and networking
To build your credibility and to establish a network of referral sources, your best tools are PR and networking. Use targeted advertising to drive business for the short term. Use PR through the media for the intermediate term and use networking for the long term.

PS #13: Know technical side
The HECM guidelines are in HUD Handbook 4235.1-Rev 1. Review this manual regularly in conjunction with HECM-related Mortgagee Letters from HUD. They are available online at www.hudclips.org. Wholesalers and major lenders have support staff, trained to help you answer technical questions. Know their names and numbers. Knowing the technical side will save you a great deal of time.

PS #14: Talk to everyone
Every homeowner or aspiring homeowner has a reverse mortgage in her future. Those who are not 62 have parents, grandparents and relatives who are, so talk to everyone about reverse mortgages. You are planting seeds.

PS #15: Explain details and disclose all programs
In your seminars and presentations to older adults and their advisors, always mention all programs; compare them fairly and accurately. An audience you just spoke with should not find out about the HomeKeeper or the jumbo programs from someone else.

PS #16: Become a resource
Position yourself and your company as a reverse mortgage resource in your market or markets. Educate yourself. You can't share what you don't have.

PS #17: Know your customer!
Know your market beyond basic demographics (age, income, available home equity, zip code, etc.). Take in their history, culture and attitudes. Know what older adults in your market would respond to and what they would resist. What works in one market may not work in another. Your marketing approach and the success of your marketing will depend on your knowledge of

Part II: Marketing reverse mortgages: It's all about education

your market. To know your local market, read the local newspapers, learn local politics (city, county and state), and talk to people, talk to people, talk to people! Understand that your market is going to change, perhaps every seven years.[1]

PS #18: Do good to do well
Do good works in your community or communities. You'll become visible, and it'll help your business. A core value of older adults is altruism.

PS #19: Make emotional connection
In your presentations to older adult groups, connect emotionally by showing, in vivid word pictures or via vignettes, how extra cash (from reverse mortgages) could:
a. Give them control and independence;
b. Enable them to give back to society;
c. Enhance their growth by making funds for continuing education available;
d. Help them live comfortably in their own home; and
e. Add to their physical, as well as emotional security, just knowing that funds are available to deal with any emergency.

PS #20: Focus on building relationships
Instead of selling features and benefits, build relationships with older adults, their children, their relatives, and their friends. Encourage prospects to bring their relatives into the reverse mortgage educational process. Build relationships through your networks and in the community to educate older adults and their advisors.

PS #21: Increase your Web presence by cross-linking
Let's say you lend in Minnesota, Iowa and Wisconsin, but do not lend in Florida, Texas and New Mexico … have your Web site cross links with a NRMLA member who operates in Florida, Texas and New Mexico, but does not do business in Minnesota, Iowa and Wisconsin.

PS # 22: Use stories
Stories should be the preferred mode of your marketing communication with older adults. Stories are more effective than features and benefits method.

Footnote
1- *Interview with Sarah Hulbert.*

Marketing postscripts

The older mind is more right-brained, making it more receptive to colorful narratives woven around key values of people 62 and older.

PS # 23: Listen, listen, listen
Older adults have stories to tell. Listen to them. It's the way you build vital empathetic bridges to them.

PS # 24: Be referable
Before you begin your networking, ask yourself two questions: Am I referable? Do I do what I say I'm going to do?

PS #25: Cultivate empathy
Empathy is the ability to walk in someone's shoes or get into another person's head and heart. How do we develop this skill? Again, it's by listening, seeking first to understand others, and by being very sensitive to their needs. It's the language of maturity. "Speaking" this "language" is crucial to your success in older adult markets.

PS # 26: The experience is the marketing
Decide that every customer you do a reverse mortgage for will have a "Wow!" feeling from pre-application to closing. Your decision will pay off.

PS # 27: Join NRMLA
Membership in the National Reverse Mortgage Lenders Association (NRMLA) offers many tangible and intangible marketing benefits. See the "Marketing Benefits of NRMLA's Membership" below:

The marketing benefits of NRMLA membership
They say membership has its privileges. Membership in NRMLA has tangible and intangible marketing value for the reverse mortgage originator. Here are some benefits:

- Listing your company on the NRMLA Web site will bring you credibility; some leads could come from Web-surfing prospects or their children.
- Membership shows you subscribe to a code of ethics and best practices that will reassure prospects when they are dealing with you.
- NRMLA conducts seminars and training across the country.
- Frequent emails and mid-month reports from NRMLA provide important data on industry trends and developments (especially rulings from HUD).

Part II: Marketing reverse mortgages: It's all about education

Data can serve as raw material for news releases in your market. NRMLA supplies information wholesale; you retail it in your marketing at local levels, with permission.
- NRMLA's membership helps individual lenders create presence in industry they cannot create on their own.
- Presence through membership leads to recognition and acceptance, leading to what Peter Bell, NRMLA's president, has called "marketing multiplier effects" for the individual lender.[2]

Chapter 10 resources
- www.reversemortgage.org
- www.nrmlaonline.org

Footnote
2- Interview with NRMLA President Peter Bell.

Marketing postscripts

Part III: Originating reverse mortgages

Part III
Originating reverse mortgages

Essentials of reverse mortgage origination I: Chapter 11

Essentials of reverse mortgage origination II: Chapter 12

Laws and regulations in Reverseland: Chapter 13

The road to Reverseland: Chapter 14

Part III: Originating reverse mortgages

Chapter Eleven
Essentials of reverse mortgage origination I

Chapter 11 objectives
After studying this chapter, the reader will be able to:
- Know three phases of the reverse mortgage application process
- Explain five goals of the pre-app phase
- Identify and discuss the "controlling" question in pre-app phase
- Know the importance of re-establishing rapport and trust before the app interview
- Explain key terms and disclosures during the app interview
- Fill out the Form 1009 completely
- Explain loan processing steps
- Know how Homekeeper origination differs from that of HECM

Gloria Neincash needs a new furnace
You are a rookie reverse mortgage specialist or loan officer. You have studied all there is to know about your mortgage specialty, and you are pretty confident in your knowledge of these unique home loans, but you haven't taken a loan application yet. And your phone rings.

It's Gloria Neincash, the 74-year-old mother of one of your most valuable customers. Mrs. Neincash needs cash to replace her boiler, and she has decided that a reverse mortgage is the most prudent way for her to finance a new furnace. How do you go about getting her the cash she needs for a new furnace?

The reverse mortgage origination steps
The steps in reverse mortgage origination include pre-application interaction, application interview, processing, underwriting and closing/disbursement.

Part III: Originating reverse mortgages

1. Pre-app interaction

The initial pre-application interaction may be in-person or by telephone as with Gloria Neincash. Whether by phone or in-person, this first contact is critical because it sets the tone for subsequent interactions. In this phase of the origination process, you want to know your prospect, establish rapport and build trust, get a "feel" for the property, walk the prospect through the process and prepare her for the application interview.

You will recall from the marketing chapters that, as a reverse mortgage originator, you should position yourself as a consultant, not a salesperson. We also advised that you should see a reverse mortgage as a solution to the needs of the prospect, not as a product to be sold. Bearing these two principles in mind, the controlling question during the pre-application interaction phase should be this: *Is a reverse mortgage appropriate for this prospect?* How this question is answered will shape the next step in your interaction with the prospect.

Let us return to the five objectives of the pre-application interaction phase of a reverse mortgage origination:

- Knowing your prospect;
- Establishing rapport and building trust;
- Getting a feel for the property;
- Walking the prospect through the reverse mortgage process; and
- Preparing the prospect for the application interview.

Know your prospect

You have known Gloria Neincash's son, Brian, for more than 10 years. He has directly brought you (and through referrals) more than $2 million in revenue over this period. You told Brian of your new specialty focus on reverse mortgages, and he promised to send you referrals as he has done in the past with your other financial services business. It helps that your first reverse mortgage prospect is Brian's mother because you come highly recommended. You still need to know Mrs. Neincash and her needs as well as you know her son's.

Now, on the phone for the first time with Gloria Neincash, you want to know her. How? You get to know her by asking questions and listening carefully and taking notes.

It is an interesting twist: Originating and marketing reverse mortgages begin at the same point—having a clear understanding of the needs of the prospect.

Establish rapport and build trust

You establish rapport and build trust with Gloria Neincash by showing a sincere interest in her and her needs. How do you do this? Again, you listen to

Essentials of reverse mortgage origination I

her, you ask questions, you give her your complete attention, you show her respect and warmth, and above all, you personify patience. Ask her to tell you her story. For example, how was life in America when she was a young girl? How did the Great Wars of the last century affect her and her family? How much was a bottle of soda or pop 50 years ago?

Also, use this initial interaction to explore her objectives further. Does she have other pressing needs in addition to the furnace? Is the furnace operable (That'll bring up other issues for homes in colder northern climates.)? Does she really need the cash from a reverse mortgage to replace the furnace? Can she get the cash from public programs she may not be aware of? Is she planning to downsize in two years? Is a home equity line of credit more appropriate? Is a reverse mortgage appropriate for Mrs. Neincash? If there are ways she can get the cash to replace her furnace without taking out a reverse mortgage, *it is your duty to tell her so, and provide her with phone numbers and contacts*. Remember, you are a consultant, not a salesperson. *After an exhaustive interview, if you determine that she does not need a reverse mortgage, tell her so and move on.*

You found out from Brian that his mother is 74-years old. Otherwise, during this initial interaction, you want to screen for age (at least 62) and for home equity. Ask questions such as, how old are you Mrs. Neincash? Is there any mortgage on your property? What is the amount? Who is the lender? The bottom line, however, is to establish rapport and build trust, or you might as well forget about moving beyond the pre-application interaction phase of the reverse mortgage origination process.

Get a "feel" for the property
You may want to start like this:
- Mrs. Neincash, you said you want to replace your furnace, is there anything else you want to replace in your home?
- Is your furnace operable?
- Is your air conditioning in order?
- How is your roof?
- Are your windows storm-proof?

The goal here is to get an indication of the shape of the collateral. Why? A reverse mortgage is a pure home equity loan which means the property must meet minimum FHA, Fannie Mae or jumbo lenders' standards. If you are meeting Mrs. Neincash at her home, you can make a quick visual inspection and take notes.

Part III: Originating reverse mortgages

You also want to know the location of the property. Is it located in urban, suburban or rural areas? If it is rural, you might have issues with wells and septic tanks which might delay the processing of the loan. By knowing the condition and location of the property, you should be able to make reasonable projections as to how long the process will take and advise the borrower accordingly.

This is also the place to probe for the legal condition of the property. Is it a property held in fee simple, a life estate, leasehold or in a living trust? If it is a leasehold, for example, find out the length of the leasehold. If it's a property held in a living trust (also called inter vivos trust), ask for the trust papers. Again, get a feel for the property.

Walk the prospect through the reverse mortgage origination process
Patiently walk Mrs. Neincash through the reverse mortgage origination process, from counseling to closing during this pre-application interaction. Why? It'll educate and reassure her; it will help build trust; and it will enhance your credibility with her.

At this point, you should give her a list of documents to bring to the application interview, such as the following*:

- Title or deed
- Copy of mortgage (or deed of trust)
- Copy of tax receipt for latest year (should have property ID)
- Medicare identification
- Social Security card/birth certificate or driver's license to verify birth date
- Homeowner's Insurance Declaration page
- Death certificate (if applicable)
- Quitclaim Deed (if a child or third party is on the title)
- Power of Attorney (POA) document
- Identification for POA
- POA validation letter (if POA attended reverse mortgage counseling in place of borrower—letter states medical reasons why homeowner couldn't perform and validates the POA)
- Trust papers (if there is a trust)
- Appraisal and credit report fees
- Reverse mortgage counseling certificate

*This list is illustrative. Your wholesaler may require other documents not listed here.**

(See Figure 11.1)

Essentials of reverse mortgage origination I

Figure 11.1
Borrower Application Checklist
(Copies Only--No Originals Except Certificate of Counseling)

* Warranty Deed

* Social Security Card

* Property Tax Statement

* Owner's Title Insurance Policy

* Homeowner's Insurance Statement, Declarations Page (except condo)

*Proof of Date of Birth (i.e. birth certificate, driver's license, passport)

*HUD/FHA (Fannie Mae) Certificate of Counseling

*Trust papers, if applicable

*Power of Attorney, if applicable

*Life Estate papers, if applicable

*Death Certificate, if applicable

Prepare prospect for application interview

Preparing Mrs. Neincash for the application interview actually began with walking her through the reverse mortgage loan origination process from counseling to closing and giving her a list of documents to bring to the interview.

The next step in readying her for the application is to give her an idea of how long the application interview will take (two hours is a good average). It's also a good idea to introduce the key documents she is going to sign, such as the first and second notes, the first and second mortgage/deed of trust, and the loan agreement (for HECM only; with HomeKeeper and the jumbo programs, there are no second notes or mortgage/deed of trust).

Manage time expectation by setting a reasonable time-frame from application interview to closing/disbursement. Forty-five to 60 days is reasonable. In addition, assess the prospect's commitment to see the process through and agree on a plan of action: Going to counseling and obtaining

Part III: Originating reverse mortgages

a certificate; getting documents to you; bringing children, grandchildren, relatives or a close advisor to the application interview; etc. Finally, set a date and time for the application interview. But you must be prepared to let your interaction with the prospect end here if you determine that a reverse mortgage is not right for her.

2. The application interview

The application interview date has arrived, and Gloria Neincash is sitting in the reception area of your office, clutching a huge manila envelope, thick with documents. Before completing the actual application forms, there are some preliminary steps you must take to ensure that the process works out smoothly. It is important to do the following:

- Re-establish rapport and trust by warmly and respectfully greeting her and recalling something you talked about during the pre-application interaction. Offer a cup of coffee, tea or a glass of water. Ask about Brian, her other children and her grandchildren. Simply make her feel very comfortable.

- If you are doing the application interview at Mrs. Neincash's home (highly recommended when feasible), do the same as above: Re-establish rapport and trust. She may offer you a cup of coffee, tea or a glass of water. Politely accept it. Look around the home for something to compliment. Spend some time looking at family pictures and ask questions about people, time, and places in those pictures on the wall: Who's this? Is this Brian as a child? Is this your wedding picture? Where were you married? Listen attentively. Make good eye contact. If she asks you about your family, share your story. If you have a wallet-size picture of your family, show her your family and comment on each member. Do not be in a hurry.

- Review the documents you asked her to bring to the application interview. If there are any missing documents, make notes of them and give her a stamped, self-addressed envelope to send them to you after the application interview.

- Ask Mrs. Neincash if she has any questions or concerns relating to the reverse mortgage process since your last meeting or interaction with her. Ask her if there any questions from the counseling session. If she has questions,

Essentials of reverse mortgage origination I

address them. If she does not, move on to Step One of the application/origination process.

Step One
Application package review*

The reverse mortgage application package should contain the following disclosures and documents:

1. Application (Truth-In-Lending): Important Terms Disclosure (state-specific)
2. HECM printouts (four pages, borrower-specific):
    a. Calculation/comparison b/w HECM and HomeKeeper
    b. Demonstration/description
    c. Amortization schedule
    d. Total Annual Loan Costs (TALC)
3. Good Faith Estimate
4. Providers' List
5. Borrower's Notifications (multiple disclosures)
6. Borrowers' Authorization
7. Servicing Transfer Disclosure
8. Excessive Fees Disclosure
9. Tax and Insurance Disclosure
10. Residential Loan Application for Reverse Mortgages (Form 1009): Four pages
11. Addendum to Application (HUD–92900A, HECM only, four pages)
12. Principal Limit Protection Disclosure

If applicable:
13. Alternative Contact (applicable if data field is not on Form 1009)
14. Homestead Advisory (applicable only if there is a spouse who will not be part of the loan)
15. Repair Acknowledgment
16. Anti-Churning Disclosure (applicable if a refinance of an existing HECM)

* This list is illustrative. Your wholesaler may require other documents not listed here

Step Two
With the borrower, Gloria Neincash, thoroughly go over all disclosures and documents in the application package. Describe and explain every disclosure and document. On HECM printout (2a) Calculation/Comparison b/w

Part III: Originating reverse mortgages

HECM and HomeKeeper, go over all the plans and explain the purpose of each plan. Line item by line item, explain the following concepts:*

A. Initial Interest Rate	M. Financed Origination Fee
B. Expected Interest Rate	N. Other Financed Costs
C. Interest Rate Cap	O. Net Principal Limit
D. Monthly Service Fee	P. Debt Payoff Advance
E. Estimated Home Value	Q. Tax and Insurance Set-Aside
F. Lending Limit	R. Net Available to You
G. Percentage	S. Cash Requested
H. Credit line Growth Rate	T. Credit line Requested
I. Principal Limit	U. Remaining Cash
J. Service Set-Aside	V. Potential Tenure Payments
K. Available Principal Limit	W. Financed Fees and Costs
L. Initial Mortgage Insurance Premium	X. Borrower Paid Costs

*See "Glossary of terms" on pages 305-310 for definition of concepts.

What if Brian's mom is not interested in an explanation because of your relationship with Brian and the warmth and trust that now define your relationship with her? As a reverse mortgage consultant, not a salesperson, you have a duty to gently and patiently insist on full disclosure and explanation. You might say, "Mrs. Neincash, these are very important documents. I'll sleep better if I thoroughly explain them to you as I am professionally obligated to do."

The objective here is to ensure that there are no surprises in store for Mrs. Neincash and other borrowers at the closing table because of failure to fully explain and disclose important terms and documents. It is important to remember that most closing officers, escrow officers or attorneys do not have the technical knowledge to explain reverse mortgages as you (the specialist) can. You are the specialist and your obligation to educate the borrower cannot be delegated or outsourced. For example, you should explain to Brian's mom why HECM has two notes and two mortgages or deeds of trust, why it has two interest rates, and why her mortgage or deed of trust may have a term of 76 years or more.

Step Three
Mrs. Neincash and you must sign and date the disclosures and application documents where indicated.

Step Four
Collect the following documents from borrower (Mrs. Neincash)*:

Essentials of reverse mortgage origination I

- Any government-issued ID to confirm birth date (typically driver's license or state ID, No pictures!)
- Evidence of a Social Security number
- Counseling certificate (original)
- Homeowners insurance declaration page
- Death certificate (if applicable)
- A check for appraisal and credit report (HECM only)
- Power of Attorney (POA) (if applicable)**
- POA validation letter (if applicable)
- Full trust papers (if applicable)**
- Copy of deed granting life estate (if applicable)**

*This list is illustrative. Your wholesaler may require other documents not listed here.

**If a trust is involved, the wholesaler usually requires the originator to have the trust papers pre-screened and pre-approved by the wholesaler's underwriting department to ensure compliance with wholesaler's underwriting guidelines. Also, the title company's approval of trust papers is required. Identification is required for POAs, trustees of trusts, remaindermen on life estates, non-borrowing spouses in homestead states (anyone signing the mortgage or deed of trust).

Step Five

Leave the following with Mrs. Neincash (borrower)*:
- Copies of all disclosures and documents signed under Step Three
- Blank credit and security instruments (HECM only)
- FHA's booklet "When Your Home is on the Line" (HECM only)
- Fannie Mae's "Reverse Mortgage, Five Steps for Safety" (HECM and HomeKeeper)

*This list is illustrative. Your wholesaler may require other documents not listed here.

Post-application

Before Gloria Neincash leaves your office or before you leave her home, let her know that the next step is the appraisal process. Inform her that your loan processor will order an appraisal of her home and an appraiser will call her to schedule an appointment. Stress the importance of the appraisal and the role of the appraiser. If you know the name of the appraiser who will be assigned to her home, give her the name. Describe for her what to expect.

Also, let her know that appraiser will flag serious repairs (roof, founda-

Part III: Originating reverse mortgages

tion) if repairs are needed to bring her home to HUD, Fannie Mae or jumbo lenders' minimum property standards. Emphasize that if repairs are structural—i.e. roof or foundation, state-licensed contractors will be asked to assess the repairs and provide estimates. And explain that structural repairs could delay or kill the loan.

Mrs. Neincash will want to know when the loan will close. Give her a reasonable time-frame, anywhere between 45 and 60 days. Understand that the worst thing you can do is to over-promise and under-deliver. Be upfront with your customers at all times, and they will reward you and your company with their loyalty.

Finally, maintain regular communication and give her frequent "status updates" throughout the process.

A note on re-disclosure

Tell Gloria Neincash to expect a stack of documents in the mail from the investor. Inform her that investors are required by law to re-disclose information you may have already disclosed to her if there is a significant change in the numbers. Say it is okay to sign and return the documents.

The Form 1009: An introduction to the residential loan application for reverse mortgages

In this section, we will go over the Residential Loan Application for Reverse Mortgages (Fannie Mae Form 1009), section by section. In each section, we will define what data is required to complete the section.

I. Type of mortgage and terms of loan

a. Mortgage applied for:
   - HomeKeeper: Backed by Fannie Mae
   - HECM: Backed by the Federal Housing Administration. If you select HECM, you also need to complete the HUD/VA Addendum (HUD-92900-A), first two pages.
   - Other: Could be the two jumbos or others that will come.

b. FHA case number (HECM): A 10-digit number used only with HECM. It is available to FHA-approved lenders through the FHA connection.

c. Lender case number: Any blend of letters and numbers used by the lender to identify the application.

d. Loan payment plans: Shows the payment plans the borrower may choose

Essentials of reverse mortgage origination I

from. The borrower can change their options at closing. I prefer to use 'cash advance options,' because 'loan payment plans' may cause some to think they have loan payment to make, creating confusion.

e. Special loan features: Specify any special loan feature. The HomeKeeper had equity share, but Fannie Mae removed it in 2000.

f. Amortization type: Select ARM or adjustable rate mortgage. If you select ARM, enter monthly or annually adjusting. Fixed-rate reverse mortgages may come soon.

II. Property information

a. Subject property address: Show the borrower's primary address, including county and zip code.

b. Legal description of subject property: Fill in the property's legal description from property tax papers or title insurance commitment. If legal description is lengthy, it should be attached to the application form.

c. Property title is held in these names: List all names on the property title.

d. Number of units: Enter "1" for single-family home, "2" for duplex, "3" for triplex and "4" for fourplex.

e. Year-built: Show construction year.

f. Estimate of appraised value: Put what borrower believes her property is worth. An appraisal will assign the current market value.

g. Residence type: Check primary, secondary residence or investment property.

h. Property title held as: Fee simple, life estate, lease hold. If leasehold is checked, you need to supply the expiration date and a copy of the lease agreement.

i. Check if title is also held as: Inter Vivos (Living) Trust

Borrower information:
   (1) Borrower's name: Enter the borrower's full legal name
   (2) Co-borrower: Show a co-borrower's name (if any)
   (3) Social Security Number: Fill in borrower and co-borrower's Social

Part III: Originating reverse mortgages

Security Numbers
- (4) Date of birth: Enter borrower and co-borrower's (if applicable) birth dates
- (5) Monthly income: Show the borrower's monthly income and, if applicable, co-borrower's monthly income
- (6) Real estate assets: Plug in the value of a borrower's real estate assets
- (7) Available assets: Enter the value of assets that can easily convert to cash
- (8) Home phone: Show the area code and phone number of borrower(s)
- (9) Years of residence at present address: How long has the borrower lived at this address; enter the number of years
- (10) Marital status: Married or unmarried? Check one
- (11) Alternative contact person: Is (or are) there any close relatives or friends? Ask the borrower to provide a name, home address and contact information of such a relative or friend.

j. Liens against the property: Is there a lien or are there liens against the property? The borrower should supply name and address of creditors in addition to the amount owed and account balance. Add unpaid balance enter in front of "Total liens to be paid."

k. Non-real estate debts: Enter the sum of all non-real estate debts.

l. Declarations: Using "yes" or "no," borrowers must complete blocks A through F. If the borrower marks "yes" in block D, a detailed explanation is required. Blocks F through H are optional for a HECM application.

m. Acknowledgment and agreement: The originator, borrower and, if applicable, co-borrower should carefully review this section, sign it and date it.

Information for government monitoring purposes: Federal regulations require completion of this section, whether or not borrower chooses to furnish information. Check the borrower's choice; visually observe race, national origin or sex. The Home Mortgage Disclosure Act (HMDA) requires this data. *(See Figures 11.2 and 11.3)*

The HUD/VA Addendum to the application

Since more than 90 percent of reverse mortgages are HECM loans, the HUD/VA Addendum (Form 92900-A) should be completed and signed by the borrower. Only the first two pages of the Addendum may be completed. Generally, the information required on the Form 92900-A can be imported

Essentials of reverse mortgage origination I

Figure 11.2
Residential Loan Application for Reverse Mortgage

Residential Loan Application for Reverse Mortgages

This application is designed to be completed by the applicant(s) with the lender's assistance. Applicants should complete this form as "Borrower" or "Co-Borrower", as applicable. Co-Borrower information must be provided when a person other than the "Borrower" (including the Borrower's spouse) is a co-owner of the real property that will be used as a basis for loan qualification or the Borrower's spouse is not a co-owner of the real property that will be used as a basis for loan qualification, but the Borrower resides in a community property state or the security property is located in a community property state.

I. Type of Mortgage and Terms of Loan

Mortgage Applied for:	FHA Case No. (HECM)	Lender Case No.
___ Home Keeper (Fannie Mae) ✓ HECM (FHA)* ___ Other _____ (specify) *Complete HUD/VA Addendum	123-456789 Loan Payment Plans: ___ Line of Credit (not available in Texas) ___ Modified Term (HECM only) ___ Tenure	3000033 ___ Term (HECM only) ✓ Modified Tenure ___ Undecided

Special Loan Features: ___ Equity Share ___ Other (specify): _____
Amortization Type: ✓ ARM (type): ___ Monthly (indicate monthly or annual)
___ Fixed Rate   Other (explain): _____

II. Property Information

Subject Property Address (street, city, state, county, and zip code): 601 108TH AVE NE
BELLEVUE, WA 98004 - KING County

Legal Description of Subject Property (attach description if necessary):
Lot 78 of Tract 1890.

Property Title is Held in These Names: (Please list all names on property title):
Gloria Neincash, a widow.

No. of Units: 1	Year Built: 1900	Estimate of Appraised Value: $200,000
Residence Type:	✓ Primary Residence	___ Secondary Residence ___ Investment Property
Property Title Held As:	✓ Fee Simple	___ Life Estate ___ Leasehold (Expiration Date: ___)

Check if title is also held as: ___ Inter Vivos (Living) Trust

III. Borrower Information

Borrower's Name (Include Jr. or Sr., if applicable)	Co-Borrower's Name (Include Jr. or Sr., if applicable)
Gloria Neincash	
Social Security Number: 123-45-6789	DOB (MM/DD/YYYY): 11/11/1931	Social Security Number:	DOB (MM/DD/YYYY):
Monthly Income: $ 500	Monthly Income: $
Real Estate Assets: $ 250,000	Real Estate Assets: $
Available Assets: $ 250,000	Available Assets: $
Home Phone (including area code): 425-456-7890	Home Phone (including area code):
Years of Residence at Present Address: 25	Years of Residence at Present Address:
Mailing Address, if different from Subject Property Address	Mailing Address, if different from Subject Property Address
Marital Status: ___ Married ✓ Unmarried (include Single, divorced, widowed)	Marital Status: ___ Married ___ Unmarried (include single, divorced, widowed)
Alternative Contact Person (name, address, phone): Brian Neincash 200 William Street Puyallup, WA 98373 253-123-4567	Alternative Contact Person (name, address, phone):

Fannie Mae Form **1009** 03/2004

Page 1 of 4

Source: **Reverse Mortgage of America, a Division of Seattle Mortgage Company**

figure 11.2 continued on page 166

Part III: Originating reverse mortgages

Figure 11.2
Residential Loan Application for Reverse Mortgage

IV. Liens Against The Property

List the creditor's name, address, and account number for all liens against the property.
NOTE: This section should not be used to list all personal liabilities, only liens against the property.

Name of Creditor	Address of Creditor	Unpaid Balance
Account Number		$
Name of Creditor	Address of Creditor	Unpaid Balance
Account Number		$
Name of Creditor	Address of Creditor	Unpaid Balance
Account Number		$
	Total liens to be paid:	$

V. Total Non-Real Estate Debts

Total Amount of Non-Real Estate Debts: $ 0.00

VI. Declarations

If you answer "Yes" to any questions a through h, Please use continuation sheet for explanation.

	Borrower		Co-Borrower	
	Yes	No	Yes	No
a. Are there any outstanding judgments against you?	☐	☑	☐	☐
b. Have you filed for any bankruptcy that has not been resolved?	☐	☑	☐	☐
c. Are you a party to a lawsuit?	☐	☑	☐	☐
d. Are you presently delinquent or in default on any Federal debt or any other loan, mortgage, financial obligation, bond, or loan guarantee? [If "Yes," give details, including date, name and address of lender, FHA or VA Case number (if applicable), and reason for delinquency/default.]	☐	☑	☐	☐
e. Do you intend to occupy the property as your primary residence?	☑	☐	☐	☐
f. Are you a co-maker or endorser on a note? (Optional for HUD)	☐	☑	☐	☐
g. Are you a U.S. citizen? (Optional for HUD)	☑	☐	☐	☐
h. Are you a permanent resident alien? (Optional for HUD)	☐	☑	☐	☐

Fannie Mae Form **1009** 03/2004

Source: Reverse Mortgage of America, a Division of Seattle Mortgage Company

Essentials of reverse mortgage origination I

Figure 11.2
Residential Loan Application for Reverse Mortgage

VII. Acknowledgment and Agreement

Each of the undersigned specifically represents to Lender and Lender's actual or potential agents, brokers, processors, attorneys, insurers, servicers, successors and assigns and agrees and acknowledges that: (1) the information provided in this application is true and correct as of the date set forth opposite my signature and that any intentional or negligent misrepresentation of this information contained in this application may result in civil liability, including monetary damages, to any person who may suffer any loss due to reliance upon any misrepresentation that I have made on this application, and/or in criminal penalties including, but not limited to, fine or imprisonment or both under the provisions of Title 18, United States Code, sec. 1001, et seq.; (2) the loan requested pursuant to this application (the "Loan") will be secured by a mortgage or deed of trust of the property described herein; (3) the property will not be used for any illegal or prohibited purpose or use; (4) all statements made in this application are made for the purpose of obtaining a residential mortgage loan; (5) the property will be occupied as indicated herein; (6) any owner or servicer of the Loan may verify or reverify any information contained in the application from any source named in this application, and Lender, its successors or assigns may retain the original and/or an electronic record of this application, even if the Loan is not approved; (7) the Lender and its agents, brokers, insurers, servicers, successors and assigns may continuously rely on the information contained in the application, and I am obligated to amend and/or supplement the information provided in this application if any of the material facts that I have represented herein should change prior to closing of the Loan; (8) in the event that my payments on the Loan become delinquent, the owner or servicer of the Loan may, in addition to any other rights and remedies that it may have relating to such delinquency, report my name and account information to one or more consumer credit reporting agencies; (9) ownership of the Loan and/or administration of the Loan account may be transferred with such notice as may be required by law; and (10) neither Lender nor its agents, brokers, insurers, servicers, successors or assigns has made any representation or warranty, express or implied, to me regarding the property or the condition or value of the property.

Certification: I/We certify that the information provided in this application is true and correct as of the date set forth opposite my/our signature(s) on this application and acknowledge my/our understanding that any intentional or negligent misrepresentation(s) of the information contained in this application may result in civil liability and/or criminal penalties including, but not limited to, fine or imprisonment or both under the provisions of Title 18, United State Code, Section 1001, et seq. and liability for monetary damages to the Lender, its agents, successors and assigns, insurers and any other person who may suffer any loss due to reliance upon any misrepresentation which I/we have made on this application.

Borrower's Signature	Date	Co-Borrower's Signature	Date
X		X	

VIII. Information for Government Monitoring Purposes

The following information is requested by the Federal Government for certain types of loans related to a dwelling in order to monitor the lender's compliance with equal credit opportunity, fair housing and home mortgage disclosure laws. You are not required to furnish this information, but are encouraged to do so. The law provides that a lender may discriminate neither on the basis of this information, nor on whether you choose to furnish it. If you furnish the information, please provide both ethnicity and race. For race, you may check more than one designation. If you do not furnish ethnicity, race, or sex, under Federal regulations, this lender is required to note the information on the basis of visual observation or surname. If you do not wish to furnish the information, please check the box below. (Lender must review the above material to assure that the disclosures satisfy all requirements to which the Lender is subject under applicable state law for the particular type of loan applied for.)

BORROWER	__ I do not wish to furnish this information.	CO-BORROWER	__ I do not wish to furnish this information.
Ethnicity:	__ Hispanic or Latino ✓ Not Hispanic or Latino	Ethnicity:	__ Hispanic or Latino __ Not Hispanic or Latino
Race:	__ American Indian or Alaska Native __ Asian __ Black or African American __ Native Hawaiian or Other Pacific Islander __ White	Race:	__ American Indian or Alaska Native __ Asian __ Black or African American __ Native Hawaiian or Other Pacific Islander __ White
Sex:	✓ Female __ Male	Sex:	__ Female __ Male

TO BE COMPLETED BY INTERVIEWER This application was taken by:	Interviewer's Name (print or type): Michael Mayberry	Name and Address of Interviewer's Employer: Seattle Mortgages
✓ Face-to face interview	Interviewer's Signature / Date	601 108th Avenue NE, Suite 700
__ Mail		Bellevue, WA 98004
__ Telephone	Interviewer's Phone Number (include area code): (800) 233-4601	

NOTE: FHA insures reverse mortgages for one to four family units under various provisions of the National Housing Act. The information contained on the loan application is collected to determine eligibility for the program as well as serve as verification of the applicant's statements. The performance function of the agency will be improved by collecting this data as determinations can be made regarding the characteristics of those borrowers obtaining HECM loans. The Public Reporting Burden for this collection is estimated to average one hour per response, including time for reviewing instructions, searching existing data sources, gathering and maintaining the data and completing and reviewing the collection of information. A response is required to obtain a HECM loan, but parties are not required to use this particular form. This information is covered by the Privacy Act.

Fannie Mae Form **1009** 03/2004

Page 3 of 4

Source: Reverse Mortgage of America, a Division of Seattle Mortgage Company

figure 11.2 continued on page 168

Part III: Originating reverse mortgages

Figure 11.2
Residential Loan Application for Reverse Mortgage

Instructions for completing the residential loan application for reverse mortgages (Fannie Mae 1009) and Addendum

1. Instructions for completing the residential loan application for reverse mortgages

For the borrower's application for a Fannie Mae conventional reverse mortgage (Home Keeper Mortgage) or an FHA-insured reverse mortgage (Home Equity Conversion Mortgage, or HECM), the lender has the option of using the Residential Loan Application for Reverse Mortgage (Fannie Mae Form 1009) or the Uniform Residential Loan Application (Freddie Mac Form 65/Fannie Mae Form 1003).

For both forms, if the mortgage applied for is a HECM, the HUD/VA Addendum (HUD 92900-A) must be completed.

The Residential Loan Application for Reverse Mortgage, Fannie Mae Form 1009, must be completed as detailed below for the Home Keeper Mortgage or the HECM:

Section I. Type Of Mortgage And Terms Of Loan
Mortgage Applied for - Check the type of reverse mortgage for which application is being made: Home Keeper, HECM, or Other type of reverse mortgage. If Other is selected, the mortgage product must be specified. If HECM is selected, the HUD/VA Addendum must be completed and attached to the application.

FHA Case No. - If the mortgage applied for is a Home Keeper, this section should be left blank. If the mortgage applied for is a HECM, the FHA case number should be entered followed by the appropriate Section of the Act ADP Code for HECMs listed below:

	HUD-Processed	Direct Endorsement
Assignment/Fixed-rate	911	951
Assignment/Adjustable-rate	912	952
Shared Premium/Fixed-rate	913	953
Shared Premium/ARM	914	954
Shared Appreciation/Fixed-rate	915	955
Shared Appreciation/ARM	916	956
Condo (Fixed)	917	957
Condo (ARM)	918	958

Lender Case No. - Indicate the case number assigned by the lender. This case number can be any combination of letters and numbers, as determined by the lender.

Loan Payment Plans - Indicate the payment plan in which the applicant is interested. The applicant can change the payment plan selection at closing.

Special Loan Features - The Equity Share Option is only available under the Home Keeper Mortgage. Other special loan features pertaining to specific reverse mortgage products must be detailed in the space provided.

Amortization Type - Indicate either fixed-rate or adjustable-rate (ARM) amortization. If ARM is selected, indicate if the adjustment will occur monthly or annually.

Section II. Property Information
Subject Property Address - The address of the applicant's primary residence–including the county name and the zip code–should be entered.

Legal Description of Subject Property - Enter the legal description of the property as shown on the title insurance commitment or survey. The legal description may be attached to the loan application if it is lengthy.

No. of Units - Enter the number of family units on the subject property. For example, "1" would be used to indicate a single-family property. "2" would indicate a duplex, etc.

Year Built - Indicate the year the property was constructed.
Estimate of Appraised Value - Enter an estimate of the property value. (An exact valuation is not necessary as verification will occur during the property appraisal process.)

Residence Type - Primary residence must be checked. Check "primary residence" and "investment property" if applicant resides in a multi-unit property with rental tenants.

Property Title is Held in These Names - List names of all titleholders to the property.

Property Title Held As - Identify how the property rights are held: fee simple, life estate, or leasehold estate. If leasehold estate is selected, enter the expiration date of the lease. If title is also held as an inter vivos (living) trust, check the corresponding box.

Section III. Borrower Information
Borrower's Name - Indicate the full legal name of the applicant, as the titleholder to the subject property.

Co-Borrower's Name - Indicate the full legal name of the co-applicant, if also a titleholder to the subject property.

Social Security Number - Enter the applicant's social security number, and co applicant's social security number, if applicable.

Date of Birth - Enter the applicant's birth date, and co-applicant's birth date if, applicable

Monthly Income - Enter the applicant's monthly income, and co-applicant's monthly income, if applicable.

Real Estate Assets - Enter total value of applicant's real estate assets.

Available Assets - Enter the amount of the applicant's available (liquid) assets.
Home Phone - Enter the applicant's home phone number, and co-applicant's home phone number, if applicable. Include the area code for each phone number.

Years of Residence at Present Address - Enter the number of years the applicant has resided at the subject property address. Provide the same information for the coapplicant, if applicable.

Marital Status - Check box that represents the applicant's marital status. If separated but not divorce, the "Married" box should be selected. Provide the same information for the co-applicant, if applicable.

Alternative Contact Person - If the application is for a Home Keeper Mortgage, provide the name, home address, and telephone number for a family member, friend, or advisor to the applicant. The contact person should be someone who has access to and/or maintains regular communication with the applicant. Provide the same information for the co-applicant, if applicable. (This information is optional for the HECM loan.)

Section IV. Liens Against The Property
The applicant must provide information on unpaid liens against the property. The name and address of the creditor(s), as well as the lien account number(s) and balance(s) owed, must be completed. The total unpaid balance of these property liens should be totaled and entered in the space provided.

Section V. Non-real Estate Debts
List the total of all debts not related to real estate.

Section VI. Declarations
The applicant and co-applicant, if applicable, must complete blocks a. through f., using "Yes" or "No" as responses. Block d. requires a detailed explanation if the response is affirmative. Blocks f., g., and h. are not required for HECM application.

Section VII. Acknowledgment and Agreement
The applicant and co-applicant, if applicable, should read this section carefully, indicate the date of signature, and sign in the pertinent blocks.

Section VIII. Information For Government Monitoring Purposes
These blocks must be completed. If the borrower chooses not to furnish any or all of this information, Federal Regulations require that the lender note that choice on the application. Federal Regulations also require the lender to note the race or national origin and sex of the applicant on the basis of visual observation or surname. This information is collected, in part, for the Home Mortgage Disclosure Act (HMDA).

2. Instructions for completing the HUD/VA Addendum (Form 92900-A)

The HUD/VA Addendum (92900-A) consists of five (5) pages, the first four of which must be completed. These four pages contain statutory and regulatory information and certifications that must be completed, signed, and dated, and included in the case binder. For lenders who are not approved for direct endorsement or have preclosing status, the documentation should be completed, signed and included in the case binder at the time of submission for firm commitment. Page five may be omitted since it is the Veteran's Administration Commitment for Guaranty and is not applicable. A copy of the Addendum must be provided to the borrower. The instructions listed below relate to completing the Addendum for the HECM Program.

PART I – Identifying Information

Section of the Act (Block 4) - Enter the same code that follows the FHA case number in Section 1 of the loan application.

Loan Amount (Block 7) - The principal limit should be entered in this block
Interest Rate (Block 8) - The Expected Average Mortgage Interest Rate ("expected rate") should be entered in the block.

Blocks 9, 10, 12a., 12b., and 20 should not be completed.

Fannie Mae Form **1009** 03/2004

Page 4 of 4

Source: Reverse Mortgage of America, a Division of Seattle Mortgage Company

Essentials of reverse mortgage origination I

Figure 11.3

HUD/VA Addendum to Uniform Residential Loan Application

HUD/VA Addendum to Uniform Residential Loan Application		OMB Approval No. VA: 2900-0144 HUD: 2502-0059 (exp. 9/30/2007)
Part I - Identifying Information (mark the type of application)	2. Agency Case No. (include any suffix) 123-456789	3. Lender's Case No. 3000033
1. ☐ VA Application for Home Loan Guaranty ☑ HUD/FHA Application for Insurance under the National Housing Act		4. Section of the Act (for HUD cases) 255
5. Borrower's Name & Present Address (include zip code) Gloria Neincash 601 108th Ave NE Bellevue, WA 98004	7. Loan Amount (include the UFMIP if for HUD or Funding Fee if for VA) $ 135,800.00	8. Interest Rate 5.95 %	9. Proposed Maturity yrs. mos.
	10. Discount Amount (only if borrower is permitted to pay) $	11. Amount of Up Front Premium $ 4,000.00	12a. Amount of Monthly Premium $ / mo.	12b. Term of Monthly Premium months
6. Property Address (including name of subdivision, lot & block no. & zip code) 601 108TH AVE NE BELLEVUE, WA 98004	13. Lender's I.D. Code 5522000004	14. Sponsor / Agent I.D. Code
15. Lender's Name & Address (include zip code) Seattle Mortgage Company 601 108th Avenue NE, Suite 700 Bellevue, WA 98004	16. Name & Address of Sponsor / Agent	
	17. Lender's Telephone Number (425) 732-3250	

Type or Print all entries clearly

VA: The veteran and the lender hereby apply to the Secretary of Veterans Affairs for Guaranty of the loan described here under Section 3710, Chapter 37, Title 38, United States Code, to the full extent permitted by the veteran's entitlement and severally agree that the Regulations promulgated pursuant to Chapter 37, and in effect on the date of the loan shall govern the rights, duties, and liabilities of the parties.

| 18. First Time Homebuyer? a. ☐ Yes b. ☑ No | 19. VA Only Title will be Vested in: ☐ Veteran ☐ Veteran & Spouse ☐ Other (specify) | 20. Purpose of Loan (blocks 9 - 12 are for VA loans only) 1) ☐ Purchase Existing Home Previously Occupied 2) ☐ Finance Improvements to Existing Property 3) ☑ Refinance (Refi.) 4) ☐ Purchase New Condo. Unit 5) ☐ Purchase Existing Condo. Unit 6) ☐ Purchase Existing Home Not Previously Occupied | 7) ☐ Construct Home (proceeds to be paid out during construction) 8) ☐ Finance Co-op Purchase 9) ☐ Purchase Permanently Sited Manufactured Home 10) ☐ Purchase Permanently Sited Manufactured Home & Lot 11) ☐ Refi. Permanently Sited Manufactured Home to Buy Lot 12) ☐ Refi. Permanently Sited Manufactured Home/Lot Loan |

Part II - Lender's Certification

21. The undersigned lender makes the following certifications to induce the Department of Veterans Affairs to issue a certificate of commitment to guarantee the subject loan or a Loan Guaranty Certificate under Title 38, U.S. Code, or to induce the Department of Housing and Urban Development - Federal Housing Commissioner to issue a firm commitment for mortgage insurance or a Mortgage Insurance Certificate under the National Housing Act.

A. The loan terms furnished in the Uniform Residential Loan Application and this Addendum are true, accurate and complete.

B. The information contained in the Uniform Residential Loan Application and this Addendum was obtained directly from the borrower by an employee of the undersigned lender or its duly authorized agent and is true to the best of the lender's knowledge and belief.

C. The credit report submitted on the subject borrower (and co-borrower, if any) was ordered by the undersigned lender or its duly authorized agent directly from the credit bureau which prepared the report and was received directly from said credit bureau.

D. The verification of employment and verification of deposits were requested and received by the lender or its duly authorized agent without passing through the hands of any third persons and are true to the best of the lender's knowledge and belief.

Items "H" through "J" are to be completed as applicable for VA loans only.

E. The Uniform Residential Loan Application and this Addendum were signed by the borrower after all sections were completed.

F. This proposed loan to the named borrower meets the income and credit requirements of the governing law in the judgment of the undersigned.

G. To the best of my knowledge and belief, I and my firm and its principals: (1) are not presently debarred, suspended, proposed for debarment, declared ineligible, or voluntarily excluded from covered transactions by any Federal department or agency; (2) have not, within a three-year period preceding this proposal, been convicted of or had a civil judgment rendered against them for (a) commission of fraud or a criminal offense in connection with obtaining, attempting to obtain, or performing a public (Federal, State or local) transaction or contract under a public transaction; (b) violation of Federal or State antitrust statutes or commission of embezzlement, theft, forgery, bribery, falsification or destruction of records, making false statements, or receiving stolen property; (3) are not presently indicted for or otherwise criminally or civilly charged by a governmental entity (Federal, State or local) with commission of any of the offenses enumerated in paragraph G(2) of this certification; and (4) have not, within a three-year period preceding this application/proposal, had one or more public transactions (Federal, State or local) terminated for cause or default.

H. The names and functions of any duly authorized agents who developed on behalf of the lender any of the information or supporting credit data submitted are as follows:

Name & Address   Function (e.g., obtained information on the Uniform Residential Loan Application, ordered credit report, verifications of employment, deposits, etc.)

I. If no agent is shown above, the undersigned lender affirmatively certifies that all information and supporting credit data were obtained directly by the lender. The undersigned lender understands and agrees that it is responsible for the omissions, errors, or acts of agents identified in item H as to the functions with which they are identified.

J. The proposed loan conforms otherwise with the applicable provisions of Title 38, U.S. Code, and of the regulations concerning guaranty or insurance of loans to veterans.

Signature of Officer of Lender	Title of Officer of Lender	Date (mm/dd/yyyy)

Part III - Notices to Borrowers. Public reporting burden for this collection of information is estimated to average 6 minutes per response, including the time for reviewing instructions, searching existing data sources, gathering and maintaining the data needed, and completing and reviewing the collection of information. This agency may not conduct or sponsor, and a person is not required to respond to, a collection information unless that collection displays a valid OMB control number. **Privacy Act Information.** The information requested on the Uniform Residential Loan Application and this Addendum is authorized by 38 U.S.C. 3710 (if for DVA) and 12 U.S.C. 1701 et seq. (if for HUD/FHA). The Debt Collection Act of 1982, Pub. Law 97-365, and HUD's Housing and Community Development Act of 1987, 42 U.S.C. 3543, require persons applying for a federally insured or guaranteed loan to furnish his/her social security number (SSN). You must provide all the requested information, including your SSN. HUD and/or VA may conduct a computer match to verify the information you provide. HUD and/or VA may disclose certain information to Federal, State and local agencies when relevant to civil, criminal, or regulatory investigations and prosecutions. It will not otherwise be disclosed or released outside of HUD or VA, except as required and permitted by law. The information will be used to determine whether you qualify as a mortgagor. Any disclosure of information outside VA or HUD/FHA will be made only as permitted by law. Failure to provide any of the requested information, including SSN, may

VA Form 26-1802a (3/98)   page 1   form HUD-92900-A (06/2005)

Source: Reverse Mortgage of America, a Division of Seattle Mortgage Company

figure 11.3 continued on page 170

Part III: Originating reverse mortgages

Figure 11.3

HUD/VA Addendum to Uniform Residential Loan Application

result in disapproval of your loan application. This is notice to you as required by the Right to Financial Privacy Act of 1978 that VA or HUD/FHA has a right of access to financial records held by financial institutions in connection with the consideration or administration of assistance to you. Financial records involving your transaction will be available to VA and HUD/FHA without further notice or authorization but will not be disclosed or released by this institution to another Government Agency or Department without your consent except as required or permitted by law.

Caution. Delinquencies, defaults, foreclosures and abuses of mortgage loans involving programs of the Federal Government can be costly and detrimental to your credit, now and in the future. The lender in this transaction, its agents and assigns as well as the Federal Government, its agencies, agents and assigns, are authorized to take any and all of the following actions in the event loan payments become delinquent on the mortgage loan described in the attached application: (1) Report your name and account information to a credit bureau; (2) Assess additional interest and penalty charges for the period of time that payment is not made; (3) Assess charges to cover additional administrative costs incurred by the Government to service your account; (4) Offset amounts owed to you under other Federal programs; (5) Refer your account to a private attorney, collection agency or mortgage servicing agency to collect the amount due, foreclose the mortgage, sell the property and seek judgment against you for any deficiency; (6) Refer your account to the Department of Justice for litigation in the courts; (7) If you are a current or retired Federal employee, take action to offset your salary, or civil service retirement benefits; (8) Refer your debt to the Internal Revenue Service for offset against any amount owed to you as an income tax refund; and (9) Report any resulting written-off debt of yours to the Internal Revenue Service as your taxable income. All of these actions can and will be used to recover any debts owed when it is determined to be in the interest of the lender and/or the Federal Government to do so.

Part IV - Borrower Consent for Social Security Administration to Verify Social Security Number

I authorize the Social Security Administration to verify my Social Security number to the Lender identified in this document and HUD/FHA, through a computer match conducted by HUD/FHA.

I understand that my consent allows no additional information from my Social Security records to be provided to the Lender, and HUD/FHA and that verification of my Social Security number does not constitute confirmation of my identity. I also understand that my Social Security number may not be used for any other purpose than the one stated above, including resale or redisclosure to other parties. The only other redisclosure permitted by this authorization is for review purposes to ensure that HUD/FHA complies with SSA's consent requirements.

I am the individual to whom the Social Security number was issued or that person's legal guardian. I declare and affirm under the penalty of perjury that the information contained herein is true and correct. I know that if I make any representation that I know is false to obtain information from Social Security records, I could be punished by a fine or imprisonment or both.

This consent is valid for 180 days from the date signed, unless indicated otherwise by the individual(s) named in this loan application.

Signature(s) of Borrower(s) - Read consent carefully. Review accuracy of social security number(s) and birth dates provided on this application.

X

X   Date signed

Part V - Borrower Certification

22. Complete the following for a HUD/FHA Mortgage.

22a. Do you own or have you sold *other* real estate within the past 60 months on which there was a HUD/FHA mortgage? ☐ Yes ☑ No

Is it to be sold? ☐ Yes ☑ No   22b. Sales Price $ 22c. Original Mortgage Amt $

22d. Address

22e. If the dwelling to be covered by this mortgage is to be rented, is it a part of, adjacent or contiguous to any project subdivision or group of concentrated rental properties involving eight or more dwelling units in which you have any financial interest? ☐ Yes ☑ No If "Yes" give details.

22f. Do you own more than four dwellings? ☐ Yes ☑ No If "Yes" submit form HUD-92561.

23. Complete for VA-Guaranteed Mortgage. Have you ever had a VA home Loan? ☐ Yes ☐ No

24. **Applicable for Both VA & HUD.** As a home loan borrower, you will be legally obligated to make the mortgage payments called for by your mortgage loan contract. The fact that you dispose of your property after the loan has been made **will not relieve you of liability for making these payments. Payment of the loan in full is ordinarily the way liability on a mortgage note is ended.** Some home buyers have the mistaken impression that if they sell their homes when they move to another locality, or dispose of it for any other reasons, they are no longer liable for the mortgage payments and that liability for these payments is solely that of the new owners. Even though the new owners may agree in writing to assume liability for your mortgage payments, this assumption agreement will not relieve you from liability to the holder of the note which you signed when you obtained the loan to buy the property. Unless you are able to sell the property to a buyer who is acceptable to VA or to HUD/FHA and who will assume the payment of your obligation to the lender, you will not be relieved from liability to repay any claim which VA or HUD/FHA may be required to pay your lender on account of default in your loan payments. **The amount of any such claim payment will be a debt owed by you to the Federal Government.** This debt will be the object of established collection procedures.

25. I, the Undersigned Borrower(s) Certify that:

(1) I have read and understand the foregoing concerning my liability on the loan and Part III Notices to Borrowers.

(2) Occupancy: (for VA only - mark the applicable box)

☐ (a) I now actually occupy the above-described property as my home or intend to move into and occupy said property as my home within a reasonable period of time or intend to reoccupy it after the completion of major alterations, repairs or improvements.

☐ (b) My spouse is on active military duty and in his or her absence, I occupy or intend to occupy the property securing this loan as my home.

☐ (c) I previously occupied the property securing this loan as my home. (for interest rate reductions)

☐ (d) While my spouse was on active military duty and unable to occupy the property securing this loan, I previously occupied the property that is securing this loan as my home. (for interest rate reduction loans)

Note: If box 2b or 2d is checked, the veteran's spouse must also sign below.

(3) Mark the applicable box (not applicable for Home Improvement or Refinancing Loan) I have been informed that ($ 200,000.00) is:

☐ the reasonable value of the property as determined by VA or;

☐ the statement of appraised value as determined by HUD / FHA.

Note: If the contract price or cost exceeds the VA "Reasonable Value" or HUD/FHA "Statement of Appraised Value", mark either item (a) or item (b), whichever is applicable.

☐ (a) I was aware of this valuation when I signed my contract and I have paid or will pay in cash from my own resources at or prior to loan closing a sum equal to the difference between the contract purchase price or cost and the VA or HUD/FHA established value. I do not and will not have outstanding after loan closing any unpaid contractual obligation on account of such cash payment;

☐ (b) I was not aware of this valuation when I signed my contract but have elected to complete the transaction at the contract purchase price or cost. I have paid or will pay in cash from my own resources at or prior to loan closing a sum equal to the difference between contract purchase price or cost and the VA or HUD/FHA established value. I do not and will not have outstanding after loan closing any unpaid contractual obligation on account of such cash payment.

(4) Neither I, nor anyone authorized to act for me, will refuse to sell or rent, after the making of a bona fide offer, or refuse to negotiate for the sale or rental of, or otherwise make unavailable or deny the dwelling or property covered by his/her loan to any person because of race, color, religion, sex, handicap, familial status or national origin. I recognize that any restrictive covenant on this property relating to race, color, religion, sex, handicap, familial status or national origin is illegal and void and civil action for preventive relief may be brought by the Attorney General of the United States in any appropriate U.S. District Court against any person responsible for the violation of the applicable law.

(5) All information in this application is given for the purpose of obtaining a loan to be insured under the National Housing Act or guaranteed by the Department of Veterans Affairs and the information in the Uniform Residential Loan Application and this Addendum is true and complete to the best of my knowledge and belief. Verification may be obtained from any source named herein.

(6) For HUD Only (for properties constructed prior to 1978) I have received information on lead paint poisoning. ☐ Yes ☑ Not Applicable

(7) **I am aware that neither HUD / FHA nor VA warrants the condition or value of the property**

Signature(s) of Borrower(s) -- **Do not sign** unless this application is fully completed. Read the certifications carefully & review accuracy of this application. Date

X

X

Federal statutes provide severe penalties for any fraud, intentional misrepresentation, or criminal connivance or conspiracy purposed to influence the issuance of any guaranty or insurance by the VA Secretary or the HUD/FHA Commissioner.

VA Form 26-1802a (3/98)   page 2   form HUD-92900-A (06/2005)

Source: Reverse Mortgage of America, a Division of Seattle Mortgage Company

Essentials of reverse mortgage origination I

from Form 1009 and other documents in the application software. An experienced FHA processor can fill in any missing information, but make sure borrower signs and dates form.

III. Processing the application

Processing consists of putting application file and supporting documentation in prescribed order for underwriting. Upon receiving completed loan application from originator, processor should do the following:

- Review the application and supporting documentation to ensure accuracy and completeness
- Check USPS to confirm address
- Order FHA case number (HECM only)
- Check to ensure parties to the loan transaction are not on LDP/GSA lists (HECM only)
- Order and review property appraisal
- Order and review title insurance
- Order and review flood certification(must be in investor's name
- Secure other documents that lender or the program requires (i.e. trust agreement, POA, borrower assistance agreement, etc.)
- Put the loan application file together in prescribed order
- Ship it to underwriting

Processing note: Once the appraisal, inspections, title and other reports come in, processor should thoroughly review these documents for potential stumbling blocks to loan approval. If there are issues (for example, a dead spouse's name still on title), processor should ensure there is a death certificate in the package. The processor should pre-underwrite the package to eliminate or minimize pre-closing conditions.

IV. Underwriting/funding

The underwriter reviews the entire application package for completeness and accuracy in line with program and investor requirements and guidelines. The underwriter pays particular attention to the appraisal and title reports. If all is well, the underwriter approves the loan. If appraisal, title report, hazard insurance and other key documents indicate additional issues, underwriter will issue conditions. The processor will work with the loan originator to ensure that underwriter's conditions are met. After conditions have been satisfied, underwriter approves loan. In cases where the loan file is weak and the underwriter determines that risks posed to investor are unacceptable, the

Part III: Originating reverse mortgages

loan application is denied. The originator should know there is a problem and inform borrower ahead.

Upon underwriting approval and a "clear to close" classification, the closing and funding departments take over. The funding department prepares the closing documents and disclosures. A date is set for closing in consultation with the borrower and the closing agent or attorney.

V. Closing/disbursement

On the appointed day and time, promissory note, mortgages or deeds of trust, loan agreement, and other key documents and disclosures are reviewed, signed, dated and notarized.

Among the disclosures, borrower reviews and signs a three-day right of rescission disclosure. Federal law gives borrower right to rescind and cancel loan during this three business day period. If borrower decides not to cancel transaction on the fourth day following closing, loan funds, typically initial draw, are disbursed by closing or escrow agent.

VI. After-closing

A "welcome kit" is usually included in the closing package sent to the closing or escrow agent. It introduces the customer to the reverse mortgage loan servicing department, complete with toll-free numbers. Six months after closing, if Gloria Neincash wants to add a monthly payment plan to her credit line, she calls the servicing department. If there is a number in her monthly statement that she doesn't understand, servicing department will explain it.

The life of a reverse mortgage begins after closing. The loan servicer takes over as the loan's guardian and primary contact for the borrower during the loan's life. Of course, you should call often to ensure all is well between borrower and mortgage servicer.

How HomeKeeper origination differs from HECM's

Below are some differences between HomeKeeper and HECM programs originators should be mindful of[*]:

1. HomeKeeper has a single national loan limit ($417,000 for 2006 and 2007).
2. With two borrowers, both borrowers' DOB affects principal limit calculation
3. Interest rate has zero impact on principal limit
4. No *term* cash advance option or payment plan
5. A complete home inspection report is required.
6. No FHA case number is assigned.

7. No MIP
8. No HUD/VA Addendum form.
9. No credit report is required.
10. No LDP or GSA lists to worry about
11. HomeKeeper important terms/Truth-in-Lending form must be used.
12. Fannie Mae Counseling Certificate must be obtained.
13. Tax service fee may be charged to the borrower on the HUD-1.
14. Title policy coverage and maximum principal amount on the security instrument must be equal to 150 percent of the principal limit.
15. One mortgage or deed of trust and one note required.
16. Appraisal only valid for 4 months; if older, value re-certification is required.

*This list is illustrative, not exhaustive.

Source: Sarah Hulbert
Chapter 12 is continuation of Chapter 11.

Part III: Originating reverse mortgages

Chapter Twelve
Essentials of reverse mortgage origination II

Chapter 12 objectives
After studying this chapter, the reader will be able to:
- Describe qualities of a reverse mortgage originator
- Identify the skills of a reverse mortgage originator
- Recognize issues and challenges in reverse mortgage origination
- Explain repair policy
- Know the purpose of a HECM refinance
- Explain HECM refinance safeguards
- Know how to calculate the total cost of a HECM refinance
- Understand the appraiser's role in reverse mortgage origination
- Appreciate NRMLA's value in reverse mortgage origination
- Know some reverse mortgage origination do's and don'ts

Paul and Irene Alexander of New Hampshire took out a reverse mortgage over five years ago. When I interviewed them for this book, they spoke glowingly of the mortgage professionals they worked with. Paul is a retired senior human resource manager with a degree in liberal arts and business, and Irene is a retired law firm receptionist. The Alexanders' encounter with a reverse mortgage professional showed the skills and qualities reverse mortgage originators should cultivate and emulate. Paul Alexander described their experience:

"My first call to Amston's 800 number was a quick one: He asked us what we owe, what the estimated current appraisal value was and how old we were. Then he sent us a "conservative" estimate. He thought we would get no cash, but would have to pay no more principal and interest.

Part III: Originating reverse mortgages

Next, the local rep called us and asked to meet with us. She was extremely kind and patient. No pressure was exerted at any time during the process. She took a $350 appraisal fee which was returned to us when we closed. It happened very quickly. A closing expert prepared the paperwork and came out to the house to sign the papers. A real class act. All three people [originator, reverse counselor and closing agent] were very professional and answered all our questions.

We ... received over $13,000 at closing in addition to the relief of paying no principal and interest for the rest of our lives. The process was smooth, not intimidating in any way, and very satisfying in its outcome. We cannot say enough good things about what happened."

Read the last sentence of Paul Alexander's statement again. It was a "Wow!" experience for them, delivered by exceptional mortgage professionals with the skills and temperament essential to serving the senior customer. Let's focus on these phrases:

- He sent us a conservative estimate
- She was extremely kind and patient
- No pressure was exerted on us at any time during the process
- It happened very quickly
- Closing expert ... came to our house to sign the papers ... a real class act
- All three people were very professional (originator, counselor and closer)
- They answered all of our questions
- The process was smooth, not intimidating, in anyway, and very satisfying in its outcome
- We cannot say enough good things about what happened

"He sent us a 'conservative' estimate." It means that he under-promised and over-delivered. The $13,000-plus they received at closing was a pleasant surprise. Under promising and over-delivering is a time-honored approach that works particularly with mature customers because the opposite, over-promising and under-delivering, can undermine trust and credibility at the beginning. Mature customers have heard too many big promises that missed the mark. They are skeptical. A conservative approach is the way to go.

"She was extremely kind and patient." This phrase needs little translation. Kindness and patience are essential qualities in a reverse mortgage originator. If kindness and patience are foreign to you, you belong in another business.

"No pressure was exerted on us at any time during the process." This part of my interview with Paul Alexander was conducted via e-mail. The emphasis on "no pressure" was his. My translation says the reverse mortgage special-

ist at Amston Mortgage was a consultant, not a pushy salesperson. So, follow the Amston Mortgage rule: Exert *no pressure* on your mature customers.

"It happened very quickly." At any age, quick service is appreciated. This was obviously a slam dunk reverse mortgage loan, with no repairs, septic/wells, termites, trusts or other time-consuming issues that reverse originators must make time allowance for.

"Closing expert ... came to our house to sign the papers ... a real class act." Again, at any age, customers value professionals who go the extra mile. Close your reverse mortgage loans on your borrower's dining table, unless they suggest otherwise.

"All three people (originator, reverse counselor, closer) were very professional." Reverse mortgage loan origination, like any mortgage loan origination, is a team effort. The originator, as the coordinator of the team, must ensure that the senior borrower receives high professional service from other members of the team, especially third party service providers such as closing agents.

"... answered all of our questions." In this case, all three professionals fulfilled their educational duties to the customers. They provided obviously satisfactory answers to questions that may have confounded the borrowers. Know your reverse mortgage programs in and out, so that you can answer your borrower's questions, or know where to find the answers.

"The process was smooth, not intimidating in any way, and very satisfying in its outcome." Every reverse mortgage originator should use this statement as their standard, their ideal and strive to construct a reverse mortgage origination experience that is seamless, simple, and satisfying.

"We cannot say enough good things about what happened." Wow! For a senior borrower to give this evaluation to a reverse mortgage lender almost two years after closing is remarkable. I don't know about you, but the Amston Mortgage model of reverse mortgage service, as documented in my interview with the recipients of that service, is my model.

Generation Mortgage Company bought Amston Mortgage in 2007.

More skills of a reverse mortgage originator

Paul Franklin of Franklin Funding, a seasoned reverse mortgage lender in Charleston, S.C., believes a reverse mortgage originator must acquire the following skills to be effective in reverse mortgage origination:

Listening skills

Seniors often have stories to tell. By listening to their stories with empathy, you will build rapport. It shows that you value and respect them. Over time,

Part III: Originating reverse mortgages

you will gain their trust. Franklin says that you cannot develop trust with every senior. In some cases, the "chemistry" just won't be there. Accept it and move on.

Ask questions
The ability to ask good questions is important because it tells the senior customer that you care about them. This ability is closely related to your listening skills. By asking good questions and listening, you develop a better understanding of your senior borrower and their needs.

Patience
Franklin says you cannot show that you are in a rush, and that your body language should be relaxed, showing diligence. As the Paul Alexander testimonial we looked at earlier indicated, senior customers value patience. As a reverse mortgage originator, you should cultivate it.

Be organized
Being organized means knowing and following an established sequence in your origination interaction with the senior customer. This skill will help you stay on task and on schedule.

Be a good planner
The skill of looking ahead and preparation for what could happen will help the reverse mortgage originator make a complex reverse mortgage process seem easy. For example, if borrower says she has a leaky roof at application, immediately arrange to have the roof inspected. Do not wait for the appraiser to ask you to do it. It saves time and simplifies the process.

Detail-lover
A healthy capacity for detail is a valuable skill in a reverse mortgage originator because there are so many pieces to the reverse mortgage puzzle. Is there something on the title report that could delay or scuttle the loan? Find out by reviewing title report, even if you have a processor. The old saw is right: The reverse devil is in the details. Make peace with details.

Task/project master
Every reverse mortgage loan file is a task or a project; as a result, a reverse mortgage originator should be project-oriented. Until project is completed (loan closed and customer satisfied), you keep at it.

Essentials of reverse mortgage origination II

Be a follow-upper and a communicator

A reverse mortgage originator should have good follow-up and strong communication skills. Follow-up and regular communications between originator and senior borrower lubricates the relationship. The reverse originator should provide weekly updates on the loan status and other matters affecting the loan. They should learn to repeat things time and again, until they register. The reverse originator should also learn to manage expectations. A good way to manage expectations is to under-promise as Amston Mortgage did with the Alexanders: "He thought we would get no cash, but would have to pay no more principal and interest." Even though, "He thought we would get no cash," they actually got more than $13,000 at closing. Their goal, their expectation, was simple: Get rid of mortgage payments for life so that they can convert mortgage payments into spending money. The bottom-line: They got more than they expected. Two years later, they are still singing the praises of their reverse mortgage originator because he proved himself a master of expectations management.

Issues and challenges in HECM origination

The way Paul Alexander describes it, their reverse mortgage origination was a slam dunk. But many reverse mortgage originations are not that simple. Issues and challenges arise that can delay closing and cause frustration. Understanding these issues and challenges, and planning to address them when they are encountered, will help the reverse originator save time and increase customer satisfaction. Prepare for the following situations:

The availability of HECM counseling

A national network of trained and HUD-approved HECM counselors is available across the country. For a list of agencies in your area of origination, log on to www.hud.gov/offices/hsg/sfh/hcc/hccprof14.cfm.

Processing a reverse application before a counseling certificate

A HECM reverse mortgage prospect gets reverse mortgage counseling from a HUD-approved counseling agency. As evidence of counseling, she is issued a counseling certificate which the lender must collect at the time of application. For various reasons, some lenders take the application and process the loan, before asking the prospect to go for the required counseling. The fees and charges incurred during the application process, before counseling, cannot be charged to the customer. FHA considers them "ineligible fees," and the lender must eat these costs. These are usually appraisal and credit report charges. Do your pocketbook a favor, follow the program guidelines: Reverse counseling before processing.

The in-person meeting

Distance between lender and borrower can be an issue in reverse mortgage origination, especially when borrower lives in a rural area. An in-person meeting with borrower is required. This requirement can be met by borrower having a face-to-face counseling, application interview or meeting face-to-face with an employee of originating company during loan process. No matter how application is taken, originating lender is responsible for certifying borrower's identity.

Living trust

A property held in a living trust (a.k.a. inter vivos trust) is eligible for a reverse mortgage. The full trust papers should be submitted to the underwriter for review. It is also important for the closing agent, attorney or title company to review and approve trust papers to avoid closing delays.

Removal from trust

A property can be removed from trust and returned to individuals if the trust does not meet HUD and lender guidelines. An originator should not recommend removal of property from trust; it must be borrower's decision.

Power of attorney

Where a power of attorney (POA) is involved, it must be a durable power of attorney, with the authority to mortgage property. To be valid, the POA must be signed before the reverse mortgage application. A copy of the POA document must be included in the loan file. To sign the application and the closing documents, the POA must receive reverse mortgage counseling. If borrower is competent, she must also attend counseling and sign the application; if not competent, a doctor's letter will be required to waive borrower's signing application.

Guardianship/conservatorship

A court-appointed guardian or conservator must be given specific authority to mortgage property with a reverse mortgage and must appear as part of vesting.[1]

Footnote

1-Reverse Mortgage Advisor, *Volume 5.2, Summer 2002, pages 5-6.*

Essentials of reverse mortgage origination II

Repair policy: FHA makes a u-turn

Once upon a time, an FHA appraisal was a dreaded document for loan officers, processors, and borrowers. It was "subject to" repairs, as opposed to "as is" appraisals for much of the residential mortgage lending world. FHA required appraisers to watch out for minor defects, such as peeling paint, missing handrails, cracked window glass and leaky faucets, etc. Where these and other light defects are present, appraisers must list them on a "VC Sheet" even if the loan is a cash-out loan like a reverse mortgage. The borrower had the choice of fixing the defects before closing or doing so after closing. They were required to get estimates from licensed contractors. It was cumbersome and time-consuming.

Well, FHA had a change of heart on Dec. 19, 2005 in Mortgagee Letter 2005-48. It threw away the old "subject to" repairs rules and joined the "as is" folks at Fannie Mae and the rest of the mortgage universe. Serious safety, health, or structural problems, such as leaky roofs or cracked foundations, must still be addressed before FHA will insure the loan. In such cases, one-and-a-half-times contractor's bid is held in escrow, and homeowner has up to six months to repair home. Underwriters must decide when a property is too dangerous for the owner/borrower because of structural problems. Mortgagee Letter 2005-48 is *required reading*. Get the full text online at www.hud.gov/offices/hsg/mltrmenu.cfm and study it. It has reduced the processing time of a HECM reverse mortgage by at least three weeks.

HECM refinance

One of the more important developments in reverse mortgages in recent years is authorization of HECM refinance (on April 26, 2004 under the American Homeownership and Economic Opportunity Act [AHEOA]). The HECM refinance law has two purposes:

a. To authorize a HECM refinance; and
b. Reduce the HECM refinance cost to borrower.

How a HECM refinance cost is reduced

The rule says the initial Mortgage Insurance Premium (IMIP) for refinancing a HECM is pegged at two percent of the increase in loan limit. For example:

a. Old loan limit = $100,000
b. New value = $150,000
c. Difference between the old and new loan limit = $50,000
d. Initial MIP of two percent is paid on $50,000, not $150,000

Part III: Originating reverse mortgages

HECM refinance safeguards

A HECM refinance contains some safeguards. The lender must provide borrower with an Anti-Churning Disclosure (HUD Form 92901). The Anti-Churning Disclosure ensures that borrower's benefit drives the refinance, not lender's profit motive.

Anti-Churning Disclosure must be given at the same time with the Good Faith Estimate if the HECM is a closed-end line of credit. For HECM loans that are open-ended lines of credit, Anti-Churning Disclosure must be given with the Truth-in-Lending Act (TILA) and Regulation Z disclosures.

A HECM refinance cost disclosure is another safeguard. The lender must provide the borrower with a "best estimate" of total cost of the refinance. In addition, the borrower must be provided the increase in principal limit, side-by-side with the old principal limit, for example, old principal limit $100,000, new limit, $150,000:

New PL $150,000
Old PL $100,000
Difference $50,000

Also, the lender should give the borrower the "best estimate" of the net principal limit under the new financing.

HECM refinance counseling waiver*

HUD regulation waives the HECM counseling requirement for a HECM refinance if the following three conditions are satisfied:

a. The borrower receives Anti-Churning Disclosure Form (HUD Form 92901)
b. Additional principal limit exceeds refinance costs five times (5-Times Rule)
c. Refinance application must be within five years of original HECM loan (Within-5-Year Rule)

*Some lenders still require counseling of all.

HECM servicer cannot stall process

HECM servicers are required to share borrower information with refinance originator as follows:

a. Maximum claim amount of the old HECM loan
b. Principal limit of old HECM loan

Essentials of reverse mortgage origination II

c. Old HECM loan pay-off amount
d. Items A-C will be fed into refinance software to complete HUD Form 92901, Anti-Churning Form.

The HECM servicer is also required to end old HECM loan and reconcile accounts before payoff.

How to calculate total cost of HECM refinance
Example:

a. Brenda Phillips, 83 years old, took out a HECM loan in June of 2002
b. The FHA loan limit (a.k.a. Maximum Claim Amount [MCA]) was $120,000
c. The principal limit (PL) amount available to her, in the 2002 loan was $72,000
d. In November 2004, Mrs. Phillips decided to refinance her 2002 HECM loan because of low interest rates and strong appreciation in the value of her home
e. The new FHA loan limit in November 2004 was $250,000
f. The new principal limit (PL) is $162,000

Calculating Principal Limit
1. New PL $162,000
2. Old PL..$72,000
3. Increase (decrease) in Mrs. Phillips PL $90,000

Calculating HECM refinance costs
FHA Upfront MIP is two percent of difference between the old (2002 FHA loan limit of $120,000) and the new (2004 FHA loan limit of $250,000):

$250,000
-$120,000
Difference between the old and new FHA loan limit—$130,000

Upfront FHA MIP = $130,000 X 0.02 = $2,600
Refinance origination fee = $130,000 X 0.02 = $2,600
Other closing costs = $2,100
Servicing set-aside = $5,500

Total estimated refinance costs to Mrs. Phillips = $12,800

Part III: Originating reverse mortgages

5-Times Test:
5 X $12,800 = $64,000

Increase in PL (see calculation of PL above) $90,000
Minus total costs times five $64,000
Difference between PL and refinance cost.............................$26,000

Conclusions
- Increase in Brenda Phillips's principal limit exceeds her total refinance cost by more than five times
- Refinance is within five years (5-Year Rule)
- Mrs. Phillips received HECM Anti-Churning Disclosure Form (HUD Form 92901)

Decision: Mrs. Phillips can skip the HECM counseling requirement; a refinance is good for Mrs. Philips.

HECM Refinance Notes
- CHUMS (FHA's underwriting system) must show the old case number.
- Check to ensure no tax and insurance delinquencies.

The appraiser's role in the reverse mortgage origination

A reverse mortgage is a pure home equity loan. A lending decision is based solely on the value and condition of property behind loan, not on credit or income as with other home equity lending. Since it is appraiser's job to assign a market value to the home and check property's physical condition, appraiser's role in reverse mortgage origination is vital.

Generally, lenders hire appraisers and borrowers pay their fees. To save borrowers appraisal cost and to find out whether it makes sense to proceed with loan, lenders ask for a free initial estimate of value. Good appraisers can come very close to the market value without doing a full-blown analysis.

With a full appraisal, the appraiser checks the home's physical condition; if serious repair issues arise, the borrower hires contractors to correct problems. When repairs are done, the same appraiser returns to certify that repairs are done. A "repair call back fee," ranging from $50-$100, depending on the custom in the area, is charged to the borrower.

To locate an FHA-approved appraiser, go to https://entp.hud.gov/idapp/html.[2]

Footnote

2-*Reverse Mortgage Advisor*, Volume 5.2, Summer 2002, pages 4 and 9.

Essentials of reverse mortgage origination II

NRLMA's value in reverse mortgage origination

In Chapter 10, we saw why one of the most important marketing moves you could make is to join the National Reverse Mortgage Lenders Association (NRMLA). NRMLA's membership has operational value for you as an originator in two vital areas, training and information.

Training

At training sessions during the year, NRMLA brings in industry and outside-industry experts to train new and experienced originators in various aspects of the reverse mortgage business.

In 2004, NRMLA initiated a monthly teleconference training/continuing education series called "Learn While U Lunch." For more information on this program, go to www.nrmlaonline.org.

Information

As a reverse mortgage originator, you need to be abreast of critical information from HUD and investors. NRMLA serves as an information conduit for HUD and investors to its members. Essential policy changes from HUD and investors are communicated to members, often with very helpful explanations and illustrations. For example, on April 23, 2004, HUD issued a Mortgage Letter on HECM refinance among other matters. Within minutes, NRMLA members had the letter via e-mail from NRMLA. That Mortgagee Letter contained information that an alert reverse mortgage originator could have used to originate a HECM refinance loan three days later.

Other information from NRMLA comes via the association's Mid-Month Report. NRMLA's "Mid-Month Report" is a summary of key industry developments e-mailed to members in the middle of the month. It contains valuable information that a reverse mortgage originator can use to stay informed and competitive.

Reverse Mortgage Advisor (now *Reverse Mortgage*, a magazine) is a publication from NRMLA distributed to its membership. It's an invaluable resource for reverse originators. Every issue includes articles written to aid members in their marketing and origination of reverse mortgages. NRMLA's password-protected Members-Only section of their Web site is a library of valuable information for the reverse mortgage originator. The HECM Handbook (4235.1-Rev.1, HUD Mortgagee Letters, HECM Activity Reports, back issues of Reverse Mortgage Advisor, and other relevant information is just a click or two away.

Part III: Originating reverse mortgages

Typically, the mid-month report, *Reverse Mortgage Advisor*, and other NRMLA information, go to the NRMLA delegate and alternate in your company. For access to these reverse mortgage marketing and origination tools, go to the NRMLA delegate or alternate in your company or go to NRMLA member Web site www.nrmlaonline.org. You must register to gain access.

The do's and don'ts in reverse mortgage origination

The guidelines below should help new originators avoid mistakes that others have made. Let's start with the do's.

Do's:
- Show respect to senior customers
- Show interest in senior customers and be genuinely interested in them
- Show patience; do things slowly
- Listen attentively to their story
- Ask questions
- Build rapport with senior customers and their relatives
- Explain all the available programs
- Know your HECM Handbook (HUD Handbook 4235.1-Rev.1), as well as HUD Mortgage Letters that from time to time modify the Handbook
- Be willing to meet with a senior customer and walk away without taking a loan application
- Be consistent
- Simplify complexity

Don'ts:
Remember flipside of all the do's.

In Chapter 13, we will discuss reverse mortgage laws and regulations.

Chapter 12 resources
A word about FHA lender Web site
A key Web site for any mortgage professional engaged in FHA lending is www.hud.gov/groups/lenders.cfm. It is a one-stop FHA-resource powerhouse. Visit it often. Get familiar with it. Take your questions there. You'll get 24/7 help.

Chapter 12 resources
- FHA appraisers: https://entp.hud.gov/idapp/html
- HECM counselors: www.hud.gov/offices/hsg/sfh/hcc/hccprof14.cfm
- NRMLA's member Web site www.nrmlaonline.org

Part III: Originating reverse mortgages

Chapter Thirteen
Laws and regulations in Reverseland

Opening quote ...
"Make sure you are using the proper disclosures."
—**James M. Milano Esq.**

"... shortcuts do not serve their purpose. Ultimately, by circumventing the system in under-disclosing or misrepresenting reverse mortgage programs, the result is non-compliance and additional burden on lenders, investors, regulatory agencies, and borrowers."
—**Sarah F. Hulbert**

Chapter 13 objectives
After studying this chapter, the reader will be able to:
- Identify federal laws and regulations affecting reverse mortgage origination
- Explain the Truth in Lending Act's Total Annual Loan Cost (TALC) disclosures requirements
- Know the importance of the HUD/HECM regulations and how to locate the HUD Handbook 4235.1–Rev. 1
- Understand RESPA disclosures for HECM reverse mortgages
- Know ECOA guidelines for taking applications
- Get some reverse mortgage compliance tips
- Learn some reverse mortgage compliance do's and don'ts
- Recognize some ethical issues in reverse mortgage lending

Virgin compliance territories
David J. Gutmann is co-CEO and general counsel with Customized Lender's

Part III: Originating reverse mortgages

Services based in Rochester, N.Y. In August 2005, I received this e-mail from him:

"I have been reading your columns in *The New York Mortgage Press* and have been extremely impressed. Not only are you raising awareness of reverse mortgages, but you are also showing that there is a need to abide by the highest ethical standards when dealing with our elderly population who may not fully understand differing mortgage products.

My company is a vendor management company, providing bundled services to the lending community, and we have been involved with the settlement of reverse mortgages over the past two years. *It is sometimes surprising to see how many people aren't aware of the benefits of reverse mortgages, or for that matter, have never heard of them,* **including attorneys.** *My office sponsored a seminar on reverse mortgages not too long ago, and* **one of the attorneys leaving at its conclusion commented that, coming in, he thought that reverse mortgages were a scam, but after hearing the presentation, he had a better appreciation of them, as well as an additional tool to help him in assisting his elderly clients** [my emphasis]."

Reverse mortgage-specific laws, regulations and compliance issues are new territories in residential real estate law practice in this country. While there is some overlap with traditional forward mortgages in some regulatory areas, seasoned legal expertise on the reverse mortgage side is thin.

Thin or not, awareness of reverse mortgage-specific laws, regulations, and compliance issues is essential to successfully marketing and originating reverse mortgages.

Some of the information and insights I will share in this chapter comes from my interview with James M. Milano Esq., a regulatory compliance attorney with the Washington, D.C.-based law firm of Weiner Brodsky Sidman Kider PC, one of only a few law firms in America with legal expertise and extensive experience in reverse mortgage practice, including counsel to NRMLA and outside counsel to a number of large and small reverse mortgage companies across the country.

Our goal is to present useful information to reverse mortgage marketers and originators. **Nothing in this chapter should be considered legal advice.** We suggest that you hire a qualified and experienced regulatory compliance attorney with experience in reverse mortgages if you need legal advice that is specific to your situation. We will briefly review the laws and regulations that originators must be aware of and comply with to do their jobs properly.

Laws and regulations in Reverseland

The federal rules
Rules and regulations abound in reverse country. The prudent reverse mortgage originator should know and follow them. Below are some pertinent ones:

- Truth-in-Lending Act (TILA)/Regulation Z (Section 33)
- HUD/HECM Regulations
- Real Estate Settlement Procedures Act (RESPA)
- Equal Credit Opportunity Act (ECOA)

In addition to these federal laws and their related regulations, some states have reverse mortgage-specific laws and regulations that reverse mortgage originators should know. For example, in the state of North Carolina, an originator must obtain "specific North Carolina reverse mortgage approval from the North Carolina Commissioner of Banks" in addition to the state's mortgage lending license in order to do reverse mortgage business. States like California, Nebraska, New York, West Virginia and Rhode Island also have reverse mortgage-specific laws. Let's briefly review the federal laws above and see how they affect origination of reverse mortgages.

Truth-in-Lending Act (TILA)
Congress passed the Truth-in-Lending Act in 1968. With its implementing rules or Regulation Z, it was designed to help borrowers know the true cost of borrowing money and to permit them to correctly compare credit costs among lenders.

In 1994, through the Home Owner Equity Protection Act (HOEPA), Congress brought all reverse mortgages under a new Truth-in-Lending requirement. This requirement is called Total Annual Loan Cost disclosure or "TALC."

The TALC rules required reverse mortgage lenders to consistently make a good faith projection of the total annual average cost of obtaining reverse mortgages, similar to original Truth-in-Lending law.

The purpose of the new law was to achieve a "grapes to grapes" comparison of reverse mortgage costs for consumers. *(See Figure 13.1 on page 192)*

Figure 13.1 shows a sample TALC disclosure form that lenders must use to comply with the 1994 rules. It summarizes loan terms and charges, including the age of the youngest borrower and the property's appraised value. A TALC rate table illustrates disclosure periods ranging from two years to

Part III: Originating reverse mortgages

Figure 13.1
TALC Chart

Your Loan Advisor
Atare E. Agbamu, CRMS
CREDO MORTGAGE INC.
5874 Blackshire Path
Inver Grove Heights, MN 55076
Phone: (866) 732-7336 Fax: (651) 389-1115

Prepared for Mr. John D Hecm and Mrs. Mary J Hecm   HUD Monthly Program

LOAN TERM

Age of Youngest Borrower:	62
Appraised Property Value:	$300,000
Initial Interest Rate:	5.80%
Monthly Advance:	$0.00
Initial Draw:	$60,000.00
Line of Credit:	$75,214.06
Length of Term:	N/A

MONTHLY LOAN CHARGE

Monthly Servicing Fee:	$35.00
Mortgage Insurance:	0.5% Annually

OTHER CHARGES

Shared Appreciation:	None

REPAYMENT LIMITS
Net Proceeds Estimated at
93% Of Projected Home Sale

INITIAL LOAN CHARGE

Other Closing Costs:	$7,602.14
Mortgage Ins. Premium:	$5,380.00

Total Annual Loan Cost Rate

APPRECIATION RATE	DISCLOSURE PERIOD (Yrs.)			
	2	11	21	29
0%	13.54%	7.80%	5.13%	3.69%
4%	13.54%	7.80%	7.15%	6.94%
8%	13.54%	7.80%	7.15%	6.94%

The cost of any reverse mortgage loan depends on how long you keep the loan and how much your house appreciates in value. Generally, the longer you keep a reverse mortgage, the lower the total annual loan cost rate will be.

This table shows the estimated cost of your reverse mortgage loan, expressed as an annual rate. It illustrates the cost for four loan terms: 2 years, half of life expectancy for someone your age, that life expectancy, and 1.4 times that life expectancy. The table also shows the cost of the loan, assuming the value of your home appreciates at three different rates: 0%, 4% and 8%.

The total annual cost rates in this table are based on the total charges associated with this loan. These charges typically include principal, interest, closing costs, mortgage insurance premiums, annuity costs, and servicing costs (but not disposition costs -- costs when you sell the home).

The rates in this table are estimates. Your actual cost may differ if, for example, the amount of your loan advances varies or the interest rate on your mortgage changes. You may receive projections of loan balances from counselors or lenders that are based on an expected average mortgage rate that differs from the initial interest rate.

**SIGNING AN APPLICATION OR RECEIVING THESE DISCLOSURES
DOES NOT REQUIRE YOU TO COMPLETE THIS LOAN**

John D Hecm   Date   Mary J Hecm   Date

Printed by Financial Freedom™ Senior Funding Corporation's Reverse Mortgage Analyzer™. Copyright © 1999-2005 11/28/05 3

Source: TALC Chart produced using Reverse Mortgage Analyzer, a registered trademark of Financial Freedom Senior Funding Corporation

Laws and regulations in Reverseland

29 years. The total cost rates align with three assumed home appreciation rates of zero percent, four percent and eight percent. An explanation of the cost of reverse mortgages and the TALC rate table is followed by a required notice in bold print: "**Signing an Application or Receiving These Disclosures Does Not Require You to Complete This Loan.**"

The TALC rate disclosure form is available in standard reverse mortgage origination software. It can be printed with most loan application forms.

The TALC Regulations can be located at 12 CFR 226.33 or Title 12 Code of Federal Regulations (CFR), Part 226.33 [Requirements for Reverse Mortgages]. To learn more, log on to www.frwebgate.access.gpo.gov/cgi-bin/get-cfr.cgi.

HUD/HECM regulations and HUD Handbook 4235.1-Rev. 1

The rules governing the FHA-insured reverse mortgage program are called the HUD/HECM regulations. To help HECM counselors, originators, processors, underwriters, closers, funders, servicers and investors understand and follow the HUD/HECM regulations, HUD created a readable manual called HUD Handbook 4235.1-Rev.1. The handbook is essential reading for any serious HECM participant.

To view and download the handbook, do the following:

- Log on to www.hudclips.org
- Select "Search or Browse All HUD Handbooks and Guidebooks"
- In the "Enter Word or Phrase" field, enter "Home Equity Conversion Mortgages"
- Hit "Submit"
- Scroll down to #16, 4235.1 "Home Equity Conversion Mortgages"

While the HUD Handbook 4235.1-Rev.1 is an essential guide for anyone involved in HECM origination, originators and processors should be familiar with their wholesale lender's operating manual and guidelines. Also, the HUD Handbook should be read in conjunction with HECM-related FHA Mortgagee Letters.

Periodic FHA Mortgagee Letters are essential reading for HECM participants because they often provide policy guidance, announce new policies, clarify existing policies and, in some cases, modify or rescind policies. See a sample FHA Mortgagee Letter below.

The HUD/HECM regulations can be found at 24 CFR 206 or Title 24 Code of Federal Regulations, Part 206. FHA Mortgagee Letters are available online at www.hudclips.org. *(See Figure 13.2 on page 194)*

Part III: Originating reverse mortgages

Figure 13.2
Sample FHA Mortgage Letter

U.S. DEPARTMENT OF HOUSING AND URBAN DEVELOPMENT
WASHINGTON, DC 20410-8000

ASSISTANT SECRETARY FOR HOUSING-
FEDERAL HOUSING COMMISSIONER

July 22, 2004

MORTGAGEE LETTER 2004-27

TO: ALL APPROVED MORTGAGEES
ALL HUD-APPROVED HOUSING COUNSELING AGENCIES

SUBJECT: Home Equity Conversion Mortgage (HECM) Program –
Delayed Effective Date for Mortgagee Letter 2004-25 Instructions

In Mortgagee Letter 2004-25, the Department of Housing and Urban Development through the Federal Housing Administration (FHA) issued guidance to mortgagees and housing counseling agencies to comply with FHA requirements for the HECM program. The effective date for compliance with those requirements was July 23, 2004. Compliance with the requirements outlined in Mortgagee Letter 2004-25 is now August 23, 2004.

If you have questions about this Mortgagee Letter, please contact your local Homeownership Center in Atlanta (1-888-696-4687), Denver (1-800-543-9378), Philadelphia (1-800-440-8647) or Santa Ana (1-888-827-5605).

Sincerely,

John C. Weicher
Assistant Secretary for Housing-
Federal Housing Commissioner

www.hud.gov   espanol.hud.gov

Laws and regulations in Reverseland

Real Estate Settlement Procedures Act (RESPA)

In 1974, Congress passed the Real Estate Settlement Procedures Act (RESPA) to make mortgage lenders and brokers give borrowers information on closing costs and mortgage servicing transfers. RESPA also forbids kickbacks and makes it a criminal offense to give or take a referral fee in a home loan transaction if no value is given for the fee. RESPA says lenders and brokers must give residential mortgage loan borrowers detailed information on settlement services and costs at the time of application. RESPA governs mortgage loans secured by one- to four-unit family houses or mobile homes.

RESPA applies to reverse mortgage transactions through the HUD/HECM regulations. Consistent with the RESPA rules, reverse mortgage originators must provide borrowers with the following disclosures at the time of application, or within three business days of the application:

- A Good Faith Estimate (GFE) of closing costs
- A Servicing Disclosure Statement (SDS)
- A Required Service Providers' List (RSPL)

(See Figures 13.3, 13.4, 13.5 on pages 196-198)

The GFE gives the borrower the lender's best estimate of the costs to close the reverse mortgage loan. The servicing disclosure statement tells the borrower whether the lender or broker has the ability, and intention, to service the loan the applicant is applying for. The statement also provides the applicant with the percentage of loans the lender or broker has transferred in the prior three years. And the required service providers' list discloses the service providers (i.e., appraisers, credit report suppliers, document preparation companies, etc.) reverse mortgage loan applicants are required to use and the providers' relationship to the lender or broker. For more on RESPA, go to HUD lenders Web site under resource below.

Equal Credit Opportunity Act (ECOA)

Enacted in 1975 by Congress, the Equal Credit Opportunity Act (ECOA), and its implementing regulation (Reg. B), forbids discrimination in the credit business on the basis of race, color, religion, national origin, sex, marital status, age (as long as the borrower has the legal capacity to enter into a binging agreement), receipt of public assistance benefits or the customer's good faith exercise of rights under the Consumer Credit Protection Act. In mortgage lending activities, lenders may not discriminate in any of these so-called

Part III: Originating reverse mortgages

Figure 13.3
Good Faith Estimate

Good Faith Estimate

Lender:
Atare E. Agbamu, CRMS
Credo mortgage Inc.
5874 Blackshire Path
Inver Grove Heights, MN 55076
Phone: (866) 732-7336 Fax: (651) 389-1115

Applicant Information
Joan Shecm
1234 Equity Street
Revmortsville, MN 55119

HECM Monthly Program

Appraised Property Value:	$300,000
Maximum Claim Amount:	$276,683
Initial Interest Rate:	6.03%
Estimated Closing Date:	May 10, 2007

Applicant's age using nearest birthday: 75

The information provided below reflects estimates of the charges you are likely to incur at the settlement of your loan. The fees listed are estimates; the actual charges may be more or less. Your transaction may not involve a fee for every item listed. The numbers listed beside the estimates generally correspond to the numbered lines or sections contained in the HUD-1 Settlement Statement which you will receive at settlement. The HUD-1 Settlement Statement will show you the actual cost for items paid at settlement.

Charges

801	Loan Origination Fee		$5,533.66
803	Appraisal Fee		$375.00
804	Credit Report		$9.14
808	Repair Admin Fee (1.5% of the repair estimate or $50, whichever is greater)		$0.00
810	Flood Certification Fee		$17.00
813	Correspondent Fee POC-L	($49.18 POC)	$0.00
814	Table Funding Fee POC-B	($375 POC)	$0.00
902	FHA Mortgage Insurance Premium		$5,533.66
1101	Settlement or closing fee		$250.00
1102	Abstract or title search		$150.00
1103	Title Examination		$130.00
1105	Document Preparation		$125.00
1108	Title Insurance		$657.52
1111	Endorsements/Conservation Fee		$100.00
1201	Recording Fees		$76.00
1204	Mortgage Registration Tax		$688.24
1302	Pest Inspection		$0.00
1303	Courier Fees		$25.00
1304	Wire Fee		$0.00
1305	Signing Fee		$0.00
1400	TOTAL SETTLEMENT CHARGES		$13,670.22

* Line items noted by an asterisk may or may not be applicable to your loan.

This Good Faith Estimate is NOT a Loan Commitment.

_____   _____
Joan Shecm   Date

_____   _____
Atare E. Agbamu, CRMS   Date

Source: Good Faith Estimate Estimate produced using Reverse Mortgage Analyzer, a registered trademark of Financial Freedom Senior Funding Corporation

Laws and regulations in Reverseland

Figure 13.4
Required Service Provider Notice (Sample)

Required Service Provider Notice (Sample)
Addendum to the Good Faith Estimate of Settlement Charges

The Lender will require you to use one of the service providers either listed below or on an attached list for the types of settlement services listed below. The Lender has no ownership interest in any of the entities listed herein or on an attachment and identifies the settlement service providers only because the Lender has regularly used or required the borrower(s) to use their services within the last 12 months. The corresponding HUD-1 number is also shown.

Item Number	Provider	Address
	TITLE COMPANY	
*The Title Company for this transaction will be selected from a list of approved companies below. The cost of the title company service is reflected on the front page of the Good Faith Estimate.*		
1101	Financial Title Company (949)220-0000	1234 Main Street, Irvine, CA, 92001
1108	Correspondent Title Co. (310)888-9900	1 Spring Strret, Los Angeles, CA 90007
	APPRAISER	
*The appraiser for this transaction will be selected from a list of appraisers who have been approved by the company pursuant to the standards set forth in the Financial Institutions Reform Recovery and Enforcement Act (FIRREA). The estimated cost for the appraisal is reflected on the front page of the Good Faith Estimate.*		
803	ABC Realtor (123)456-7890	123 Realtor Dr. Small Town, CA 90001
803	QSF Appraisal Co. (323)888-9999	22 Main Street, Small Town, CA 90005
	CREDIT CERTIFICATION	
*The cost to obtain a consumer credit report will range from $8.00 - $65.00 per credit report.*		
804	Correspondent Credit Co. (800)444-5555	123 Crdit Co Address
	FLOOD CERTIFICATION	
*The cost to obtain a flood report will range from $14.00 - $25.00 per flood report.*		
810	Correspondent Flood Company (800)000-9999	234 Flood Co. Address
	DOCUMENT PREPARATION	
*The cost of document preparation will range from $125.00 - $135.00 per closing package.*		
1105	BayDocs (888) 297-3627	1683 Novato Blvd. Suite 3 Novato, CA 94947
1105	First American Nationwide Document (800) 892-6678	4500 Cherry Creek South Dr. Ste 1100 Denver, CO 80246
	COURIER – MESSENGER – MAIL	
*The cost of courier services will range from $45.00 - $55.00 per package.*		
If an express delivery service is required for your reverse mortgage request, the Company will select an express mail service provider from a list of approved companies. The cost of the express mail service is reflected on the Good Faith		

Initial _____ Date _____ Initial _____ Date _____

Source: Required Service Provider Notice (Sample) produced using Reverse Mortgage Analyzer, a registered trademark of Financial Freedom Senior Funding Corporation

Part III: Originating reverse mortgages

Figure 13.5
Servicing Disclosure Notice

Servicing Disclosure Notice

NOTICE TO FIRST LIEN MORTGAGE APPLICANTS: THE RIGHT TO COLLECT YOUR MORTGAGE LOAN PAYMENTS MAY BE TRANSFERRED. FEDERAL LAW GIVES YOU CERTAIN RELATED RIGHTS. IF YOUR LOAN IS MADE, SAVE THIS STATEMENT WITH YOUR LOAN DOCUMENTS. SIGN THE ACKNOWLEDGEMENT AT THE END OF THIS STATEMENT ONLY IF YOU UNDERSTAND ITS CONTENTS.

Because you are applying for a mortgage loan covered by the Real Estate Settlement Procedures Act (RESPA) (12 U.S.C. Section 2601 et seq.) you have a certain rights under federal law.

This statement tells you those rights. It also tells you what the changes are that the servicing for this loan may be transferred to a different loan servicer. "Servicing" refers to the collecting of your principal, interest and escrow account payments, if any. If your loan servicer changes, there are certain procedures that must be followed. This statement generally explains those procedures.

Transfer practices and requirements
If the servicing of your loan is assigned, sold, or transferred to a new servicer, you must be given written notice of that transfer. The present loan servicer must send you notice in writing of assignment, sale or transfer of the servicing not less than 15 days before the effective date of the transfer. The new loan servicer must also send you notice within 15 days after the effective date of the transfer. The present servicer and the new servicer may combine this information in one notice, so long as the notice is sent to you 15 days before the effective date of the transfer. The 15 day period is not applicable if a notice of prospective transfer is provided to you at settlement. The law allows a delay in the time (not more than 30 days after a transfer) for servicers to notify you, upon the occurrence of certain business emergencies.

Notices must contain certain information. They must contain the effective date of the transfer of the servicing of your loan to the new servicer, the name, address, and toll-free or collect call telephone number of the new servicer, and toll-free or collect call telephone numbers of a person or department for both your present servicer and your new servicer to answer your questions. During the 60 day period following the effective date of the transfer of the loan servicing, a loan payment received by your old servicer before its due date may not be treated by the new loan servicer as late, and a late fee may not be imposed on you.

Complaint Resolution
Section 6 of RESPA (12 U.S.C. Section 2605) gives you certain consumer rights, whether or not your loan servicing is transferred. If you send a "qualified written request" to your servicer, then your servicer must provide you with a written acknowledgement within 20 business days of the receipt of your request. A "qualified written request" is a written correspondence, other than notice on a payment coupon or other payment medium supplied by the servicer, which includes your name and account number, and the information regarding your request. Not later than 60 days after receiving your request, your servicer must make any appropriate corrections to your account, or must provide you with a written clarification regarding any dispute. During this 60 business day period, your servicer may not provide information to a consumer reporting agency concerning any overdue payment related to such period or qualified written request. A business day is any day in which the offices of the business entity are open to the public for carrying substantially all of its business function.

Damages and Costs
Section 6 of RESPA also provides for damages and costs for individuals or classes of individuals in circumstances where servicers are shown to have violated the requirements of that Section.

Servicing Transfer Estimates
1. The following is the best estimate of what will happen to the servicing of your loan:
   A. ☐ We may assign, sell or transfer the servicing of your loan while the loan is outstanding.
      We are able to service mortgage loans and we
         ☐ will service your loan
         ☐ will not service your loan
   B. ☐ haven't decided whether to service your loan ☒ We do not service mortgage loans and we have not serviced mortgage loans in the past 3 years
      ☒ We presently intend to assign, sell or transfer the servicing of your mortgage loan
      ☒ You will be informed about your servicer

2. For all of the mortgage loans we make in the 12 month period after your mortgage loan is funded, we estimate that the percentage of such loans for which we will transfer servicing is between:
   ☐ 0 to 25%   ☐ 26 to 50%   ☐ 51 to 75%   ☒ 76 to 100%
   This estimate ☒ does ☐ does not include assignments, sales or transfers to affiliates or subsidiaries.

3. We have previously assigned, sold, or transferred the servicing of first lien mortgage loans.
   This is our record of transferring the servicing of first lien mortgage loans we have made in:

Year	Percentage of Loans Transferred
2004	100%
2005	100%
2006	100%

   This estimate ☒ does ☐ does not include assignments, sales or transfers to affiliates or subsidiaries.

Acknowledge of Mortgage Loan Applicant(s)
I/We have read and understood the disclosure; and understand the disclosure is a required part of the mortgage application as evidenced by my/our signatures below:

_____ _____ _____ _____
Applicant   Date   Applicant   Date-

_____ _____ _____ _____
Applicant   Date   Applicant   Date

Source: Credo Mortgage Inc.

prohibited bases, i.e., race, color, age, sex, etc.

ECOA sets the rules for gathering and using information in the loan application process. While it is not clear that present reverse mortgage programs, which were created specifically for people 62 and older more than a decade after enactment of ECOA, were anticipated in the rules, it is wise to act as if they do. After all, reverse mortgages are mortgages first. Also, it is good business to have clear written policies of non-discrimination based on the *prohibited basis.*

It is prudent to observe the following ECOA guidelines when taking reverse mortgage applications:

- Do not give an opinion on the likelihood of a borrower's approval on a loan request. Under ECOA, an opinion on the possibility of approval actually triggers an application whether or not an actual application has been taken;
- Encourage all borrowers to apply and provide them with loan program information;
- Notify borrowers that they have a right to receive a copy of their property's appraisal used in the lending process provided they have paid for it;
- Give applicant a written notice of denial if there is a loan turndown; and
- Find out from borrower if the reverse mortgage loan application is for "joint credit," i.e., between the borrower and a spouse or someone else.

As far as reverse mortgages are concerned, James Milano says, the more pertinent federal laws are TILA and the HUD/HECM regulations.

Compliance tips for reverse mortgage originators*
*Interview with James M. Milano, The Mortgage Press, *February and March 2005*

On ads
- Design an ad that is professional with an effective marketing message.
- Have a competent attorney review it.
- Once the ad is legally reviewed, it can be used repeatedly.
- If the ad changes, it should be reviewed again.
- Many states have advertising requirements that their licensees must follow.

On balloon
- Lenders should disclose that there will be a balloon payment at the end of a reverse mortgage transaction.

Part III: Originating reverse mortgages

On treatment of points and interests

- The tax treatment of points and interests can be complex. Reverse mortgage originators should advise their senior borrowers to consult with a reverse mortgage-savvy tax advisor.
- Originators should not advise seniors that they can deduct their interest payments because that may not happen until the reverse mortgage loan matures.
- Saying reverse mortgage proceed is tax-free is a fair and accurate statement, but always qualify your statement by asking seniors to consult their tax advisor.

On the cost of non-compliance

- Jumping the gun on HUD's reverse mortgage counseling could result in loans that are uninsurable and unsaleable.
- Forfeiture of the origination fee may result if the loan is improperly originated and the borrower backs out.
- Loss of lending license is a possibility if a state audits uncover serious violations of state laws.
- TILA violations could carry statutory penalties, plus actual damages that the plaintiff can prove plus attorney's fees.
- Repeated violations of HUD/HECM rules could result in being barred from originating HECMs.

And as NRMLA's General Counsel, James A. Brodsky, has said: "If you are not in the HECM business, you are not in the reverse mortgage business."

On avoiding compliance issues

- Subscribe to regulatory compliance services.
- Review available resources from state and federal regulators.
- Attend NRMLA meetings. It is the "marketplace of ideas" in the emerging reverse industry.
- Hire a qualified and reverse mortgage-experienced attorney.
- Visit state and federal regulatory Web sites (see resources below).

On state regulations

As state regulators become more knowledgeable about reverse mortgages and the reverse mortgage industry, originators can expect audits from state regulators. As a reverse mortgage or aspiring reverse mortgage lender or broker, you need to pay attention to reverse mortgage compliance issues some states' laws may bring about. Such issues may include the following:

Laws and regulations in Reverseland

- Reverse mortgage-specific licensing/approval requirements.
- Terms and conditions [of loan] requirements
- Lien ranking requirements
- Prohibition of certain practices (for example, California's Senate Bill 1609, effective Jan. 1, 2007, among other provisions, forbids "tying an annuity to a reverse mortgage or soliciting annuities to reverse mortgage borrowers during the rescission period after closing"[*Reverse Mortgage Advisor*, Vol. 9.3, Fall 2006, page 4, visit www.nrmlaonline.org for more on this potential wild regulatory fire.])

Some of these states' issues may or may not be relevant to HECMs because they are regulated by federal/HUD rules. As a general caution, check with a qualified attorney. In consulting with your lawyer, you should use the following questions as guide:
- Do I need approval to do reverse mortgages specifically?
- Are there any reverse mortgage-specific disclosures requirements that I need to know about?
- Are there any specific provisions that need to be in the loan documents for reverse mortgages originated in this state?

Some compliance do's and don'ts

Do's
- Be licensed to do mortgages in the state where you operate in unless you qualify for an exemption. Your regular traditional forward mortgage license should do in most of the states.
- Comply with your state's reverse mortgage-specific laws or requirements where they exist because a number of states have reverse-specific laws (i.e. California law cited above); a qualified attorney should be able to tell you if your state has specific reverse mortgage licensing or approval requirements.
- Use the proper disclosures. HECMs require early disclosures and documents. Some states have specific disclosure requirements for reverse mortgages. Again, ask a competent attorney for guidance.
- Be certain you have a separate independent agreement between your company and the senior customer if you are acting as a non-FHA-approved broker or advisor.

Don'ts
Obviously the don'ts are the flipside of the do's:
- Acting as an advisor or a broker without a written independent agreement between your company and the senior is a no-no.

Part III: Originating reverse mortgages

- Operating without being properly licensed either generally or under some state-specific reverse mortgage law is another no-no.
- Meeting with customers and taking applications without giving required disclosures and documentation is not smart.

Ethics in reverse mortgage marketing and origination

Submitted by Sarah Hulbert, president, Senior Financial Corporation. Ms. Hulbert has 16-plus years of experience in reverse mortgage marketing, origination and management. She also chairs NRMLA's Ethics Committee.

As the reverse mortgage industry continues its expansion, it is critical that all lenders pay special attention to the laws and regulations that govern our industry. We provide an important financial tool to senior homeowners, one that we want to make sure continues to become increasingly accessible to our customers.

In this busy world, some individuals may perceive our industry guidelines as an inconvenience to both themselves and the borrower. In some cases, this perception may be correct. However, there are valid reasons for these guidelines. There is a fine line when it comes to compliance, and it's a dilemma faced by all reverse mortgage lenders. How do you continue to provide superior customer service while abiding by the rules and regulations set forth by the governing agencies? The key to this is knowledge, because in-depth knowledge and understanding of program guidelines enable us to create systems that are compliant and customer-friendly.

Make sure the importance of compliance with rules and regulations is stressed to all employees in your company, especially those in the "trenches" working with the borrowers. They are likely to experience the most frustration with seemingly confusing program requirements. Sometimes, this frustration can lead to decisions that are made with the best intentions. They see a shortcut as justifiable because it streamlines the process for the borrower. In most cases, however, these shortcuts do not serve their purpose. Ultimately, by circumventing the system in under-disclosing or misrepresenting reverse mortgage programs, the result is non-compliance and additional burden on the lenders, investors, regulatory agencies and borrowers.

As reverse mortgage marketers and originators, we should strive to do the following on a daily basis:
- Educate ourselves, our employees and our customers
- Do things the right way from an ethical and a regulatory perspective
- Put the best interest of our customers first
- Take pride in the fact that we are providing a valuable service to senior homeowners

By following these simple guidelines, we will maintain the strong foundation we have built as an industry ... a foundation that will support significant growth in the years to come.

In Chapter 14, we discuss how to get into reverse mortgages.

Chapter 13 resources

- www.nrmlaonline.org/nrmla/ethics/conduct.aspx
- www.hud.gov/groups/lenders.cfm
- For access to compliance information nationally: www.thomas-law.com
- TALC Regulations: www.frwebgate.access.gpo.gov/cgi-bin/get-cfr.cgi

Part III: Originating reverse mortgages

Chapter Fourteen
The road to Reverseland

Chapter 14 objectives
After studying this chapter, the reader will be able to:
- Know how to get into reverse mortgage origination
- Explain the levels of participation in reverse mortgage origination
- Know the requirements for approval as correspondent and wholesaler
- Know how to get into reverse mortgages without FHA approval
- Know where to place loans or find a lender
- Know where to find program rules and guidelines
- Know where to find reverse mortgage leads
- Know where to find information about reverse mortgages

Getting into reverse mortgage origination
A frequent question from readers of my regular column on reverse mortgages in *The Mortgage Press* is, "How do I get into reverse mortgages?"

There are three ways to get into reverse mortgages. You can get into reverse mortgages as:

- A correspondent broker/lender
- Retailer
- Wholesaler

A correspondent broker/lender
Any FHA-approved mortgage broker or lender can become a correspondent broker/lender. A correspondent lender is a step up the FHA-HECM food chain from the advisor. For more information on how to become an FHA lender, please visit www.hud.gov/groups/lenders.cfm.

A correspondent-sponsoring wholesaler may have an FHA application package

Part III: Originating reverse mortgages

ready for you. The wholesaler may provide guidance to help you get FHA approval. You can go directly to the FHA. In addition to FHA correspondent approval, the wholesale lender must approve as a correspondent before you can begin originating reverse mortgages for wholesaler. Here are some of the major lenders*:

- Wells Fargo Bank NA (https://www.wellsfargo.com/mortgage/reversebrokerin/program/index)
- Financial Freedom Senior Funding Corporation (www.financialfreedom.com)
- Bank of America (http://reversemortgage.bankofamerica.com)
- World Alliance Financial (www.worldalliancefinancial.com)
- Liberty Reverse Mortgage (www.libertyreversebroker.com)
- Omni Home Financing (www.omnihomefinancing.com)
- First Mariner Bank (www.1stmarinerbank.com)
- MetLife Bank (www.metlifebank.com/reversemortgage.do)
- Urban Financial Group (www.urbanfinancialgroup.com)
- Academy Mortgage Corporation (www.academymortgage.com/index.php)
- Generation Mortgage Company (www.generationmortgage.com/wholesale/default.aspx)
- American Reverse Mortgage (www.americanreverse.com)
- M&T Bank (www.mandtreversemortgage.com)
- Pacific Reverse Mortgage (www.pacificreversemortgage.com)
- AAA Reverse Mortgage (www.1staam.com)
- Equipoint FinancialNetwork (www.mortgagefit.com/equipointfinancialnetwork)
- Stay In Home Mortgage (www.stayinhome.com)
- James B. Nutter and Company (www.jamesbnutter.com)
- Griffin Financial Mortgage (www.griffinloans.com)
- Live Well Financial (www.livewellfinancial.com)

*This list is not exhaustive. These are top-20 volume leaders as of May 2008, according to HUD data.

Some sponsoring wholesalers classify their correspondents depending upon the level of contracted service received from the sponsor. For example, some correspondents originate the loan and turn over processing, underwriting, closing, funding and servicing to the wholesaler. This may be the prudent path for a correspondent without experienced reverse mortgage processors.

Some correspondents originate, process and turn over underwriting, funding and servicing to the sponsor. This may be the ideal way for correspondents with skilled processors. Others originate, process, underwrite, fund and sell the closed loans to the wholesaler, including servicing rights. This may be the better route for correspondents with skilled staff and the capital to fund loans.

Steps to a reverse mortgage correspondent
See Appendix 3(b) for Requirements for Correspondent Approval
- Identify a sponsor/wholesaler, visit www.nrmlaonline.org
- Find out the reverse mortgage programs they offer
- Find out about the sponsor by interviewing the current correspondents they are working with
- At the www.reversemortgage.org Web site:
    - Click "Find NRMLA member reverse mortgage lender in your state"
    - Use the drop-down list to identify your state or any state
    - Click "Go" and pick any lender
    - Call the listed representative
    - Find out if they are a correspondent representative
    - Make sure they are not a retail rep of a sponsor/wholesaler
    - Ask for their boss's phone number
    - Talk with their boss about their correspondent experience
    - Find out what their values are? Are they square with yours?

Sponsor-wholesaler:

- Make a decision on choice of sponsor
- Ask for their correspondent package
- Fill out the application and return it with the required supporting documentation and a fee where applicable
- If approved, schedule training with sponsor's trainer for your staff
- After initial training, you may begin originating reverse mortgages

Who are the correspondent-sponsoring reverse mortgage wholesalers in America?
Please see list of top-20 lenders on page 206. The list is not exhaustive and not all lenders may have correspondent-sponsoring programs.

Where to find a lender/place loans
The wholesalers listed above are your available sources for funding loans. Go to their Web sites and call their wholesale representatives.

Part III: Originating reverse mortgages

What does a reverse mortgage correspondent get paid?
- Full origination fee less any fees to wholesaler for contracted services to correspondent
- A small service released premium based on the age of the borrower
- A percentage of borrower's initial draw (This is a new income scream; it probably reflects premium pricing wholesalers get for HECMs in the secondary market.)

(See Figure 14.1 on page 209)

Initial training and support
Wholesalers provide their correspondents initial training and support to get them started in reverse mortgage origination. Training usually covers the following areas:

- Reverse mortgages
- Reverse mortgage origination software
- Reverse mortgage origination
- Reverse mortgage processing
- Reverse mortgage marketing
- Compliance

They also have specialized staff dedicated to correspondent support that the correspondent's staff can call on to answer questions and provide guidance during business hours.

Ongoing training and support
In addition to initial training for their correspondent's reverse mortgage staff, wholesalers provide ongoing training and support to their correspondents through:
- On-site or online presentations
- Scheduled annual or semi-annual sales/marketing events
- Weekly updates on reverse interest rates
- Periodic updates on their policies or relevant FHA or Fannie Mae policies

A reverse mortgage wholesaler
Any Fannie Mae-approved seller/servicer can become a wholesaler. A seller/servicer originates, processes, underwrites, funds and sells reverse mortgage loans to Fannie Mae.

> *The road to Reverseland*

Figure 14.1
Correspondent Fee/Sample Calculations

Youngest borrower age 83 with a $35 servicing fee = $420 Correspondent Fee

Youngest borrower age 75 with a $35 servicing fee = $525 Correspondent Fee

Youngest borrower age 75 with a $30 servicing fee = $450 Correspondent Fee

Youngest borrower age 62 with a $30 servicing fee = $450 Correspondent Fee

Source: Financial Freedom Senior Funding Corporation

Fannie Mae is a secondary market investor. It is one of the largest investors for the industry's flagship program, FHA's HECM and its own product, the HomeKeeper. The seller/servicers may sell the servicing rights or service the loan themselves. To become a Fannie Mae seller/servicer, your company must meet these requirements*:

- Have a net worth of at least $250,000
- Show ability to originate reverse mortgages to FHA and Fannie Mae standards
- Demonstrate capabilities to service reverse mortgages
- Have reverse-mortgage-experienced and trained staff in place
- Have reverse mortgage systems and processes in place
- Be FHA-approved to originate HECMs

This list is illustrative. Fannie Mae may change requirements at any time. For information on how to become a Fannie Mae seller/servicer, go to www.efanniemae.com.

Although Fannie Mae now has competition as a HECM investor, having the status of a Fannie Mae-approved seller/servicer is very valuable. If there is one lesson we can take from the credit crunch of 2007/2008, it is that when the credit chips are down, we can count on Fannie Mae (thanks to its connection to Uncle Sam) for liquidity.

HUD/FHA has its own requirements that lenders or mortgagees must also meet before they can originate HECMs. These requirements are in HUD Handbook 4060.1 Rev-2.

The requirements for lender or mortgagee approval are extensive, and it may be prudent to hire an experienced attorney specializing in the HUD/FHA lender-approval process. However, to get an idea, visit www.hud.gov/groups/lenders.cfm.

Part III: Originating reverse mortgages

HUD Handbooks should be read in conjunction with HUD Mortgagee Letters. Mortgagee Letters are used to announce HUD policy changes. They often modify contents of Handbooks. To obtain updated HUD rules, it is necessary to search for Mortgagee Letters relating to the subject of a HUD Handbook and read them together.

What do wholesalers do?

Reverse mortgage sponsor/wholesalers do the following*:

- Sponsor, train and support their correspondent and retail channels of production
- Provide their correspondents reverse mortgage origination software
- Provide origination forms/documentation to correspondent and retail channels
- Originate loans via their correspondent and retail channels of production
- Process and underwrite loans
- Fund and insure loans
- Sell and service loans
- Provide technology support for their correspondent and retail channels

This list is illustrative.
Source: Reverse Mortgage of America

How do wholesalers get paid?

Their income is derived from:

- Origination fees from their retail channels
- Servicing fees
- Interest income
- Premium pricing (gain on sale)
- Underwriting fees charged to broker
- Miscellaneous fees charged to borrower (courier fees and others)

How to get into reverse mortgages without FHA approval

A common and frequent question I receive from readers of my regular column around the country is, "Can I do reverse mortgages without FHA approval?" The answer is yes and no. Let's look at the "yes" part first.

As we saw with advisor programs of the major reverse mortgage lenders, you can "participate" in the front-end advisory part of the FHA reverse mortgage program (HECM) and be paid without FHA approval. But, you do not originate HECM loan and your compensation is pegged

The road to Reverseland

at 25 percent of the origination fee. The 25 percent advisory fee is industry standard. It has the tacit approval of industry's guardians, HUD and Fannie Mae.

In addition to the advisor program, the other way you can get into reverse country without FHA's approval is through some jumbo product. Each lender has its own requirements for approving advisors for its program. To originate Seattle Mortgage's The Independence Plan, your company must be an approved correspondent of Seattle Mortgage and it must be able to offer the product in your state. And to be a Seattle Mortgage correspondent, you must be FHA-approved; so, you must be an FHA-approved lender to offer The Independence Plan. While processing of The Independence Plan is non-FHA, the "process is nearly identical to the HECM loan." Use the resources below to find out more.

Where to find reverse mortgage leads

Just about any person you come across is a potential source of reverse mortgage leads, and you should let them know that you are a reverse mortgage originator. Beginning reverse mortgage originators can generate leads from the following sources*:

- Banks and bankers (small community banks)
- Accountants
- Certified Public Accountants (CPAs)
- Elder law attorneys
- Financial planners
- Insurance agents
- Real estate agents
- Mortgage brokers
- Mortgage bankers
- Doctors
- Doctors' offices waiting rooms
- Geriatric social workers
- Geriatric care managers
- Nurses
- Home healthcare providers
- Undertakers
- Rabbis
- Pastors

This list is illustrative. Think up others.

Part III: Originating reverse mortgages

Where to find program guidelines

For originators, the guidelines for the FHA reverse mortgage (HECM) are located in HUD Handbook 4235.1 Rev. 1 and in HECM-specific Mortgagee Letters that FHA issues from time to time. To find the HUD Handbook, go to www.hud.gov/offices/adm/handbks_forms/index.cfm.

Again, the Handbook must be read in conjunction with HECM-specific Mortgagee Letters.

In Chapter 15, we will learn from some reverse mortgage borrowers' profiles.

Resources

- www.aarp.org
- www.hecmresources.org
- The HUD HECM homepage:
  www.hud.gov/offices/hsg/sfh/hecm/hecmhome and
  www.hud.gov/groups/lenders.cfm
- www.fanniemae.com/homebuyers/findamortgage/reverse
- www.hud.gov/offices/adm/hudclips/letters/mortgagee/index.cfm
- www.hud.gov/offices/adm/handbks_forms/index.cfm

The road to Reverseland

Part IV: Enhancing freedom: The essence of reverse mortgages

Part IV
Enhancing freedom: The essence of reverse mortgages

Beyond our wildest imagination:
Profiles in satisfaction: Chapter 15

Part IV: Enhancing freedom: The essence of reverse mortgages

Chapter Fifteen
Beyond our wildest imagination: Profiles in satisfaction

Opening quote ...
"I think we're rich. We don't have any money, but our lives are rich. That's what the reverse mortgage has done for us. It has literally taken the shackles off our hands and allowed us to do things that we wouldn't otherwise have been able to do. Do we have a lot of money? No. But do we have richness in our lives and happiness? Beyond our wildest imagination! And most of that is due to the reverse mortgage."
—**Paul K. Alexander, Hampstead, N.H.**

Chapter 15 objectives
After studying this chapter, the reader will be able to:
- Appreciate the range of life-enhancing experiences extra cash from reverse mortgages can make possible for older adults
- "Catch" the reverse mortgage "bug"

One of the most rewarding aspects of marketing, originating, studying and writing about reverse mortgages is listening to the stories of reverse mortgage consumers. The extra cash from reverse mortgages often brings major changes into their lives. Their stories are always fascinating, instructive, and redeeming. Read the opening reflection by Paul Alexander again.

As veteran reverse mortgage lender, Paul Franklin of Franklin Funding in Charleston, S.C., has said, "you have to believe in the good reverse mortgages can do" if you are going to market and originate them successfully. By the time you finish reading the stories that form the core of this chapter, you will become a believer. You will catch the reverse bug, and perhaps even "infect"

Part IV: Enhancing freedom: The essence of reverse mortgages

others with it. As we spread the reverse bug in our various circles of influence, we will bring an awareness that will help our elders throw off the "shackles" of financial worry in the liberating years of their lives.

In addition, we will catch a glimpse of the promise of these revolutionary mortgage finance tools for retirees for all-time.

Florence Patricia "Pat" Schrantz: "I'm financially covered ..."

Patricia Schrantz

Florence Patricia "Pat" Schrantz was born in St. Paul, Minn. She grew up, went to school, and completed two years of college in Minnesota's capital city.

A mother of three children and grandmother of six, Pat retired from Wells Fargo as a personal banker in 2001. In 2002, George, her husband of 42 years, died.

With George gone, Pat had to confront a hard question: Could she afford to live, in the manner she was used to, in her suburban St. Paul home? She knew she wanted to live in her home, but the expense of maintaining her home, relative to her income, worried her. She consulted an experienced and knowledgeable financial advisor. My "financial advisor" had said earlier on after my husband died that there was no way I could financially stay here because we didn't have much accumulated wealth such as stock market funds or other outside savings.

"So, that was basically it for me. This person didn't feel that I could stay here on my monthly income. Yet, that's what I wanted to do and this is where I wanted to be," Pat said.

Pat's desire to continue living in the home she shared with her late husband was what led her to explore the reverse mortgage option.

"When I made the decision that I truly want to stay here, somehow or another, reverse mortgage came up.

"I first remember discussing it with my niece out in Seattle. Shortly after I got home from that trip, my daughter, who lives in Virginia Beach, Va., sent me an article that she had read about reverse mortgages.

"My children were actually the ones who encouraged me to check into the situation. They were very supportive. They are not interested in the inheritance side at all. They do well, all three families. They don't want me to feel like there is any burden at all incumbent on myself toward their retirement," said Pat.

Beyond our wildest imagination: Profiles in satisfaction

Accompanied by her son-in-law, Pat went to required HECM counseling. The counseling session with a HUD-approved reverse mortgage counselor was instructive and reassuring.

"I was encouraged at what I learned. I was pleased with the interview I had with the HUD representative and her input. She clarified any questions I had regarding reverse mortgages: "That it wasn't a mortgage where I was going to be giving up the deed to my home, that the bank wasn't going to own my home. I was pleased to know that there was a cap as far as the limit, so that you couldn't use all of the equity in your home and then get yourself into some kind of a huge financial burden.

"My bottom line is that I'm trying to protect the assets I have here in my home to such a degree that it could possibly benefit my grandchildren sometime in the future as far as helping them with college.

"The point is that I wanted to shelter what I do have to a degree, and I felt like when I understood and learned more about reverse mortgages, that it gave me all those benefits," Pat said.

Following the required reverse mortgage counseling, Pat called me to begin the loan application process. I took her application in November 2004, and we closed her reverse mortgage in her living room just a few months later in January 2005.

I asked Pat how she felt after going through the reverse mortgage loan process and getting the loan.

"I am feeling great about the whole thing. I know I can stay here. And if something happens like if I need to buy a different car, if I need to replace the furnace, any of those unforeseen things, I can afford them," she said.

Retirement in 2001, the death of her husband in 2002, and the expert pronouncement of a trusted financial advisor that she could not live in her home, financially speaking, brought Pat Schrantz much stress. The extra cash from the reverse mortgage has made a difference in Pat's life.

"Well, I think my only way of explaining it is that it's taken away any of the concern, worry or stress of staying here. If I want to buy a couple of cans of paint to paint my bathroom, if I want to hire somebody to do it, I feel like I can do that now without such a worry about having to put so much money away every month out of my monthly income toward the possibility of some disastrous thing, such as furnace going out or having to replace an air conditioner.

"What the reverse mortgage has provided me was the huge benefit of knowing that any event or some unseen happening that I have to use money to replace something in my home, the funds are going to be there.

"I don't have to worry about how I'm going to come up with the funds. In

Part IV: Enhancing freedom: The essence of reverse mortgages

the meantime, my monthly income, rather than half of it being set aside to be saved for that purpose, can be used to take my grandchildren to a movie or to the zoo, or take them shopping ... that sort of a thing.

"That's the way I want to live. I'm financially covered, because I have prudently used some of the equity in my home and set that aside for those possible unfortunate situations. If those possible unfortunate situations don't arise in the 10 or 15 years that I hope to be here, at least then, that equity is still all there. But, it's given me peace of mind to know that I don't have to worry."

Durfee Bedsole and Odile Besseau: "Now our dreams can become a reality"

Odile Bessea and Durfee Bedsole

Durfee Bedsole was born in Atlanta, Ga. She grew up in California, earned a degree in journalism from the University of California at Berkley in 1955, and worked for CBS Television as a publicist in the 1960s. Along the way, she sold real estate, married and raised two children.

Now an American citizen, Odile Besseau was born in Brittany, France. A governess in her native country, she acquired excellent French culinary skills before moving to her dream country in 1972. Upon her arrival in the United States, she put her French culinary expertise to work in Los Angeles.

Odile's French kitchen skills and Durfee's business acumen brought both women together in California several years ago. They later moved to Texas to start a "country French restaurant," as Durfee describes it. Their restaurant was very successful. They sold it a few years ago, paid cash for a log home and retired. In 2003, Durfee and Odile decided to take out a reverse mortgage on their log home. Durfee's exhilarating account of the impact of the extra cash from the reverse mortgage on their lives in retirement follows:

By way of introduction, I am 70 years of age in 2004, and share a log home with my business partner/chef, Odile, who is 64. We both divorced our husbands many years ago. We came to east Texas 13 years ago and opened a country French restaurant. We enjoyed tremendous success, but decided to retire seven years ago. Our combined income is approximately $1,700 per month from Social Security.

After paying homeowners insurance, car insurance, life insurance, Medicare supplements, utilities, gasoline, car maintenance, lake community dues and normal expenses to survive, like food and clothes, there was never anything left over to play with. We had no savings account for emergencies, no travel money, no luxuries.

A few years ago, I was sitting on my back porch, admiring the view of the neighbor's pastureland with gorgeous quarter horses roaming at dusk. The sunset was spectacular. I was absolutely in awe. What a lucky person I am. I started to count my blessings—my house and car are paid for, I'm debt free, I have my health, two grown children on the West Coast and two beautiful grandchildren, and close friends who are there for me. But I started wondering, is this all there is?

Suddenly, it hit me while I sat here enjoying the sunset and gloating over my health and good fortune: My retired friends are traveling all over the world, going on cruises, getting manicures, pedicures, going to the big city for concerts, plays, ballgames, buying fancy clothes and jewelry, and eating out in fancy restaurants. And here I sit, living their lives vicariously. Maybe they handled their money more wisely than I did; maybe they have tremendous pensions; maybe they have annuities, stocks, bonds, you name it. Big deal! We have none of that. But we do have a house that is paid for! I wasn't born yesterday. Isn't that called equity? And I am sitting on it while others are sitting on deck chairs in the Bahamas! Why not have my cake and eat it too?

Just about that time, I read about reverse mortgages in the local paper. "I want that," I cried. But how do I get that? Most people, including bankers here, either never heard of them or didn't want to hear about them. For a year I talked to bankers or anyone who would listen, to find out about these reverse mortgages. Finally, my banker referred me to a Web site to read a column written by someone at the *Dallas Morning News*. He said to try W.R. Mortgage and gave me the e-mail address of Clive Hambrook, their Starkey reverse mortgage manager. Bingo!

Well, it worked! Not without some diligence on all our parts, getting an appraisal, a survey, termite inspection, credit report, title report and filling out lots of paperwork. Was it worth it? You bet!

Now I know what you are thinking, what about the children and grandchildren? What about their inheritance? First of all, we still have plenty of

Part IV: Enhancing freedom: The essence of reverse mortgages

equity left, even after the mortgage. Both of my kids are thrilled that, at last, I have some money to "play" with, and now I can visit them. I can send them presents and money for special things if they need it. They are completely supportive and have always been. Don't they want me to enjoy the fruits of my labors? Their inheritance is me ... now ... not after I'm gone.

So, what was the first thing we did with the money? I bought a computer, started putting collectibles on eBay and have had so much fun doing it. Then, we immediately signed up for a Mahjong Cruise on the biggest cruise ship out of Miami, Navigator of the Seas (Royal Caribbean). The ship is 15 stories high, two football fields long, and has an ice rink. Then, we went to California on a whim to attend a birthday party for an 80-year-old ... five days of fun and visiting, including a reunion with my old cronies from CBS. Then, I received a note from my niece in California that her daughter was marrying in October, and I had to come! So, back to California I went, twice in one year. Without the reverse mortgage, I would have missed two very important events.

As if this wasn't enough travel for one year, Odile was anxious to visit her sisters in France. Can we afford it, she asked? Silly question! She went ahead of me for four weeks, and I joined her for two weeks after my great niece's wedding. I said I would go on the condition that we spend one of the two weeks in Paris. Voila! Done! She had been a nanny for a family of five children in the 1960s, and she arranged with one of the grown girls for us to stay with her and her family in their three-bedroom Paris apartment. This is about as good as it gets in Paris!

She also enlisted her sister who works for Air France to drive us around town for a day. Like Mr. Toad's Wild Ride! Up to Montmartre, then speeding along the Champs Elysees to the Arch de Triomphe, and down to the Louvre for lunch under the pyramid. One day, we went to the famous Pere Lachaise Cemetery, and I actually touched the graves of so many famous people—Edith Piaf, Moliere, Sarah Bernhardt, Chopin, Balzac, Oscar Wilde, Colette, Gertrude Stein, Victor Hugo, etc. The climax of the trip was Odile's sister's 60th birthday party in Brittany, which lasted from 1:00 p.m. to 1:00 a.m. The French really know how to party! Flying home on Air France, we were able to reflect on our good fortune while sipping an after-dinner liquor: Coffee, tea or Grand Marnier? Not a difficult question for world travelers to answer!

As I write this, I am thinking of visiting my children in California and Oregon together with attending my 50th college reunion. My high school class of 1951 is planning a cruise next year. Mark the calendar.

And, oh yes, I've had a few manicures, a pedicure and went to my first Cal (UC Berkeley) football game since I graduated in 1955! We took some good friends out to dinner at a fancy restaurant last year and can now treat ourselves to an occasional lunch, Starbucks coffee or a new book. I went to my first book signing and actually bought the book with author's autograph. We still have two CDs that mature in the next few years and a special savings account just for emergencies. We have tickets to community concerts, and we are able to make a small contribution to the local art museum each year.

I almost forgot … we just bought the lot next to us to protect our peace and tranquility.

None of the above would have been possible without our reverse mortgage. Now, our dreams can become a reality. I still sit out back and watch the horses at sunset, listen to the birds, crickets and cicadas, watch the herons as they swoop down on the pond. Is this all there is? Yes, and a whole lot more.

(Atare's Note: Durfee and Odile now live in Oregon, and are still raving about the reverse mortgage's impact on their lives).

Paul and Irene Alexander: "A godsend to us"

Irene and Paul Alexander

Paul Alexander was born in Kane, Pa. in 1934, a little town of less than 4,000 nestled in the Allegheny Forest. As he describes it, Kane is "pretty remote, pretty quiet and pretty wild, a beautiful place with a lot of deer and bear."

While working and raising a family with his wife, Irene, he earned a college degree at night. He retired as a senior human resource manager seven years ago.

Irene Alexander was born in Lynn, Mass. Like her husband, she finished her education at night, while raising a family. She retired as a receptionist for a law firm more than three years ago.

Similar to Durfee, I first "met" Paul and Irene on the pages of *Reverse Mortgage Advisor* [Summer 2004], a publication (now called *Reverse Mortgage*, a magazine) of the National Reverse Mortgage Lenders Association (NRMLA). I obtained their contact information from NRMLA and called them.

Part IV: Enhancing freedom: The essence of reverse mortgages

On the family events that led them to decide on reversing their forward mortgage:

"Well, my wife retired. She had been working for a couple of years two days a week. Before that, she worked full-time most of her adult life. And I was lonely at home without her. When she came home without a job, I was delighted. I didn't want her to work anymore," said Paul.

"Paul was also afraid that if anything should happen to him (Paul had a stroke in 2002), I wouldn't be able to stay here in our lovely condo. And by doing a reverse mortgage, we felt I would be able to stay here," Irene said.

"When I did the numbers before we got this reverse mortgage, I had a terrible fear that she would have to sell this place and move out. In which case, she will be paying $800 to $1,000 for rent per month or maybe even more, and she wouldn't be in her home. She'll be in some small, dingy apartment, rather than in the beautiful sunlit and surrounded-by-woods townhouse that we're in now."

Paul and Irene have three grown children. What was their reaction to their parents' decision to do a reverse mortgage?

"They really didn't have a reaction," said Irene.

"They understand what we did and why we did it. None of them are looking to us to leave them any money. They don't expect anything. They are very successful in their own lives," Paul added.

What benefits or experiences have they derived from their decision to go the reverse mortgage route? How has it impacted the quality of their lives in retirement?

"The most important thing is the $10,000 it puts in our pocket annually, because we don't have to pay our mortgage, and it allowed us to go to Florida, last year (winter 2003-2004) for three months, this year (winter 2004-2005) for four months, and next year, for how many months, we don't know. But that is the major difference.

"We would have not been able to afford that. We would have been stuck up here in this cold northern climate, which is not as cold as Minneapolis, but certainly cold. And it was bitter last winter, as a matter of fact, while we were gone. So, that's the benefit. It really makes a difference in our lives. We love going to Florida, it's like a long vacation for us.

"We're both so excited and anxious to go, that it's hard to believe," Paul said.

Irene sees the benefits and experiences a little differently from her husband.

"It's a feeling of security, as far as after the scare with Paul two years ago when he had his stroke. If anything happened to him, I would be able to stay

Beyond our wildest imagination: Profiles in satisfaction

here in our townhouse with no mortgage to pay.

"And secondly, just being able to go south in the wintertime was so good for both of us. We just absolutely loved it! The nice, warm sunshine and going to a beautiful beach, it's just great," she said.

I mentioned that it is interesting how they responded to the same question.

"She was interested in the security aspect of this (reverse mortgage). Most likely, she'll outlive me by a number of years.

"I mean, it makes me feel good knowing that she is secure in this place. She only has to worry about her taxes. We got a reduction in our taxes of several hundred dollars this year (2004). It means more money in our pocket.

"I don't have to write a check every month. That's a big deal. I don't have to write a check for my principal and interest. I can spend that money I would have been sending to the bank. It's just glorious! It's just wonderful … absolutely wonderful," Paul said.

Beginning in the 1950s, Paul and Irene Alexander have been volunteering for worthy social causes all their lives. As he describes it, they were "peaceniks" and "pretty left-wing in those days." In the 60s and 70s, they were civil rights workers, deeply involved in civil rights movement. In business, Paul was an affirmative action program manager for a very large company and ran seminars on the issue. He has been a founding member of a community action program. He has served as a district chairman of the Boy Scouts of America, and has served as an officer and vice chairman of his credit union.

In retirement with the extra cash and monthly mortgage-payment freedom that a reverse mortgage brings, Paul and Irene now have the freedom to recover the volunteerism of their young and adult lives.

"From a contribution basis, that's what we're talking about. We are able to concentrate on contributing to other people's quality of life, as well as our own. Our primary concern is not ourselves, but it's also outward, of the outreach that we're able to have. The fact that we can work 12 hours each week to help people who need it is important to us psychologically.

"Now, we are not earning any money doing that. We just get satisfaction from it. It is very nice to be able to do that.

"If we had to work to pay our mortgage, that's a different story. We wouldn't be able to make those contributions," Paul said.

I commented that, for them, a reverse mortgage has been a liberating financial tool in retirement, freeing them to do the things they really want to do, not the things they have to do.

"Absolutely right! Absolutely right! So, that's what we're talking about when

Part IV: Enhancing freedom: The essence of reverse mortgages

we say it is not just that we're saving money and able to go to Florida and she (Irene) is secure. It has also given us freedom. So, it has expanded our horizons to be able to make contributions," said Paul.

Paul and Irene Alexander are thinking about doing volunteer work during their long Florida vacations.

"Our reverse mortgage was a godsend to us, and it has changed our lives," Paul said.

Beyond our wildest imagination: Profiles in satisfaction

Part V: A new frontier in mortgage lending

Part V
A new frontier in mortgage lending

The new mortgage cheese: *Chapter 16*

Part V: A new frontier in mortgage lending

Chapter sixteen
The new mortgage cheese

Opening quote ...
"Change happens. They keep moving the cheese."
—**Spencer Johnson, M.D.**

Chapter 16 objectives
After studying this chapter, the reader will be able to:
- Know that reverse mortgages represent change for residential mortgage lending
- Gain a better understanding of the reverse mortgage/long-term care connection
- Know what to do to prepare for the new mortgage lending opportunity

Aging demo equals mortgage opportunity
In Spencer Johnson's 1998 book *Who Moved My Cheese?*, he uses cheese as a metaphor for the things we want in life. We can safely assume that mortgage originators want to produce more mortgage loans to generate the income they need to sustain their families and their businesses. More originations equal more cheese for mortgage professionals and vice-versa. Reverse mortgages, combined with America's aging population, represent a major change for residential mortgage lending: They give mortgage originators more residential mortgage loans to originate in the later half of a mortgage consumer's life circle. The home equity-rich but cash-poor aging homeowner can now eat her cake and have it: Own and live in her home, get cash from the "bank" and make no payments for life. It is what social scientists would call a paradigm shift or new worldview in mortgage lending.

For traditional forward mortgage lending, the growing aging demographic and related shrinkage in the younger home-buying population mean low

Part V: A new frontier in mortgage lending

growth for years. Marketing expert David B. Wolfe, co-author of the seminal book, *Ageless Marketing,* says, "The traditionally all-important 25- to 44-year-old age group, which in the past contributed more to the gross domestic product {GDP} than any other 20-year age group, is shrinking. It will be smaller by 4.3 million people in 2010 than it was in 2001."

Within the dwindling 25- to 44-year-old cohort is the 35- to 44-age bracket. This 10-year age group (35- to 44-year olds) traditionally drives housing and housing-related spending in the U.S. economy. Forward mortgage origination is linked to the fortunes of the housing industry. In the 1990s, the 18- to 34-year old age group decreased by more than eight million people.

By contrast, growing aging population equals high growth for the reverse mortgage side. Wolfe Resource Group estimates that the 45- to 64-year old age group will jump by 16 million members by 2010. Besides the larger numbers of older people, older Americans also own their homes in larger numbers. Harvard University's Joint Center for Housing Studies says 82 percent of seniors between the ages of 65 and 74 owned their homes in 2003, up from 80 percent in 1993. In this 10-year period, the homeownership rate grew from 74 percent to 78 percent among our elders, age 75 and older.

A study by the National Council on Aging (NCOA), "Using Your Home to Stay at Home," finds that seniors age 62 and older own $953 billion in home equity, ready for origination through reverse mortgages. This is just a slice of the new mortgage cheese for residential mortgage professionals.

In June 2007, NRMLA and the Hollister Group LLC, a consulting and financial analytics firm, published the Reverse Mortgage Market Index (RMMI). It put the potential reverse mortgage market at $4.3 trillion. Hollister Group statisticians observed that even with zero home price appreciation between 2007 and 2030, senior home equity will grow to $9 trillion!

At 2.3 percent home value increase, senior home equity will be $19 trillion. And at the usual 4.7 percent home price appreciation, available home equity could top $37 trillion by 2030, less than 22 years away.

The RMMI numbers, growing origination volumes since 2002 *(See Figure 16.1),* and less-than-one-percent market penetration suggests boundless business opportunities in reverse mortgage lending.*

As of May 2008, the value of outstanding HECMs stood at about $39 billion. Add, say $4 billion for proprietary jumbo reverse, we have about $43 billion. Out of $4.3 trillion (let's say, $3.9 trillion because of recent dive in property values)! That is still a tiny market penetration!!

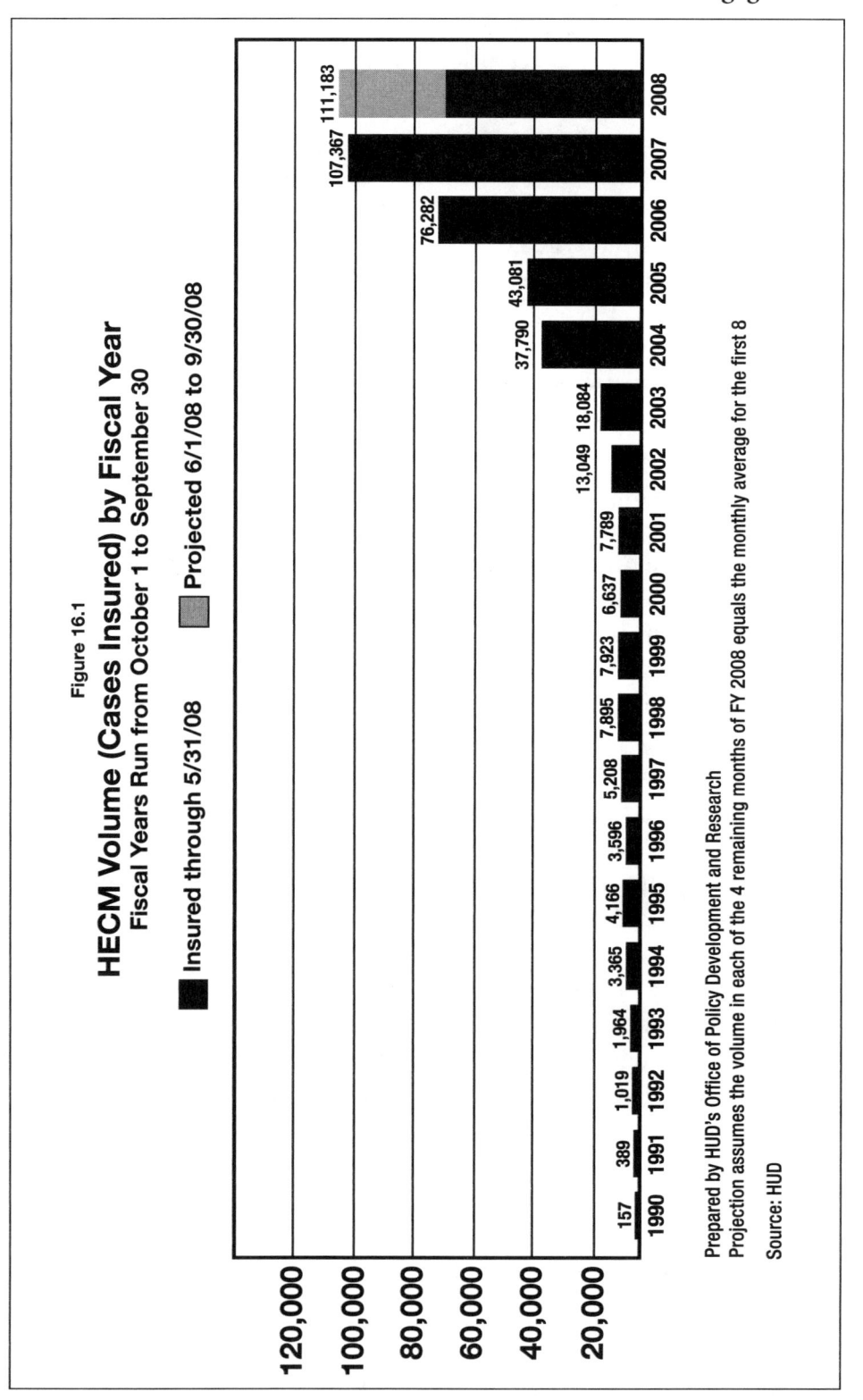

The new mortgage cheese

Figure 16.1
HECM Volume (Cases Insured) by Fiscal Year
Fiscal Years Run from October 1 to September 30

■ Insured through 5/31/08   ▨ Projected 6/1/08 to 9/30/08

Fiscal Year	Volume
1990	157
1991	389
1992	1,019
1993	1,964
1994	3,365
1995	4,166
1996	3,596
1997	5,208
1998	7,895
1999	7,923
2000	6,637
2001	7,789
2002	13,049
2003	18,084
2004	37,790
2005	43,081
2006	76,282
2007	107,367
2008	111,183

Prepared by HUD's Office of Policy Development and Research
Projection assumes the volume in each of the 4 remaining months of FY 2008 equals the monthly average for the first 8

Source: HUD

233

Part V: A new frontier in mortgage lending

Reverse mortgages and the healthcare economy

The engine that will drive the U.S. economy in the 21st century is healthcare, not the automobile. Again, you don't have to be a rocket scientist to figure it out. We have a huge aging population. As people grow older, they tend to consume more healthcare products and services. To finance these products and services, they will need extra cash, especially older folks on a fixed retirement income. Healthcare experts agree that the most expensive healthcare service will be long-term care. Now, just what is long-term care and what does it have to do with reverse mortgages?

Long-term care, or LTC, consists of non-medical services and support a person needs to cope with ongoing challenges arising as a result of a stroke, fall, heart disease, Alzheimer's, arthritis, osteoporosis, and other chronic conditions. These services can be provided at home, in a nursing home or in an assisted-living facility.

Long-term care expert Barbara Franklin says there is a 50 percent chance that everyone will need some long-term care during their lifetime. Needless to say, that probability increases with age. Where does reverse mortgage come into the long-term care picture?

Reverse mortgages and LTC meet at the cash register. LTC can be expensive. According to the 2007 MetLife Market Survey, the average daily cost of a nursing home stay nationally is $213 or $77,745 a year. Since an average nursing home stay is about 2.5 years; that is $194,363. Assisted living averages $2,969 a month or $35,628 a year nationally. Home care is just as costly. Home care attendants in the Twin Cities metro area range from $10-$12 per hour. For a person who needs 24-hour, round-the-clock care at home, that is $288 per day or $105,000 annually. Barbara Franklin says the average rate in the Charleston, S.C. area is about $15-$17 per hour. For 24-hour care, that is $360 a day or $131,400 a year. That does not include the cost of maintaining the home. So, whether it is nursing home, assisted-living, or home care, the price tag can be huge; and it could be (and has been) financially devastating for families who have not planned for it through saving, investment or insurance. Unquestionably, LTC expenses are the biggest financial risk facing every older homeowner.

The government wants out

In the U.S. today, most of the cost of LTC is borne by Uncle Sam and the state governments through Medicaid. Originally created in 1965 to meet the medical needs of the poor, Medicaid, by default, has become the financier of last resort for almost everyone who failed to plan for LTC. Matt Salo, director of

The new mortgage cheese

the National Governors Association's Health and Human Services Committee, says about Medicaid costs:

"... Medicaid, just this past year [2004], became for the first time, the single largest expenditure in state budgets. It exceeded K through 12 [education] and is now the largest part of state budgets."

By some account, states spend an average of 38 percent of their Medicaid dollars on "long-term care and more than half of that on nursing homes, which costs approximately $57,000 per patient annually."

As former chairman of the National Governors Association, former Virginia Gov. Mark Warner offers this caution:

"... the Medicaid system is going to bankrupt all of the states, and indirectly, then lead to further deficit problems at the federal level over the next decade ..."

With record national budget deficits stemming from the war on terrorism and other factors, with more than 77 million baby boomers barreling down the LTC pipeline in the decades ahead, Gov. Warner's warning shows that government-financing for LTC is fiscally unsustainable. To avert potential financial meltdown, the federal government has been looking for ways to encourage people to plan for their own LTC needs. State governments are scrambling to find ways to control Medicaid before it's too late.

With the size of available home equity as shown by the NCOA numbers, reverse mortgages could be (and has to be) a part of federal and state governments' plan to manage ballooning LTC costs. In a 2003 statement, the head of Centers for Medicare and Medicaid Services (CMS), a unit of the U.S. Department of Health and Human Services (DHHS), hinted at Uncle Sam's thinking:

"The encouragement of reverse mortgages as a means of private sector financing of long-term care expenses for the elderly is a priority issue for DHHS, CMS."

The upshot is that Uncle Sam's emphasis on personal responsibility for LTC planning and financing may lead to policies that could strongly encourage use of home equity, thus boosting the demand for reverse mortgages. A possible policy path may be a requirement for house-rich older adults to use reverse mortgages to get LTC financing first before turning to public

Part V: A new frontier in mortgage lending

funds through Medicaid. Such a policy may include incentives to push reverse mortgages use by waiving, reducing, or subsidizing government-controlled fees in the reverse mortgage origination process.

Actually, a provision in a 2000 federal law calls for the Federal Housing Administration to waive its two percent upfront insurance fee for older adults who use all the proceeds of their HECM loan to pay for LTC insurance. This requirement is problematic because it's too restrictive. Reverse mortgage and LTC industry thought-leaders now agree it was a mistake. The Deficit Reduction Act of 2005 [DRA, see my conversation with LTC authority and reformer Stephen Moses in Appendix 1] is a modest step in the right direction.

Follow the new mortgage cheese

With the RMMI numbers, the life-cycle extra-cash needs of a huge aging population, and Uncle Sam's interest in reverse mortgages as a means of LTC financing, you don't have to be a genius to see that the future of residential mortgage lending is in reverse-land. And you don't have to be gloomy about the prospects for traditional forward mortgage originations either.

There will always be forward mortgages, but the market will shrink. The competition for the shrinking forward mortgage origination pie could be fierce and nasty if trends at the bottom of refinance booms hold true. Look at it this way: As residential mortgage originators, what we are losing due to a demographic shift on the younger end of the life cycle, we are gaining on the mature side. The humongous demographic shift underway is actually a boon to residential mortgage originators because of reverse mortgages.

That brings us to the real issue.

The real issue for us mortgage professionals is whether we are aware that the supply of the old residential mortgage cheese, once so plentiful when boomers were predominantly in the 35- to 44-year old demographic, is dwindling. As a parallel issue, are we fully cognizant of the immense size of the new mortgage cheese? Regular readers of my column are because I get their e-mails and phone calls often. The more important issue for those who are aware is one of preparedness to seize the new origination opportunity.

Opportunity favors the prepared

The French chemist who gave us the idea of heating milk to destroy bacteria or pasteurization, Louis Pasteur, was reported to have said that opportunity "favors the prepared mind." If you accept the view that America's aging population presents a compelling residential lending opportunity for mortgage professionals, then you must ask some serious questions of yourself as a mortgage professional. Are you prepared for the new mortgage cheese?

Or, are you hoping, against overwhelming objective demographic evidence that the old forward mortgage cheese will always be available in the quantity our industry is used to? What must you do to prepare for the new mortgage cheese?

Ten reverse-readiness questions

The reason mortgage professionals get calls about reverse mortgages is simple: Reverse mortgages are first and foremost, mortgages. The consuming public rightly assumes that mortgage professionals know about mortgages, forward or reverse. It follows that mortgage professionals should begin by seeking information about reverse mortgages and educating themselves to answer some basic questions such as the following:

- What is a reverse mortgage?
- How does someone qualify for a reverse mortgage?
- What programs are available?
- What are the benefits and features?
- What are the costs?
- Who are the lenders?
- What is the process?
- Where can I get more information?
- How can I get into reverse mortgages?
- What does reverse mortgage mean for my business?

As consumers are becoming more aware of the benefits and flexibility of reverse mortgages, mortgage professionals, on whom they depend for informed consultation, ought to be ahead of the knowledge curve, if they aspire to retain their customers' confidence and business. It's about being competitive. It's about growth.

Think reverse to move forward

The first step is awareness. The next is to think reverse. Why? The new masters of the marketplace, consumers who are 40 and older, will expect and demand that you think reverse. What does it mean to think reverse? For me, thinking reverse means becoming fully aware of the opportunities and challenges reverse mortgages represent for aging consumers as well as for mortgage professionals.

Part V: A new frontier in mortgage lending

Let's see what two aging consumers who think reverse know that others may not.

John Solace is an assumed name for an 80-year-old retired high school math teacher who called me about reverse mortgages some months ago. After normal pleasantries, I asked him what his objectives were for seeking a reverse mortgage. He said, "Atare, I want to get rid of my mortgage payments. I have done counseling and picked your name from a list the counselor gave me." Translation: I have done my homework on a reverse mortgage. Let's get on with an appointment.

At 80 (his ailing wife was 79), John Solace recognized they were unlikely, in their lifetime, to pay off their forward mortgage principal balance of $133,000 at seven percent with a PITI (Principal, Interest, Taxes, Insurance) of $1,139. He knew that the cash-munching monthly payment was reducing their fixed retirement income of about $4,000 by 28 percent. So, their decision to "reverse" their mortgage put an extra $10,618 in their pocket every year. Besides paying off their cash-draining forward mortgage principal, the reverse mortgage loan left the couple an extra $12,000 in a growing reverse mortgage creditline for their use when needed.

Another aging consumer who thinks reverse is a single Minneapolis man. Let's call him Peter Oddmeister. Mr. Oddmeister was looking to retire in July of 2006 when he turned 62. He called me up in early May of 2006 to find out more about reverse mortgages. He said he does not expect much retirement income because all of his working life, he did "a lot of odd jobs." He is retiring early because of back problems. Peter Oddmeister says he expects to use a reverse mortgage to supplement his retirement income. He has no children.

Although he had called to know more about reverse mortgages, it was clear to me after our 15-min. telephone conversation that he has an intuitive grasp of the value of these loans. At a gut level, he knew that a reverse mortgage is central to his retirement cash-flow plans. It is the reason he could imagine early retirement from "a lot of odd jobs" at 62 to nurse his ailing back.

Peter Oddmeister is emblematic of the reverse mortgage customer of the 21st century and a reason to be bullish about the prospect of these remarkable financial tools. During our conversation, it was clear he has no inhibitions about the judicious use of debt (reverse mortgage) to take out the accumulated equity in his home for a better retirement. Oddmeister and Solace are examples (see Chapter 15 for more) of what I mean by consumers who think reverse. They actually moved forward financially.

Pros are thinking reverse

A mortgage professional who thinks reverse is similar to this New York mortgage banker and regular reader of my column who sent me the following comment:

"I have read your articles about reverse mortgages with great interest and appreciate your information and insight. I believe that with the shrinking refinance market, along with rising interest rates, *it will become necessary for mortgage professionals to diversify the manner in which they do business* [my emphasis]. Additionally, I feel that reverse mortgages provide an opportunity to help older Americans to confront their financial needs, while maintaining ownership of their homes.

I would appreciate it if you could assist me in understanding how to proceed. We are a mortgage banker licensed in seven states and are about to expand into seven additional states. We are quite capable at sub-prime and conventional mortgages. I would assume that there are unique characteristics to reverse mortgages, and need to know who the best investors are, permissible fees, rules and regulations, underwriting guidelines, etc."

It's interesting that this obviously reverse thinking New York mortgage banker used words such as "shrinking refinance market" along with "rising interest rates." He mentions the necessity of product diversification. Reverse mortgages are not as interest-rate-sensitive as forwards. He says reverse mortgages "provide an opportunity to help older Americans to confront their financial needs, while maintaining ownership of their homes." Our New York mortgage banker has the right motivation and focus. He's thinking reverse and seeking understanding first.

Another example of a mortgage professional who thinks reverse is this mortgage broker from Maryland:

"The subject of reverse mortgages is very much misunderstood and feared by many of the folks I've spoken with. In my efforts to attempt to explain reverse mortgages, I realize I first need to be educated on the subject. Can you help me?"

Here is an astute mortgage broker who realizes that mortgage professionals need to educate themselves on reverse mortgages if they are going to be explaining it to older adults and their advisors.

Part V: A new frontier in mortgage lending

It's not just core mortgage originators who are thinking reverse these days. Other mortgage-affiliated professionals are doing the same as this e-mail I received from a title attorney shows:

"It was a pleasure to read your recent article in *The Massachusetts Mortgage Press*, and you expressed many of the concerns that we have just recently been discussing about the changing market here in our office. I just suggested this week that we start doing roundtable discussions about both reverse mortgages and age 55 and over residential communities.

My question: What is a good resource for information about handling reverse mortgages? Our agents, all of whom are attorneys, are starting to see more and more reverse mortgages, so we are issuing more and more title insurance policies that insure them. Any suggestions that you might have for good information about reverse mortgages would be greatly appreciated."

Astute insurance agents are also thinking reverse as a May 2005 article in *Life Insurance Selling* suggests. Understandably unaware of the double cost of using reverse mortgages to buy insurance products and the suitability of such products for many elders, the author (an insurance salesman with 17 years of experience) attempts to show his fellow insurance agents how they can use reverse mortgages to "separate the producer from the rest of the [life insurance] crowd" and "benefit [producer] with some nice commission checks in his [her] pocket."

Isn't it interesting that insurance professionals are looking to use their knowledge of this innovative mortgage lending product to 'differentiate' themselves and make money? I say, "What are you waiting for Mr. Mortgage Professional?"

Ginnie Mae thinks reverse

Ginnie Mae, a secondary market giant in FHA and VA mortgages, launched a HECM-mortgage-backed security in 2007. This historic initiative was championed by Ginnie Mae's former president Robert M. Couch. For mortgage lenders and brokers who are yet to think reverse, Mr. Couch offers these words:

"I would tell them to take some time to look at the growth rate of this product; and take time to look at the demographic changes that are coming in the marketplace, where the population is aging at a fairly rapid clip.

The new mortgage cheese

And when you look at those two factors together, it makes a fairly compelling case that if you don't get involved in reverse mortgages, you are going to miss a substantial opportunity."

These capable financial services professionals know clearly that the way forward is for them to think reverse. Besides offering mortgage professionals non-cyclical program diversification and other opportunities, reverse-mortgage competency gives them added tool to build business relationships with other financial and non-financial professionals whose businesses may depend on cash flow from reverse mortgages. For example, on the non-financial front, a new industry has emerged to help older adults "age in place." They include home-modification specialists, home designers, contractors, home care providers, etc. The financial side counts insurance agents, financial planners, and long-term care specialists among others. The extra cash stream from reverse mortgages could provide sustenance for many businesses and give the reverse mortgage originator unsurpassed opportunity for professional networking.

Understanding mature markets

My January 2005 column began as follows: "The new lords of the marketplace are watching us. How well do we know them?"

The new masters of the marketplace, including the mortgage lending marketplace, are consumers who are 40 and older. They surpassed the 39 and younger group in 1989 and they continue to grow. Part of thinking reverse is paying attention to this demographic, for the survival of most businesses will depend on understanding these groups and how to make marketing connections with them. In his book, *The Longevity Revolution*, Theodore Roszak said:

"The marketing trend away from youth and toward age is irreversible."

Please read the above statement again. A revolution has begun in the American marketplace. Youth, defined here as those between 18 and 39, is now lagging in numbers and buying power behind age. Age or maturity is defined as those who are 40 and older.

Our marketing establishment [Madison Avenue] is still struggling to make sense of the revolution that is underway. Most are in denial, but some are seeing the demographic light and its implications for the old, youth-dominated marketing worldview. For mortgage lending professionals, we must re-

Part V: A new frontier in mortgage lending

turn to the question: How well do we know the new bosses of the marketplace? There is no substitute for this knowledge if we want our marketing communication to be effective in this new age. That is why David B. Wolfe asks in his groundbreaking book, *Ageless Marketing:*

"Without an understanding of aging and aging customers, how can a marketer be successful in marketing to the New Customer Majority?"

To win in this new marketing era, where the old rules of youth-centered and product-focused marketing no longer apply, *we must begin with a superior understanding of aging and aging customers.* This should be a no-brainer, right? Well, wrong. The people who make creative decisions on Madison Avenue still don't get it. Just study most of their ads and other marketing communication work.

Knowledge of aging and aging customers required to craft persuasive marketing communication must be deeper than traditional demographic details—age, income, available home equity, spending patterns, zip codes and all data that can be programmed into a customer relationship management (CRM) system. What is needed to figure out second-half customers cannot be fed into CRM systems. Although CRM and other marketing tools are still useful, the well-documented failures of traditional marketing thought and techniques in corporate America suggest fresh thinking for mortgage professionals and others in the reverse mortgage arena.

Any reader who has come this far with me ran into some of this new thinking in Part II (Chapters 6-10).

In *Who Moved My Cheese*? Spencer Johnson teaches that change is a constant. Mortgage professionals know (and thrive on) change. Every day, the market is changing and graying. Older-adult consumers now rule the marketplace. While reverse mortgages were designed for people 62 and older, many 40-plus (or younger) have older parents and relatives. And every homeowner who expects to retire someday has to know about reverse mortgages, for they have become essential in our retirement kit. *Can you afford to be ill-informed about the new mortgage cheese?*

Resources

- www.agelessmarketing.com
- www.centerltc.com
- www.aoa.dhhs.gov
- www.ncoa.org
- www.hud.gov/offices/hsg/comp/rpts/hecm/hecm0508.xls

The new mortgage cheese

Think Reverse!

Appendix

Think Reverse!

Appendix 1
DRA 2005: Medicaid rule change and reverse mortgages

A conversation with Stephen A. Moses of the Center for Long-Term Care Reform

If you are marketing and originating reverse mortgages, pay attention to Medicaid, Medicaid eligibility, and long-term care (LTC) finance issues. It's about keeping an eye on the forest and the big issues that could drive demand for reverse mortgage for decades.

For over 40 years, Medicaid, a federal/state program designed to help the poor, has been paying for LTC for most people the U.S. That is about to change because it is eating up states' budgets. Some experts say if the pace of Medicaid financing for LTC goes unchecked, it could bankrupt the states. Others argue that government financing is the solution.

Stephen Moses

With 78 million baby boomers coming down the LTC financing pipeline in the next 20 years, federal and state government planners are concerned. So, Uncle Sam has changed the rules. The new rules are in the Deficit Reduction Act of 2005 (DRA 2005).

They say you are responsible for your LTC financing unless you are truly poor. Personal responsibility for LTC financing means alternative financing. That is where reverse mortgages come in. And that's why we should add Medicaid, Medicaid eligibility, and LTC financing know-how to our education.

To help us understand the implications of DRA 2005 for the reverse mortgage industry, I share with you a conversation with Stephen A. Moses.

Mr. Moses, president of Seattle-based Center for Long-Term Care Reform, is one of America's leading authorities on LTC financing issues.

Mr. Moses has been involved in healthcare financing issues at state and federal levels since 1979. His research and advocacy influenced the design of Medicaid rules in the Omnibus Budget Reconciliation Act of 1993 (an earlier federal law), as well as the Deficit Reduction Act 2005.

A frequently quoted and consulted author and speaker, Mr. Moses is a one-man crusader for long-term reform in the U.S. He has spoken before Congress and two-thirds of U.S state legislatures.

Atare E. Agbamu: Stephen, why is DRA 2005 important for the reverse mortgage market?
Stephen A. Moses: Until now, Medicaid exempted home equity with no limit. One could own a home, including all contiguous property, regardless of value. This could be a 10,000-acre ranch in Montana, Bill Gates's big house on Lake Washington in Seattle or any other mansion, and you can qualify for Medicaid. There were other income and asset restrictions, but those were avoided as well.

AEA: What has changed is that there is now a limit of half $500,000 in home equity for people to retain and still qualify for Medicaid.
SAM: Now, that's still a very high level. Medicaid is a means-tested public assistance program. And to retain the value of $500,000 and get the government to pay for your LTC, which can be very expensive, especially in a nursing home, is extremely generous.

In Britain, they allow $36,000 in home equity to be exempted to qualify for publicly-financed LTC. In Germany, they have a 10-year look back on the transfer of assets, whereas we have only moved the look back period to five years in this country. The irony is that America, with a supposedly free-market capitalist healthcare system, is far more generous than the so-called socialized healthcare system in Western Europe.

If people can't exempt unlimited home equity, they would be less likely to hide money in home equity to qualify for Medicaid, a common practice until now. And if they do have home equity in excess of $500,000, they are far more likely to take out a reverse mortgage to reduce their equity down to the allowable level of $500,000 and use the proceeds from the reverse mortgage either to supplement their income so they can buy LTC insurance or to pay for community-based services to help them remain in their home and delay or prevent nursing-home institutionalization and Medicaid dependency altogether.

So, it is a very, very positive development [DRA 2005]. It sends the message to the public that LTC is a personal responsibility: that you can no longer preserve unlimited assets and get the government to pay for your LTC; that,

Appendix 1

therefore, you should plan to pay for your own LTC. The best way to plan is early planning with private insurance. Failing that, if one gets to be 62 and eligible for reverse mortgage, that's an excellent way to ensure that one can pay one's own way.

AEA: Why should reverse mortgage lenders support the effort to educate the American public on the new Medicaid limits on exempt home equity? How should reverse mortgage lenders go about this educational process?
SAM: First of all, they should educate themselves. Reverse mortgage lenders are no more knowledgeable about the effect of Medicaid eligibility in the past on the marketability of their product than are LTC insurance industry agents and officials. Very few people who are marketing reverse mortgages or LTC insurance understand that the primary reason their products have not sold very well in the past is that Medicaid was readily available to cover the single biggest risk the elderly faced financially. People could ignore the risks, avoid the premiums for private insurance, wait until they get sick, shelter all of their income and assets, including their home equity and get the government to pay for their LTC. As long as that was true, it's little wonder that most people didn't prepare for LTC, didn't buy insurance, and didn't tap the equity in their home. *Why would you tap the equity in your home if it isn't at risk for your single biggest cost?*

Reverse mortgage lending has taken off in the last few years, but it hasn't been driven by LTC expenses. It's been largely a function of interest rate collapse, and seniors are dipping into their home equity in order to retain their income levels and normal standard of living.

Now that Medicaid doesn't protect an unlimited level of home equity, the public needs their product [reverse mortgage] much more than was ever the case. Once they understand it themselves, they should begin educating the media about this reality. The reporters who are writing many positive articles lately about how to use reverse mortgages to retain a decent lifestyle will also be talking about the importance of using home equity to ensure access to quality LTC, particularly in the home.

This new law will mean nothing unless the states implement it, the feds enforce it, the media publicizes it, and reverse mortgage lenders and insurance agents sell it. *It's critical, at every stage, that the industry is involved in marketing the products that can help people get access to quality LTC and that they are out aggressively promoting all of those laws: Encouraging states to implement the rules, the feds to enforce them, the media to publicize them, and their salespeople to sell them. Otherwise, if we don't get the public awakened to*

Think Reverse!

the importance of planning for LTC, even using their home equity, we are going to see the age wave crest and crash on us over the next 10 or 15 years in a way that will likely wipe out many of the supports that have been there in the past.

Medicare has a $60 trillion unfunded liability. We've just added Medicare Part D, which is another $8 trillion that is completely unfunded for the future. The Social Security program has $10 trillion unfunded liability. Medicaid, the primary funder of LTC in this country, is not even calculating the unfunded liability there because the money comes directly out of general funds and there is no trust fund. Never mind that is phony, but Medicare and Social Security, at least, have trust funds ... Medicaid doesn't.

We've got a whole house of cards here. Government entitlements that have anaesthetized the public to the risk of LTC are about to come tumbling down over the next 20 years, and smart people would be preparing now for that eventuality particularly in the area of LTC. **These are things that reverse mortgage lenders need to understand. They need to train their salespeople on the fiduciary responsibility to their clients to explain these facts of financial life.** *As they do so, more people will see the light and buy their products. But if it [the education] isn't done, consumer behavior won't change.*

AEA: So, it is not just enough for reverse mortgage marketers and originators to know about reverse mortgages. What should the LTC financing curriculum be for reverse mortgage lenders?
SAM: The simplest and most direct way to do that is to retain the Center for Long-Term Care Reform, through me, to speak at their conferences, to write for their publications, and to do op-ed articles for local newspapers. It's basically education. Without being immodest, there is nobody in the country who understands it better than I because I've done nothing but this since the early 1980s when I was a career U.S. government employee of the Health Care Financing Administration, doing the early studies that identified the problem of Medicaid planning. And I have been working ever since to give Medicaid back to the poor and to get everybody else planning responsibly.

If people understand the importance of planning for LTC, more people will take out reverse mortgages, but that isn't going to happen unless the salespeople understand what has changed in Medicaid law and unless they convey that reality to their clients.

I am making the observation that while you don't want to use this new change as a scare tactic, you do have a fiduciary responsibility to the public to warn them that the rules have changed and that they will be personally responsible in the future for their LTC. They should be preparing, through insurance and the use of

Appendix 1

home equity [reverse mortgages], to pay their own way for LTC. The benefits go beyond avoiding any penalties or consequences that are in the law.

It is well known that Medicaid has a dismal reputation for problems of access, quality, reimbursement, discrimination, institutional bias, loss of independence, welfare stigma, and so on. When people understand the problems associated with ignoring LTC until it's too late and then depending on Medicaid, I think an increasing number of them will use their home equity [reverse mortgages] and buy insurance, rather than ending up in nursing homes.

AEA: It appears that most of those who will be attracted to home equity, based on the $500,000 cut-off, will be those in the upper income or upper asset brackets, right?
SAM: No, it shouldn't be at all. What this should be is a way to convey to the public that home equity is now at risk. They place the limit this year at $500,000, but as I said, in England [UK], the limit is $36,000. I think there is every possibility that next year, Congress can take it to $250,000, and a year after that may be to $50,000.

The message the public should receive is that while the rules remain very generous, the whole trend is in a downward direction toward preserving Medicaid as a safety net for the poor, and conveying the message to the public that they need to plan.

If I were of an age where I was concerned about long-term care now, and I had a home even with $250,000 (which will still be exempt for purposes of Medicaid); if I needed the income from that home through a reverse mortgage to supplement my income so that I can afford private insurance, and I was still healthy and medically qualified, it would be a very sensible reason to take out a reverse mortgage in anticipation that Medicaid won't be there in the future for me.

AEA: And you think that the limit will keep dropping from $500,000 over the next several years, right?
SAM: They have to. Medicaid is bankrupting the states. They can't go on providing expensive nursing home care for affluent seniors. All you have to do is look at the writing on the wall.

AEA: Was there anything in the legislative history of DRA 2005 that suggests a lower limit in 2007 and in coming years?
SAM: The National Governors Association recommended most of the changes that ended up in the Deficit Reduction Act, and their recom-

Think Reverse!

mendation was to take the Medicaid home-equity exemption to $50,000. The Governors were recommending it this time around. The legislators, you know, it's a very politically sensitive thing. There was a lot of opposition. And they got as low as they could get it on this round; but, believe me, they are going to be fighting to get it lower in the future. Either that or Medicaid would collapse entirely.

AEA: You said the states recommended $50,000. So is that an indication of what is coming?
SAM: Yes, that's what I think! I think people are pretty naive if they expect Medicaid to go on paying for two-thirds of residents and 80 percent of all patient days in nursing homes. It's just too expensive, and it cannot continue. Trends that cannot continue will not work, as one wag once said.

AEA: You talked about LTC Partnerships in your LTC Bullet. What do you mean by LTC Partnerships?
SAM: LTC Partnerships was a program promoted by the Robert Wood Johnson Foundation going back to the late 1980s. *It's an incentive to buy more LTC insurance, thereby forgiving Medicaid's spend down liability.*

The way it usually works is this (a little different in New York): If you bought $100,000 worth of insurance and used it up. Then, instead of having to spend down to $2,000 of assets to qualify for Medicaid, you could retain $102,000.

Now, in 1993 when Congress mandated estate recoveries; that's if you were on Medicaid, the state was required to go into your estate and recover the costs of care provided to you.

Congressman Henry Waxman, who at that time chaired the House Energy and Commerce Committee, refused to exempt the partnerships that have already been set up from the estate recovery requirements. So, while they could continue to exempt the money up-front for purposes of eligibility, they could not exempt it from the estate recovery requirements. Because of that change, no more partnerships took effect, in essence eliminating the incentive that was there to preserve assets by buying insurance.

Now, that restriction has been lifted. States can exempt not only the money on the front end, but also on the back-end from estate recovery. It means that the four LTC Partnerships that exist now can be expanded in any state in the country that wants to set one of these programs as long as they meet the requirements in the law: They have to be in concord with rules of the National Academy of Insurance Commissioners, they have to be IRS-qualified LTC insurance policies, and so on.

The insurance industry fought hard for the expansion of the partnerships. I think it is not nearly as important as the Medicaid eligibility changes for a simple reason: Why would anybody buy insurance to avoid a Medicaid spend down liability that doesn't exist in the first place.

AEA: What do you mean by '"spend down liability?"
SAM: Technically, the way Medicaid is always presented is that, you can only retain $2,000 in assets. Other than that, you must "spend down" your own money for your LTC until you become impoverished.

The reality is that there is no limit on how much income or assets you can have and still qualify for Medicaid LTC. You determine income eligibility by first deducting from a person's income, the cost of private nursing home care, co-insurance and deductible for Medicare, co-insurance and deductible for the Medicare supplemental policy, and all of the medical expenses seniors pay for that Medicare doesn't cover, like foot care, eye care, dental care and pharmaceuticals. And if they still don't have enough income to pay for everything, they are eligible for Medicaid.

Then the assets; while, technically, you can only retain $2,000, you can have a home and all contiguous property regardless of value. That was true until the DRA [2005]. Now, it's limited to $500,000. But, you can still retain a business, including the capital and cash flow of unlimited value, an automobile of unlimited value, pre-paid burial funds of unlimited value for every member of the family, not just the Medicaid recipient and spouse, unlimited home furnishings. In essence, as long as you hold the assets in exempt form, there is no limit on how much you can have in assets and qualify for Medicaid.

While the DRA has created some additional restrictions on the diversion and divestment of assets, it doesn't really get to all of the methods people can use to retain assets and qualify Medicaid.

AEA: What is the way forward then in terms of creating incentives for people to use reverse mortgages?
SAM: Well, any number of things they can do to incentivize people to use home equity for LTC insurance and home equity for long-term care. A lot of these ideas are being talked about similar to the partnerships for LTC insurance where you give people an extra benefit if they use home equity to purchase LTC; but they do cost money. The reason they tend not to pass is that the Congressional Budget Office (CBO) scores them as being very expensive.

Think Reverse!

The CBO doesn't take into consideration the ultimate savings down the line.

If they did, they might be more likely to pass those incentives. But here is the critical thing: No amount of incentives is going to encourage people to buy LTC insurance or take out reverse mortgages as long as they can ignore the risk, avoid the premiums, and wait until they get sick, shelter the home, and get Medicaid to pay for their LTC. *It is the Medicaid eligibility stuff that is critical.*

And as I said before, we've made some progress on that, but we still have a long way to go to make sure Medicaid is a safety net for the poor and not a hammock for the upper-middle class. And if we do that, whether or not we get tax incentives and other publicly-financed incentives for these products [reverse mortgages and LTC insurance], people will buy them.

AEA: So, the key, to repeat what you've just said, is to make Medicaid eligibility more restrictive, right?

SAM: Well, to target Medicaid to the genuinely needy. If you do that, you will save more than enough money to pay for the incentives to get other people to plan for long-term care. We just have way too many people depending on welfare for LTC and way too few people planning responsibly to pay their own way. And those are directly related.

It's a fact that for 40 years, we've been able to just ignore care and get the government to pay; that has caused low market penetration of reverse mortgages and LTC insurance. If you get Medicaid out of the business of giving away [long-term care] for free what we'd like people to do for themselves, you'll see people taking out reverse mortgages and buying long-term care insurance.

AEA: What do you think is going to happen if people don't get the message about the relationship between Medicaid and reverse mortgage sales?

SAM: If people don't get the message, we'll just continue on the course we've been on, Medicaid will collapse and a lot of poor people will be hurt. The baby-boomer generation will have no way to pay for LTC, except through their home equity [through reverse mortgages]. They won't buy insurance. When the time comes, Medicaid won't be there for them, and they will have to use their home equity.

Regardless of whether we solve the problem through responsible public policy or just leave it alone and let Medicaid collapse, both the reverse mortgage industry and the LTC insurance industry are going to explode in popularity because that will be the only way to pay for decent LTC.

The tragedy is that a lot of poor people will get hurt. A lot of young people

Appendix 1

won't get inheritances from their baby-boomer parents similar to what baby-boomers parents are getting from their World War II generation parents.

AEA: What do you say to people who say premiums for LTC insurance are just way, way out for most people in their 70s? They will not be able to get the right policy at the right price because they may have pre-existing conditions and other factors that could disqualify them from getting a better policy.

SAM: Well, you can't buy fire insurance when your house is in flames, and you, obviously, can't buy LTC insurance when you already have Alzheimer's. Most people who make those kinds of arguments are totally unrealistic about economics. And the idea that you can now transfer this risk to government programs that are already bankrupt, just covering what they have already covered is just so economically and philosophically irresponsible that it's, frankly, kind of sickening.

The reality is, a vast majority of people can afford LTC insurance if they purchase it at the most appropriate time of their lives. It's cheaper when they are younger. But if they are raising a family, well, then, maybe later on if incentives are in effect. The children, if they are in responsible positions, can supplement the parents to afford LTC insurance.

The main thing is that there should be an incentive to buy it and an incentive to use home equity if they don't have the other resources to afford it. Those incentives have not been there in the past, and as a consequence, both the LTC insurance and the reverse mortgage industries have been under-developed.

Those incentives are developing, through small steps taken by the Deficit Reduction Act of 2005. There will be more restrictions in the future. So, you will see people re-evaluating the risk, such that they're willing to pay more toward the purchase of LTC insurance. As they see the need for it and, as the need becomes real, they'll be more likely to tap their home equity to help them afford it.

In your 70s, long-term care insurance gets expensive. I purchased it for my parents in their mid-70s in 1989. I've paid the premiums ever since, because I don't think they should have to pay the premiums on insurance that protects my inheritance. And I have a policy for myself and my wife that I've paid for 10 years. I am part of the solution.

I pay my taxes in order to preserve Medicaid as a safety net for the poor. What I resent is paying taxes that support people who hire attorneys to get rid of their assets in order to take advantage of a program that's supposed to be for the poor. They've basically ruined Medicaid as a safety net for the poor.

Think Reverse!

And my mission and the mission of my organization, the Center for Long-Term Care Reform, is to give Medicaid back to the poor and encourage everyone else to plan responsibly for long-term care, which they can and should afford to do if they put the proper priority on that risk.

AEA: Do you have any closing remarks for reverse mortgage lenders?
SAM: I think they should wake up, smell the coffee, take it upon themselves to learn more about the relationship between public and private LTC financing and, then, get involved in publicizing this and educating their sales people so that we can get the word out to the public that LTC is a risk for which they need to take responsibility in the future.

Appendix 1

Think Reverse!

Appendix 2(a)
7-Point ReverseTalk™ imagination: Profiles in satisfaction

Objective

To help reverse mortgage originators and their senior audiences focus on the experiences the extra cash from reverse mortgages can make possible.

Point One/Two Questions

At this moment, what experiences would you like to have? Or, what things would you like to do if you have some extra cash? Please list them under Point Two.

1. _____
2. _____
3. _____

Point Three/Why

Why would you like to do or experience these things? Please list your reasons below:

1. _____
2. _____
3. _____

Point Four/When

Please state when you would like to have these experiences or to do these things? Please write dates by your list in Point Two above.

Think Reverse!

Point Five/RM Talk
A reverse mortgage gives you the extra cash you need. You keep legal and physical control of your home. And you make *no* monthly mortgage repayments for the life of the loan.

Point Six/Reaction
How about some questions on reverse mortgages for me?

Point Seven/Sharing
How about a volunteer who wants to share their list with the group?

© 2007 ThinkReverse LLC/Atare E. Agbamu

Appendix 2 (a)

Think Reverse!

Appendix 2(b)
Presenter's Guide 7-Point ReverseTalk™

Objective
To help reverse mortgage originators and their senior audiences focus on the experiences the extra cash from reverse mortgages can make possible.

Point One/Two Questions
At this moment, what experiences would you like to have? Or, what things would you like to do if you have some extra cash? Please list them under Point Two. [You are framing the conversation around possible experiences. You are appealing to the "more introspective/more autonomous" bent of second-half customers.]

Point Two/List [Enhances focus]

1._____
2._____
3._____

Point Three/Why
Why would you like to do or experience these things? Please list your reasons below: [Focuses on experiences with reasons]

1._____
2._____
3._____

Think Reverse!

Point Four/When
Please state when you would like to have these experiences or to do these things? Please write dates by your list in Point Two above. [Focuses on the experiences with time frames.]

Point Five/RM Talk
A reverse mortgage gives you the extra cash you need. You keep legal and physical control of your home. And you make *no* monthly mortgage repayments for the life of the loan. [Conveys the essence of reverse mortgages in plain English, in three sentences.]

Point Six/Reaction
How about some questions? [Stimulate discussion. Initiate conversational reciprocity.]

Point Seven/Sharing
How about a volunteer who wants to share her list with the group? [Reinforces focus on the experiences.]

© 2007 ThinkReverse LLC/Atare E. Agbamu

Appendix 2 (b)

Think Reverse!

Appendix 2(c)
How to garner broadcast coverage on a conservative budget

Recognize news

Even though reverse mortgage companies are changing lives and building communities every day, the truth is that the actual work that we do—hundreds of faxes and phone calls to support truckloads of paperwork—Is simply not glamorous or novel. Therefore, the person responsible for promoting your company must be able to distinguish between information that is newsworthy and information that should be distributed to company insiders and associates only.

To determine if your company information is newsworthy, ask yourself these questions:
- Is this an industry first?
- Is this company information evidence of an industry trend?
- Will this information dispel commonly held misconceptions?
- Will this information affect individuals not related to my company or the mortgage industry?
- Is this information something that even my competitors would be interested in knowing?
- Is this information timely, innovative or unique?
- Does this information provide a complete story about our company or company leader?
- Will this information impact the public's safety, health or purchase decisions?

If you can answer "yes" to two or more of these questions, then your story is most likely worth sending to your local media. Keep in mind that televi-

Think Reverse!

sion stations are most interested in stories that have a visual element to them.

Your company information is likely not newsworthy if you can answer "yes" to *any* of the following questions:
- Are my competitors offering the same class/product/level of service (and perhaps just calling it by a different name)?
- Has the media aired a story similar to this in the past six months?
- Is this information about a branch of my company that is located outside of the targeted media market?

Write a broadcast news release

When preparing your story for broadcast media, follow the basic journalism process by answering the questions *Who? What? Where? When? Why?* and *How?* in the lead sentence(s) of your press release. Next, indicate, using simple terms, why this information is newsworthy, who it will affect and how. Consider including a quote from your company spokesperson. State the name(s) of the spokesperson who will be available for interviews, along with that individual's title and a brief description of the role that they play within your company. End your news release with a boiler that includes basic company information. (See Sample Press Release, Appendix 2[d])

Write a cover letter

Along with your news release, it can be helpful to send a cover letter that supplements the information in your news release. For instance, if your company has just started offering reverse mortgages and you would like to appear on a morning television program to talk about it, you would want to send a cover letter that answers the question, "Why will this station's viewers be interested in hearing my story?" Your letter may include statistics on homeownership levels among senior citizens, or facts and figures that support the need for extra income at various stages of life. Your cover letter should set the stage for your press release, demonstrating the importance of the news that you are about to announce and indicating how this news will affect the industry or the public (See Sample Cover Letter).

Your cover letter should be engaging and informative, and offer your company/company spokesperson as the expert on your suggested topic in your industry. Often, on-camera personalities will use information from your cover letter as their introduction of you and the news that you are there to discuss.

Know your local media

Nearly every media market across the nation has access to more than one channel for local network television news. Television stations, like mortgage companies, try to distinguish themselves from their competition in the local market. As a viewer, you can probably name which station only covers hard news such as murders, fires and elections, and which station includes lifestyle stories about local heroes and charities in their news coverage. Generally, hard news stations will not cover stories submitted by mortgage companies, with the exception of stories that involve the unfortunate and rare instances of fraud.

Once you have identified which stations only cover hard news and which stations include lifestyle stories, evaluate the content of your news release. Was your company just named "Mortgage Company of the Year" by a nationally recognized consumer organization, or is one of your loan officers being recognized by a local elementary for five years of volunteer service? It would be appropriate to pitch the former story to both types of news stations, while the latter may be best suited for stations that include lifestyle stories.

The pitching process

When offering a story for potential inclusion in an upcoming television or radio broadcast, often called "pitching a story," the first step is to prepare an informative news release and cover letter. This written communication serves as an introduction of your story idea to a producer as well as an invitation to conduct an interview.

Once you have sent your news release to the television or radio station, your company spokesperson MUST be available to answer any questions that the producers and news directors may have. If a news station is interested in covering your news release, they will most likely arrange to interview your spokesperson by contacting whoever is named as the primary contact at the top of your news release. Your primary contact person should have direct access to your spokesperson at all hours of the day.

Interviews generally take place at a location of your choosing, or on-site at the broadcast news studio.

The producer or station representative will tell you where to be and what time to arrive. While it can be helpful to arrive early, do not arrive more than 15 minutes prior to your interview. News segments are timed to the minute, and station representatives will not have the time or the staff to attend to you for long periods of time.

If the interview is not live, the reporter will want to video or audiotape you while taking notes on your responses to questions. When finished with the interview, the reporter will edit their work and prepare it for broadcast. To

Think Reverse!

find out when your story will air, ask the reporter before he or she leaves the interview location. Request a business card or phone number where you can reach the interviewer with any pertinent information that you may have forgotten during the interview.

Who to pitch

Unlike newspapers, which have a reporter assigned to cover just about every industry, broadcast outlets have relatively few assignment reporters. Your local television station may have a crime reporter, an education reporter and a government reporter, but they most likely do not have anybody assigned specifically to mortgage stories.

When pitching the your local network television stations, you will most likely target a morning news program for to discussion-style announcement or the evening news program for hard news story.

If your goal is to appear on a morning television news show, follow these easy steps:

1. Call the television station and ask for the name, number and fax number of the morning show producer. Some stations are reluctant to give out this information. In that case, contact a public relations consultant who can provide you with a list of local media, including contact information, for a small fee.

2. E-mail or fax the morning show producer your cover letter and press release. If you have not received a response from the producer within two days, leave a voice message that includes your story suggestion and contact information.

3. Most often, a producer will only return your follow-up call if he or she is interested in including your information in an upcoming segment.

If your goal is to have your information covered on the evening news, follow these easy steps:

1. Call the television station and ask for the name, number and fax number of the news assignment editor. Again, some stations are reluctant to give out this information, but a public relations consultant can provide you with a media list for a small fee.

2. E-mail or fax the news assignment editor your cover letter and press

release. If you have not received a response from a reporter within two days, leave a voice message that includes your story suggestion and contact information.

3. Again, you will only be contacted if the television station is interested in including your information in an upcoming segment.

If your goal is to have your information covered on a radio news program, follow these easy steps:

1. Call the radio station and ask for the name, number and fax number of the news director.

2. Call the news director and introduce your story idea. Offer to fax or e-mail additional information. If you have not received a response from the news director within two days, leave a second voice message that includes your story suggestion and contact information.

3. Be sure that your messages are brief and clearly state your story idea. Radio stations will determine whether you will be a good interview subject, in part, by evaluating how well spoken you are on the telephone.

Select a spokesperson

Once you have prepared your story for media distribution, you will need to identify a spokesperson who will respond to interview requests. Your spokesperson should be approachable, well spoken and fully informed about the information that you are announcing. It is imperative that your spokesperson be able to relay your key messages in a clear, concise manner, using one or two sentences, as broadcast producers are looking to air a sound byte rather than a complete summary of an event.

Your spokesperson for general news announcements should hold a top-level position within the company. If your company owner or CEO is not comfortable in front of a camera or not fond of public speaking, consider another senior employee. If one of your loan officers wins a national award, then consider making both the loan officer and your company CEO available for media interviews.

Your primary contact person must have access to your spokesperson around the clock–even nights and weekends. If that much time passes before the reporter has contact with your spokesperson, then your story will

Think Reverse!

probably be passed up for another one that had interviews and answers readily available. Deadlines are the nature of the news business. They are short-term and definite.

Identify key messages

Before your interview or before you invite a reporter into your office, identify two key messages that will serve as talking points during the interview. If you want the public to know that your company is, for example, "the most trusted mortgage company in the state," then you will have to verbalize that quite often during your interview. Do not be afraid to repeat yourself. The news story will only include what you offer the reporter, so bring each question back to one of your key messages.

The following is a sample interview between a reporter and a broker. The key messages are:

1. "Company X is the most trusted mortgage company in the state."
2. "Reverse mortgages provide consumers with financial freedom."

Reporter: So, tell me how reverse mortgages work.
Broker: Reverse mortgages provide consumers with financial freedom by …

Reporter: Will reverse mortgages be the best solution for everybody?
Broker: Well, Company X is the most trusted mortgage company in the state because we always match the customer with the best product to meet their needs. And, while reverse mortgages provide many consumers with financial freedom, we work with each family to make sure that they get what is best for them.

Reporter: Is Company X the first company to offer reverse mortgages in this state?
Broker: I cannot answer that with much certainty, but I can tell you that our state trusts Company X to provide the most up-to-date products as soon as they become available.

Reporter: How many people in our state do you suppose will benefit from a reverse mortgage?
Broker: Reverse mortgages can provide financial freedom to over … people in our state.

Did you notice how the broker managed to use one of their two key messages in each of their responses? Bringing most questions back to one of your key messages may feel uncomfortable and repetitive at first, but it will become second nature through practice. The best-trained public speakers use this method, including politicians, airline spokespersons, and lawyers.

Preparing for the interview

- Practice interviewing aloud, using questions that the interviewer may ask. You may request a list of the questions that will be asked during the interview, but the news media is under no obligation to provide you with that information.

- If the reporter asks questions about something that you do not know or a topic that you prefer not to comment on, do not hesitate to say, "I don't know the answer to that," or "Perhaps we should schedule another interview to discuss _____." Do not say "no comment."

- Don't ramble. Keep your answers concise and stick to your messages to ensure that your interview reflects what you want the public to know.

- Understand that the interview begins when the reporter arrives. There is no such thing as "off the record." Stick to your messages, even when the camera is not rolling.

- For a television interview, wear formal business attire in traditional shades. Be aware of things that may not look good on camera, such as eyeglasses and patterned clothing.

- Respond to the person who is asking the question and not to the cameras.

- Avoid gesturing. Too much "talking with your hands" comes across on camera as over-animated and foolish. If necessary, keep one hand on your lap and one hand on the arm of the chair.

- Always be forthright and honest.

Media etiquette

- Pitch only what is newsworthy. Sending news releases about everyday events, donations and/or decisions will prove more irritating than informative for reporters.

Think Reverse!

- Send your news release to the person most likely to cover the story. Do not send multiple faxes or e-mails to station staff members in hopes that one of them will want to interview you.

- Calls from the media may come at any time of day. Make sure that your company spokesperson is available for phone calls and interviews at any hour.

- Return phone calls and e-mails immediately. If you happen to miss a phone call, it is imperative that you return it immediately. Do not expect that a producer who showed interest in your story to wait 24 hours.

- Understand that the media is interviewing you because it is their job to do so. Do not expect a producer, news director or reporter to spend an extended period of time with you. Their work is finished when they have what they need for their story, and not when you have told them everything that you want them to know.

- Stick to the subject that was identified in your news release, unless the reporter inquires about another topic that you feel comfortable talking about.

- Never offer gifts or incentives to media representatives, no matter how small. A sincere verbal or written "thank you" will demonstrate your appreciation for their time and attention to your story without compromising their perceived objectivity.

- Do not expect to see, hear or edit the story before it is broadcast.

Follow-up

After your story has been broadcast, it is acceptable to send the reporter or producer a note of appreciation or leave them a voice mail if you feel that the coverage was good. If there are inaccuracies in the reporting (a statistic or the spelling of a name), you may request that the reporter correct it in future broadcasts, but do not expect the station to re-run the story or make a public announcement correcting the mistake. If you have serious concerns about how your information was presented, contact the news director to open the door for conversations about future coverage.

Appendix 2 (c)

Submitted by: Rebecca White Selby

Rebecca White Selby is owner of White Consulting, a public relations and marketing consulting firm in the Twin Cities. She is public relations advisor to the Minnesota Mortgage Association.

Think Reverse!

Appendix 2(d)
Sample press release

[Insert: Company Logo Here]

FOR IMMEDIATE RELEASE **Contact: Rebecca White Selby**
Phone #: (888) 888-8888
E-mail@address.com

PEOPLE FOR GREAT COMPANIES NAMES COMPANY X "COMPANY OF THE YEAR"

MINNEAPOLIS (Insert Date)—The not-for-profit consumer group, People for Great Companies (PFGC) has named Company X "Company of the Year" for their mortgage industry work, and will recognize Company X with an award on Feb. 10 at the Main Hotel in Mortgageville, Minn.

Each year, the PFGC "Company of the Year" receives a $25,000 grant to continue their corporate involvement in the local community. Company X is the eleventh winner of the award and grant.

"The citizens of Mortgageville can rest assured that we will continue to offer them our volunteer time and our charitable donations for the projects that we have supported in the past as well as new endeavors," said Company X CEO Ronald Incharge.

Incharge, a former loan officer and author of *Mortgages in Mortgageville* is available to speak on topics, including *How to make your company great*, and *How to explain the mortgage process in simple terms.* Please call (888) 888-8888 to arrange an interview.

###

[Indicates the end of the news announcement]

[Boiler]
Company X is the leading reverse mortgage company for community involvement in the Midwest. Led by CEO Ronald Incharge, Company X maintains branch offices in Reversetown, HECM City and ReverseMortgageland, with its headquarters in Mortgageville, Minn. Company X can be reached at (888) 888-8888.

Appendix 3(a)
A different customer: A personal perspective

Lawrence Jensen, CFP is a reverse mortgage specialist in Walpole, Mass. A Certified Financial Planner (CFP), Larry originated forward mortgages for many years before deciding to focus on reverse mortgages. He has a perspective that we can all learn from, so I asked him to share some issues he has had to deal with as a reverse mortgage originator and marketer.

Atare:
Some of the issues I have had to deal with include the following:

- **Overcoming suspicion**
- **Establishing trust**
- **Dealing with a lack of urgency**
- **Pace**—Seniors move slowly
- **Justifying fees**
- **Illness**—Had an appointment cancelled due to a stroke
- **Competing family members**—Those who want mom and dad to enjoy versus those who are concerned about their inheritance
- **Skeptical professionals**—More and more CPAs, lawyers and financial planners are buying into reverse mortgages, but many are still not there yet
- **Collaborative sales**—I encourage bringing all interested parties to the appointment, but sometimes this process stretches out the sales cycle due to not being able to get everyone together
- **Feeling like I am an island**—The community of those involved in the reverse mortgage industry is small, so it can be lonely
- **Prospecting**—You must turn over many stones to find one good prospect.

In spite of these issues, I am still very optimistic about my future in the reverse mortgage industry.

Larry

Larry is clearly a passionate believer [Lesson #5, Chapter 9].

Think Reverse!

Appendix 3(b)
Reverse mortgage correspondent requirements

Below is a list of documentation and information the prospective correspondent must provide to Seattle Mortgage as part of their application for approval as a correspondent of Seattle Mortgage Company's Reverse Mortgage Program.

Once approved, Seattle Mortgage provides comprehensive training, both at the time of initial approval as well as follow-up training as needed going forward.

Application checklist

Please attach the following information with the submission for approval by Seattle Mortgage Company's Reverse Mortgage Division:

- Completed and signed application form.

- Copies of business license(s) for each state in which reverse mortgage loans will be originated by this organization ("Applicant").

- A copy of Trade Name or d/b/a approvals for names which the Applicant may use to originate reverse mortgages (if applicable).

- A copy of Applicant's Certificate of Good Standing from the Secretary of State of the state of Applicant's formation.

- A copy of the past two year's audited financial statements.

- Copies of letters of approval from FHA and Fannie Mae (if Fannie Mae-approved).

Think Reverse!

- A listing of branch locations and a list of those who may be originating reverse mortgages in each location.

- Resumes of key individuals within Applicant including those of branch managers in areas where reverse mortgages will be originated.

- A copy of Applicant's Articles of Incorporation or equivalent organizational document, if other than a corporation.

- A brief summary of Applicant's business plan with regards to the implementation of a reverse mortgage program (i.e., staff, projected volume, marketing, etc.).

- Application fee, payable to Seattle Mortgage Company (not required until after approved).

Applicant information

Applicant name: _____
Mailing address: _____
Street address (if different): _____
Name of primary contact for Reverse Mortgage Program: _____
Phone #: _____
Fax #: _____
E-mail address: _____
Year applicant founded: _____
Number of branches: _____
Any other names under which has done business: _____
_____

Principals/Officers: _____
Name: _____
Title: _____
Briefly describe applicant's mortgage lending area by county or state:
_____
_____

Appendix 3 (b)

Approvals: _____

a. FHA ID#: _____

Type of Approval (i.e., supervised, non-Supervised, Loan Correspondent, Delegated Underwriting): _____

b. Fannie Mae ID#: _____

Business information

Loans closed (year to date):

Number	**Dollar volume**
(a) _____	Government:_____
(b) _____	Conventional:_____

Approximate number of loans serviced (if applicable): _____

Approximate dollar amount of loans serviced (if applicable): _____

Has the applicant or any employee thereof ever been suspended by FHA?
❏ Yes   ❏ No

Has the applicant or any employee thereof ever been suspended or had servicing removed for cause by an investor?
❏ Yes   ❏ No

Has the applicant had any unfavorable findings in any audit examination or report by Fannie Mae, HUD or any regulatory or investigative agency within the last three years?
❏ Yes   ❏ No

If the answer to any of the preceding three questions is "yes," please attach a detailed explanation.

Does the applicant have experience selling reverse mortgages?
❏ Yes   ❏ No

Think Reverse!

If yes, how many years experience: _____

If yes, how many loans were closed in the last 12 months?
- HECMs: Number of loans: _____   Dollar amount: _____
- Fannie Mae: Number of loans: _____   Dollar amount: _____

References

Please list three investors to whom the applicant has sold production on a servicing released basis:

1. Name: _____
Address: _____
Contact: _____
Phone #: _____

2. Name: _____
Address: _____
Contact: _____
Phone #: _____

3. Name: _____
Address: _____
Contact: _____
Phone #: _____

Please list information on applicant's primary banking institution:

Name: _____
Address: _____
Contact: _____
Phone #: _____

Certification and signature

The undersigned hereby certifies that the information provided in this application is true and correct to the best of his or her knowledge and accepts the statements made herein.

Appendix 3 (b)

It is understood that Seattle Mortgage Company may make reference inquiries and, at its own expense, order credit reports and perform independent background investigations regarding applicant. Applicant hereby consents to such investigation, and authorizes its financial institutions, those who have previously purchased loans from applicant and others to provide information concerning past experience with applicant to Seattle Mortgage Company, its designees and agents. Applicant hereby releases all such parties from all liability for any damage that may result from furnishing such information.

Legal name of applicant:_____

Authorized signature:_____

Print name and title:_____

Date: _____

Source: Reverse Mortgage of America/Seattle Mortgage Company

Think Reverse!

Appendix 3(c)
What happens when the last surviving reverse mortgage borrower dies?

Upon notice of the death of a 'last surviving borrower,' the lender's servicing staff responsible for loan termination should do the following:

1. Send out 'due and payable' notice.

2. Ask for response within 30 days.

3. Notify the estate that the loan must be paid off within six months from date of death (can be extended up until one year before payment).

4. HUD says foreclosure can begin 30 days from the day 'due and payable' notice was sent and must start within one year of death.

5. Interest and monthly servicing fees continue to be charged until loan is paid off.

Think Reverse!

Appendix 4(a)
Does John Neincash need mortgage payments?

By Atare E. Agbamu, CRMS

The names mentioned in this article have been changed to preserve anonymity.

A few months ago, Karen Docless, a very likeable and effective account executive with one of America's leading financial behemoths, came to our office to "train" us on some of their "new" mortgage products.

At one point in her 45-min. presentation, she recounted how she helped 79-year-old John Neincash refinance by putting him into one of their new no-doc, no-income products. Karen Docless was at her self-congratulatory best. She really believed she had helped this septuagenarian get financing that could have been hard for him to obtain under normal home mortgage underwriting rules.

Predictably, I asked her whether she considered a reverse mortgage for Mr. Neincash. She said she didn't. Then, she added, "Atare, I really needed that loan." Good-naturedly, we laughed it off. She continued with her training.

Although I admire Karen Docless for her strong people skills and her effectiveness as an account executive, I was bothered not only by the mortgage product she admitted giving to a 79-year-old man, but also by her reason for doing it: " ... I really needed that loan."

For an elder customer who's probably already pressed for cash, does it make sense to tie him to a mortgage loan with a monthly payment obligation? You don't have to be a genius to figure out how John Neincash will fare with his no-doc cash-out refinance.

He will soon begin returning the cash back to the lender in monthly payments. Between his daily cash needs and his monthly repayment obligation to the lender, he may run out of cash and his ability to make repayments to his lender. He will miss payments. A default will happen and foreclosure will soon follow.

Think Reverse!

Mortgage product suitability (or putting the John Neincashes of America into mortgage products that take their needs, age and total financial situation into consideration) is going to be one of the biggest challenges for the mortgage industry in the 21st century. It will make "predatory lending" look like a picnic. A June 2005 United Press International report stated that homebuyers are being lured into "choosing risky mortgages like adjustable-rate and interest-only" loans. Is every adjustable-rate, interest-only and no-doc loan unsuitable or risky? It depends on the needs and circumstances of the borrower.

As a professional mortgage originator, you must decide what mortgage product is suitable for your borrower based on your borrower's needs and financial situation, not yours. If a borrower insists on going against your professional judgment and product recommendation, you should require them to sign a statement absolving both you and your company of responsibility for any adverse consequences.

What mortgage programs are there for seniors 62 and older who need cash from their homes, but do not want or cannot afford the burden of monthly mortgage repayments? Reverse mortgages! Only reverse mortgages! Are reverse mortgages suitable for every senior borrower? No. Should every senior borrower (62 and older) who calls you up or comes into your office for a mortgage know about reverse mortgages? I believe they should.

As mortgage loan officers in a marketplace with a growing senior population, we have a duty (as with our non-senior customers) to ask a simple question of ourselves before we recommend a mortgage product to a customer: Is this loan suitable for this borrower?

In an evolving marketplace with customers that have abundant home equity yet are lacking in extra cash, reverse mortgage programs may be the most suitable solution that mortgage brokers and lenders can use to meet the long-term, extra-cash needs of America's expanding senior population.

For suitability and sound strategic reasons, mortgage brokers and lenders should consider adding reverse mortgages to their product offerings. They should also think about training their origination staff in reverse mortgages so that they can better evaluate reverse mortgage candidates and make appropriate program recommendations. It is what I call *reverse-readiness*. It could be your most astute marketing and business move.

Failing to be reverse-mortgage-ready may suggest gross insensitivity to the needs of our flourishing senior customers at best. At worst, it could expose

Appendix 4 (a)

mortgage lenders and brokers to potential legal and financial risks. I believe reverse mortgage know-how is a competitive advantage in 21st century mortgage lending. Are you reverse-ready?

Think reverse. Move forward.

Reprinted from The Mortgage Press Ltd. (August 2005)

Think Reverse!

Appendix 4(b)
Harvesting cash for the golden years: To HECM or to HELOC?

By Atare E. Agbamu, CRMS

Peter Forward, an industry colleague in the Twin Cities, called me to inquire about a reverse mortgage for his mother.

"My mother needs a reverse mortgage, and 'Laura' at 'Gopher Country Mortgage' says I should talk to you," he said.

I reviewed the basics of the program with him, collected some data about his mother's needs, and suggested that he make an appointment for his mother to meet with a reverse mortgage counselor. I advised him to accompany his mother when meeting the counselor.

Approximately two weeks after our initial conversation, I followed up with a phone call to find out whether his mother had received the required counseling. He said the counseling had been completed, but he decided against a reverse mortgage for his mother due to the "high cost" and the amount of equity she could pull out. Instead, he confidently told me, "I put her in a home equity line of credit (HELOC) where she can access more equity and pay 'less cost.'" The reverse mortgage product, in this case, is the government-insured Home Equity Conversion Mortgage (HECM).

Every HECM originator, sooner rather than later, will encounter a Peter Forward. A Peter Forward is a mortgage professional or trusted financial advisor to a potential reverse mortgage borrower. Peter Forwards have a superficial grasp of these unique home loans, yet they are in a position to influence the decisions of reverse borrowers for better or for worse. Peter's decision for his mother raised an important question that we will address in this article: On a value-cost basis, how does a HECM compare with a HELOC?

Both HECMs and HELOCs are financial tools for squeezing cash out of a home. To secure the cash stream, a lender puts a lien on the house; the borrower

Think Reverse!

retains full ownership and possession rights. HECMs were created for borrowers 62 years and older; HELOCs were designed for borrowers of all ages who can meet standard credit and income qualifications. HECMs are government-insured loans with capped variable interest rates; HELOCs are private-sector products with uncapped and capped adjustable interest rates. With HECMs, a borrower's other assets are safe from the lender's reach in case the lender lends more than the equity in the property; with HELOCs, a borrower has no such protection.

Except for minimal credit checks for federal loan defaults, no income or credit is needed to qualify for HECMs, and no monthly repayment is needed; and to qualify for HELOCs, borrowers must pass credit, income and monthly repayment-ability tests. With HECMs, the unused portions of the credit line grows larger every month according to a unique formula; and the unused portion of HELOCs remain stagnant, subject to the cash-corroding impact of inflation. Failure to make monthly payments is not an issue with HECMs because there are no monthly payments to make; however, in the case of HELOCs, missed payments can result in default and foreclosure.

As part of a system of built-in protection for elders, HECMs require free consumer education from a HUD-approved reverse mortgage counselor before an application can become effective; HELOCs have no such built-in safeguards for a potentially vulnerable segment of the population. Indeed, HECMs total costs drop lower and lower after five years, but no such claim can be made for HELOCs.

There's no question that HELOCs are valuable loan products with very low initial costs for borrowers with strong income, good credit and financial savvy. However, it is apparent from the foregoing HECM-HELOC comparison that HELOCs are not suitable for cash-strapped seniors who cannot afford to lose their homes. Also, HECMs are not for every senior. For seniors who plan to sell and move on or who have other means of generating retirement funds for short-term use, there may be less expensive (and probably more risky) alternatives in forward mortgage lending.

Peter Forward's mother is in her late 70s with probably more than 15 years left and a long-term need for cash. In my opinion, Peter made the classic penny-wise, dollar-foolish decision choosing a HELOC instead of a HECM for his mother. As informed reverse mortgage originators, we must continue to stress the incomparable value of HECMs and other reverse mortgage programs to our forward-thinking colleagues ... Let's think forward on reverse!

Reprinted from The Mortgage Press Ltd. (July 2004)

Appendix 4 (b)

Think Reverse!

Bibliography

Think Reverse!

Bibliography

1. *AARP*, "Beyond 50.03: A Report to the Nation on Independent Living and Disability." Washington, D.C. AARP, 2003.
2. *AARP*, "Home Made Money." Washington, D.C.: AARP Foundation, 2003.
3. Alvig, Mark R. and Petracek, Thomas M. *A Practical Guide to Successful Estate Planning*. North Branch, Minn.: Specialty Press, 1999.
4. *Administration on Aging*, "Profile of Older Americans: 2003." Washington, D.C.: Administration on Aging, 2003.
5. Barletta, Martha. *Marketing to Women*. Chicago, Ill.: Dearborn Trade Publishing, 2003.
6. Beckwith, Harry. *Selling the Invisible*. New York, N.Y.: Warner Books, 1997.
7. Carter, Jimmy. *The Virtues of Aging*. New York, N.Y.: Ballantine Publishing Group, 1998.
8. Congressional Record–House, Dec. 14, 2005. H11586.
9. Culligan, Matthew J. and Greene, Dolph. *Getting Back to the Basics of Public Relations & Publicity*. New York, N.Y.: Crown Publishers Inc., 1982.
10. DeSimone, Anna. *Reverse Mortgages*. Washington, D.C.: MBA Real Estate Finance Press, 1998.
11. Dilen-Schneider, Robert L. with Mary Jane Genova. *The Critical 14 Years of Your Professional Life*. Secaucus, N.J.: Carol Publishing Group, 1997.
12. Dychtwald, Ken. *Age Power*. New York, N.Y.: Jeremy P. Tarcher/Putnam, 1999.
13. *Fannie Mae*, "Money from Home." Washington, D.C.: Fannie Mae, 2004.
14. *Federal Register*. Vol. 69 No. 58, March 25, 2004/ HUD 24 CFR Part 206 "Home Equity Conversion Mortgage (HECM) Program, Insurance for Mortgages to Refinance Existing HECMs."
15. Green, Brent. *Marketing to Leading-Edge Boomers*. New York: Writers Advantage, 2003.

16. Goleman, Daniel. *Emotional Intelligence.* New York: Bantam Books, 1995.
17. HUD. "2000 HECM Report." Washington, D.C.: HUD Policy Development & Research, 2000.
18. HUD. "2003 HECM Report." Washington, D.C.: HUD Policy Development & Research, 2003.
19. HUD. "Options for Elderly Home Owners." Washington, D.C.: HUD Policy Development & Research, 1989.
20. HUD. "Handbook 4235.1 Rev – 1: Home Equity Conversion Mortgages."
21. *Joint Center for Housing Studies of Harvard University.* "State of the Nation's Housing: 2002."
22. *Joint Center for Housing Studies of Harvard University.* "State of the Nation's Housing: 2003."
23. *Joint Center for Housing Studies of Harvard University.* "State of the Nation's Housing: 2004."
24. *Joint Center for Housing Studies of Harvard University.* "State of the Nation's Housing: 2005."
25. *National Council on the Aging.* "Using Your Home to Stay at Home™." Washington, D.C.: NCOA, 2005.
26. *National Reverse Mortgage Lenders Association.* "Testimony by Jeffrey S. Taylor, CMB to Commission on Affordable Housing and Health Facility Needs for Seniors in the 21st Century." 2002.
27. Raines, Franklin D. "Remarks to Mortgage Bankers Association's 88th Annual Convention," Toronto, Canada, Oct. 15, 2001.
28. Restak, Richard M. *Older & Wiser.* New York: Simon & Schuster, 1997.
29. Ries, Al and Laura Ries. *The Fall of Advertising & The Rise of PR.* New York, N.Y.: Harper Business, 2002.
30. Reverse Mortgage to Help America's Seniors Act, Washington, D.C.: Congressional Record–House, 2005.
31. Roszak, Theodore. *Longevity Revolution.* Berkeley, Calif.: Berkeley Hills Books, 2001.
32. Scholen, Ken. *Your New Retirement Nest Egg (2nd Edition).* Apple Valley, Minn.: NCHEC Press, 1995.
33. Scholen, Ken. *Reverse Mortgages for Beginners.* Apple Valley, Minn.: NCHEC Press, 1998.
34. Trout, Jack. *Trout on Strategy.* New York, N.Y.: McGraw-Hill, 2004.
35. Whitenack, Rhonda. *Older Americans: Aging Well and Living Well.* Good Age, June 2004.
36. Wolfe, David B. and Robert S. Snyder. *Ageless Marketing.* Chicago, Ill.: Dearborn Trade Publishing, 2003.

Bibliography

Glossary of terms

Think Reverse!

Glossary of terms

Adjusted Property Value
Fannie Mae's national loan limit or the portion of appraised value of borrower's property used in deciding principal limit for HomeKeeper reverse mortgage.

Available Principal Limit
Principal limit minus service fee set-aside.

Cash Account Advantage
A proprietary reverse mortgage indexed to six-month LIBOR with no lending limits better suited for higher-end (jumbo) properties.

Creditline
A reverse mortgage cash advance plan that allows a borrower to control the timing and amount of loan advances (a.k.a. line of credit).

Deferred Payment Loans
A type of home loans from local governments used for repairing or improving homes (a.k.a. public reverse mortgages).

Estimated Home Value
Borrower's estimate of her home's value at application before an appraisal. Borrower may say her home is worth $100,000, based on knowledge of neighborhood home values.

Equity Choice
Equity choice allows a borrower to limit the percentage of home value used as collateral for a Cash Account Advantage loans. Borrower may shield between 10 and 50 percent of home value from use as security for loan.

Think Reverse!

Expected Interest Rate
Interest rate used to decide a HECM loan's principal limit. It is the 10-Year Treasury note plus a margin. It can be locked.

Falling Equity
A reverse mortgage is a falling-equity home loan; as borrower receives cash and lender's interest and fees accrue, home equity falls. It's an equity-consuming loan.

Fannie Mae
HECM loans' largest secondary market investor.

FHA
Federal Housing Administration (FHA), a unit of the U.S. Department of Housing and Urban Development (HUD).

Five-Times Rule
In HECM refinance, it is a HUD rule that says lender must ensure that additional principal limit (benefit to borrower) exceeds total refinance costs at least five times. See Within-Five-Years Rule.

Generation Plus
A proprietary reverse mortgage indexed to one-month LIBOR with no lending limits, better suited for higher-end (jumbo) properties.

Gentleman Farm
A non-professional, hobby-type farm.

Ginnie Mae
It's a federal agency within HUD. It guarantees payment of principal and interest to investors who buy securities backed by FHA (including HECMs) and VA loans.

HECM 100
An FHA-insured proprietary monthly HECM with a margin of one percent, owned by BNY Mortgage Company.

Home Equity Conversion
It's the idea of turning home equity into cash, with borrower making no

Glossary of terms

monthly repayments. Every reverse mortgage is a home equity conversion loan.

Home Equity Conversion Mortgage (HECM)
The FHA's reverse mortgage program.

HomeKeeper
Fannie Mae's proprietary reverse mortgage program.

HomeKeeper for Home Purchase
Fannie Mae's reverse mortgage that the borrower can use to buy a home and avoid monthly mortgage payments for the life of the loan.

Initial Interest Rate
The monthly or annually adjusting rate applied to a HECM borrower's loan balance (a.k.a. applied interest rate).

Initial Mortgage Insurance Premium
An insurance premium a HECM borrower pays to FHA for insuring the loan. It's two percent of the lending limit or appraised value of the home.

Lending Limit
The maximum a reverse lender would lend. For FHA's HECM, it's the county-by-county limit (a.k.a. Maximum Claim Amount or 203[b] limit); for Fannie Mae's HomeKeeper, it's the adjusted property value or Fannie Mae's annual loan limit; for jumbos, there are no limits.

Loan Agreement
A key document a reverse mortgage borrower signs at closing in addition to the note and the mortgage (deed of trust).

Loan Balance
Unpaid balance of a reverse mortgage loan; it's the principal plus accrued interest, servicing fees and other charges.

Loan Proceeds
Cash advances to a borrower via a reverse mortgage.

Loan Termination
End of a reverse mortgage life circle; the lender's lien is fully paid (a.k.a. maturity).

Think Reverse!

Lump Sum
A large loan advance to a reverse mortgage borrower on funding date.

Mortgage
A legal document making a home available to a lender as a security for a loan.

National Reverse Mortgage Lenders Association (NRMLA)
The reverse mortgage industry's trade group.

Net Principal Limit
The total credit available to a borrower at origination minus loan costs.

Non-Recourse Loan
A loan, such as a reverse mortgage, where lender must use home value as security for the loan; a borrower's other assets are protected by law.

Origination Fee
The fee a borrower pays to get a loan.

Partial Repayment
It's a feature in Fannie Mae's HomeKeeper reverse mortgage creditline. It allows borrower to partially repay borrowed cash and redraw another time.

Payment Plan
How a reverse mortgage borrower gets cash from the loan. Available plans are term, tenure, creditline, or a combination of term and creditline, or tenure and creditline.

Payment Suspension
A feature of Fannie Mae's HomeKeeper reverse mortgage which gives borrower an option to suspend cash advances from lender to conserve equity.

Principal Limit
It is total credit available to a borrower at origination before loan costs.

Principal Limit Protection
A feature in HECM loans that protects borrower's principal limit against higher interest rates for 120 days from the date borrower signs application. If expected interest rate is lower at closing, borrower gets lower rate.

Glossary of terms

Property Inspection
A professional look at the inside and outside of a property to assess its condition.

Property Tax Deferrals
A type of home loans from local governments used for paying property taxes (a.k.a. public reverse mortgages).

Reverse Mortgage
A non-recourse home loan that provides borrower (62 and older) tax-free cash advances; borrower keeps physical and legal control of her home and makes no monthly mortgage payments for as long as she lives in the home.

Rising Debt
A reverse mortgage is a rising-debt loan because borrower receives cash, but makes no monthly repayments; by contrast, a forward mortgage is a falling-debt loan.

Reverse Select
A proprietary reverse mortgage indexed to the prime rate with no lending limits better suited for higher-end (jumbo) properties. It also has a fixed-rate feature.

Servicing
Essentially, babysitting the loan—making payments to borrower, responding to borrower's requests, sending monthly statements to borrower, reporting to investor, monitoring property, handling loan termination and other issues.

Servicing Fee
A monthly fee borrower pays to cover costs of servicing loan.

Servicing Fee Set-Aside
For HECM and HomeKeeper reverse mortgages, non-cash, equity set-aside for servicing fees.

Tenure
Fixed monthly cash advances for as long as borrower lives in her home.

Term
Fixed monthly cash advances for a specified number of months.

Think Reverse!

The Independence Plan
A proprietary reverse mortgage with no lending limits better suited for higher-end (jumbo) properties.

Total Annual Loan Cost (TALC) rate
The projected total annual average cost of a reverse mortgage expressed as a single rate; it allows for an apples-to-apples comparison of reverse mortgage programs.

Within-Five-Years Rule
In a HECM refinance, the HUD rule that says refinance must be within five years of the original HECM loan.

Glossary of terms

Think Reverse!

Endnotes

Think Reverse!

Endnotes

Introduction
Stephen R. Covey, *The 8th Habit* (Free Press, 2004), xi.

Chapter 1
1. Ken Scholen, *Reverse Mortgages for Beginners* (Apple Valley, Minn.: NCHEC Press, 1998), pages 108-123. For more reverse mortgage history, visit www.reverse.org.

Chapter 2
1. Ken Dychtwald, *Age Power* (Tarcher/Putnam, 1999), page 1.
2. Rhonda Whitenack, *Older Americans: Aging Well and Living Well* (Good Age, June 2004), page 4.
3. Heather C. McGhee and Tamara Draut, "Retiring in the Red: The Growth of Debt Among Older Americans" (January, 2004) www.demos.org/pubs.
4. AARP's "Home Made Money" (2003), pages 20-21. www.aarp.org/revmort.

Chapter 3
1. www.efanniemae.com/lc/publications/borrowers/pdf/moneyfromhome.pdf.

Chapter 4
1. Fannie Mae Selling and Servicing Guide, 3.B.6, page 11.
2. Fannie Mae Selling and Servicing Guide, 3.B.3, page 10.
3. Fannie Mae Selling and Servicing Guide, 3.B.4, page 10.

Chapter 5
1. Interview with Jim Mahoney of Financial Freedom Senior Funding Corporation, *The Mortgage Press*, August 2004.
2. Interview with Jim Mahoney of Financial Freedom Senior Fund Funding Corporation, *The Mortgage Press*, August 2004.

Think Reverse!

Chapter 6

1. David B. Wolfe with Robert E. Snyder, *Ageless Marketing* (Dearborn Trade Publishing, 2003), page 47.
2. Ibid., page 163.
3. Ibid., pages 166-167.
4. Ibid., page 169.
5. Ibid., page 169.

Chapter 7

None

Chapter 8

1. Interview with Sarah Hulbert of Reverse Mortgage of America/Seattle Mortgage Company, June 18, 2004.
2. David B. Wolfe with Robert E. Snyder, *Ageless Marketing* (Dearborn Trade Publishing, 2003), page 250.
3. Attributed to Joseph Pine and James Gilmore (authors of the *Experience Economy*) in *Ageless Marketing*, page 262.
4. Ibid., page 262.
5. Matthew J. Culligan and Dolph Greene, *Getting Back to the Basics of Public Relations & Publicity* (Crown Publishers Inc., 1982), page 1.
6. Interview with Sarah Hulbert of Reverse Mortgage of America/Seattle Mortgage Company, June 18, 2004.
7. Matthew J. Culligan and Dolph Greene, *Getting Back to the Basics of Public Relations & Publicity* (Crown Publishers, Inc., 1982), page 27.
8. Ibid., pages 16-17.
9. Ibid., page 41.
10. Ibid., pages 42-44.
11. Interview with Peter Bell of the National Reverse Mortgage Lenders Association (NRMLA).
12. *Merriam Webster's Collegiate Dictionary (10th Edition)*, page 780.
13. *Webster's New World Dictionary*, page 395.
14. Robert L. Dilen-Schneider with Mary Jane Genova, *The Critical 14 Years of Your Professional Life* (Carol Publishing Group, 1997), page 78.
15. Interview with Paul and Barbara Franklin of Franklin Funding, Charlestown, S.C., May 19, 2004.

Chapter 9
1. Interview with Barbara Franklin of Franklin Funding, Charleston, S.C., Dec. 27, 2004.
2. Interview with Peter Bell of NRMLA, May 7, 2004.
3. Interview with Paul Franklin and Barbara Franklin of Franklin Funding, Charleston, S.C., May 19, 2004.
4. Jack Trout, *Trout on Strategy* (McGraw-Hill, 2004), page 77.
5. Ibid., page 81.
6. Interview with Alfred Sanchez of ADS Mortgage Corporation, Albuquerque, N.M., Sept. 3, 2004.
7. My editor, Eric C. Peck of *The Mortgage Press* is the originator of the "Got Reverse?" idea.

Chapter 10
1. Interview with Sarah Hulbert of Reverse Mortgage of America/Seattle Mortgage Company, June 18, 2004.
2. Interview with Peter Bell of NRMLA, May 7, 2004.

Chapter 11
None

Chapter 12
1. Interview with Paul and Irene Alexander, Nov. 19, 2004.
2. *Reverse Mortgage Advisor*, Vol. 5.2, Summer 2002, pages 5-6.
3. Ibid., pages 4-9.

Chapter 13
None

Chapter 14
1. Interview with Jeffrey S. Taylor, CMB of Wells Fargo Home Mortgage, *The Mortgage Press*, September 2004.
2. Interview with James R. Mahoney of Financial Freedom Senior Funding Corporation, *The New York Mortgage Press*, August 2004, pages 36-37.
3. Ibid., page 37.

Chapter 15
1. Interview with Paul and Irene Alexander, Nov. 19, 2004.

Think Reverse!

Chapter 16

1. David B. Wolfe with Robert E. Snyder, *Ageless Marketing* (Dearborn Trade Publishing, 2003), page 21.
2. Ibid., page 21.
3. *National Council on the Aging.* "Using Your Home to Stay at Home™." (Washington, D.C.: NCOA, 2005), page 41.
4. Atare E. Agbamu, "The Reverse Mortgage/Long-Term Care Connection," *The California Mortgage Press* (January 2004), page 18.
5. Ibid., page 18.
6. "LTC Bullet: Governors Get Going on LTC Reform, " April 19, 2005, Center for Long-Term Care Financing, www.centerltc.com (New name: Center for Long Term Care Reform).
7. Ibid.
8. Center for Long-Term Care Financing, LTC Bullets, November 2003.
9. Atare E. Agbamu, "Marketing Reverse Mortgages 101: It's All About Understanding Mature Prospects," *The California Mortgage Press* (January 2005), page 33.
10. Theodore Roszak, *Longevity Revolution* (Berkeley Hills Books, 2001), page153.
11. David B. Wolfe with Robert E. Snyder, *Ageless Marketing* (Dearborn Trade Publishing, 2003), page 314.

Endnotes

Think Reverse!